When I was riding my mountain bike I felt like I was headed in some direction. Even when I was hopelessly lost in the woods I knew that I was going somewhere. At least I was in charge. Myself. I determined left or right. I decided fast or slow. To keep going or to pause. And there was no shame if I got bruised or bloodied. No guilt if I was stronger than someone else. And those achievements affected everything else. Just like on a mountain-bike ride where I could yell, "No, this way!" and jump off onto a path separate from the pack....

Marla Streb competes as a world-class downhill mountain-bike racer. During her career as a biomedical researcher, she fell in love with cycling. She has appeared on *The Today Show* and on the cover of *Outside,* and is sponsored by Luna Bar and Red Bull. She lives in San Geronimo, California.

THE LIFE STORY OF A
DOWNHILL
GRAVITY GODDESS

MARLA STREB

A PLUME BOOK

PLUME
Published by the Penguin Group
Penguin Group (USA) Inc., 375 Hudson Street, New York, New York 10014, U.S.A.
Penguin Books Ltd, 80 Strand, London WC2R 0RL, England
Penguin Books Australia Ltd, 250 Camberwell Road, Camberwell, Victoria 3124, Australia
Penguin Books Canada Ltd, 10 Alcorn Avenue, Toronto, Ontario, Canada M4V 3B2
Penguin Books India (P) Ltd, 11 Community Centre, Panchsheel Park, New Delhi – 110 017,
India
Penguin Books (N.Z.) Ltd, Cnr Rosedale and Airborne Roads, Albany, Auckland 1310,
New Zealand
Penguin Books (South Africa) (Pty) Ltd, 24 Sturdee Avenue, Rosebank, Johannesburg 2196,
South Africa

Penguin Books Ltd, Registered Offices: 80 Strand, London WC2R 0RL, England

First published by Plume, a member of Penguin Group (USA) Inc.

First Printing, November 2003
10 9 8 7 6 5 4 3 2 1

℗ REGISTERED TRADEMARK—MARCA REGISTRADA

LIBRARY OF CONGRESS CATALOGING-IN-PUBLICATION DATA

Streb, Marla.
Downhill : the life story of a gravity goddess / Marla Streb.
p. cm.
ISBN 0-452-28458-9 (trade pbk.)
1. Streb, Marla. 2. Cyclists—United States—Biography. 3. All terrain cycling. I. Title.

GV1051.S77A3 2003
796.6'2'092—dc21
[B]
2003054717

Printed in the United States of America
Set in Sabon
Designed by Leonard Telesca

Dedication

To my brother Mark, an inspiration always.
And to another Mark, a guy I also love,
but obviously in a different way.

Acknowledgments

I'd like to thank my agent
Robert Preskill and editors
Gary Brozek and Laura Blumenthal.

Author's Note

To make identification easier for the reader,
in this book as I have done in my own journal
entries, I have changed the spelling of my boyfriend
Mark's name to Marc.

Contents

Introduction

Five Minutes Down

Santa Cruz V-10 mountain bike. (*Author*)

I am not supposed to be doing this. But I am trying my hardest anyway. My name is Marla Streb. I am thirty-six years old. I ran away from what I was supposed to do, so that I could do what I really wanted. I used to be a normal woman with a promising career as a research scientist, but a mountain-biking bug bit me, and I changed.

Who would have guessed?

Riding a bike down a mountain should be so simple. Just let go and let gravity do its thing. Rip down mountains, in dirt and mud, through rocks and green trees at speeds of up to sixty miles an hour. Fly through the air. Bounce off boulders. Work around or through every obstacle to maintain control.

Thick in the syrup now, my body quivers, moves slightly, before the last start beep becomes a noise. The forward momentum for a fraction of a second here, even before the race begins, could make all the difference later when the race is over. I'm standing on the pedals, balanced, in the starting gate. And though the starting sequence is governed by an electronic brain, I try my best to anticipate that fifth and last high-pitched tone, usually a G-sharp, that screams: Race! Static balance transforming into forward motion; I push down with my right pedal, and then my left, lumbering past the timing beam swinging each foot into a tight circle and churning my legs faster and faster, clicking through the gears of my bike's drive train. Upright, my legs pumping, pulling with all the strength of my arms on the handle bar, compelling this nearly forty-five-pound bicycle down the hill as fast as I can make it.

Just a few sounds are heard. Maybe my heart banging away inside my chest and the wind frantically swirling through the vents of my helmet. I can't hear the roar of the crowds if I am racing in Europe, or the silence of its absence if I am racing in the United States. The world slows down and I know the trail, often no wider than my shoulders, in front of me. Then, I slip into a silence where there is no clanging chain slap or whirring drone of knobby tires.

A typical downhill race lasts for about five minutes. This mental one, self-guided imagery, is just beginning. I have spent the last ten years of my life preparing and training to transform these five-minute vignettes into a reality.

From South Africa, Japan, Sweden, and Slovenia, to all over North America, I've circled for these five-minute spurts of adrenaline. I train year-round, three or four hours a day on my bike and more in the weight room, or on a motorcycle—trail running for endurance. Wood chopping and dirt digging a jump course in my backyard for upper body conditioning. Yoga for increased flexibility and balance. Icy cold mornings. Sweltering hot afternoons. Hours of phone calls and e-mails to sponsors, race organizers, and training partners. I declare on my tax forms that my bikes are tools, that injuries are business expenses, and that my boyfriend, Marc, is a dependant. In reality, I'm the one who's dependent. I live for those sweet gravity-induced minutes.

Until I started on this path I was lost. Riding a bike off this cliff, committing to this venture wholeheartedly, has made all the difference. Mountain biking saved me from the insanities of inane

Launching myself downhill, playing with gravity. (*Paul McKenzie courtesy of Clif Bar*)

suburban life. It steered me away from too much tequila. Mountain biking has transformed food into fuel, and compromise into opportunity. It's given me the resolve to ride out the ups and downs. Downhilling has left permanent marks on me, a few even the darkest panty hose can't hide. I now possess more confidence. I'm physically stronger than I ever thought I could be. And I've earned the admiration of my peers, even if they are just muddy, sweaty, rain-soaked, Lycra-clad bike geeks some of the time.

Always, my eyes are around the next turn, on the other side of a jump. I am floating, like in those dreams where you can never run fast but merely hang in the air just above the earth. I almost have to fight to remain connected to the ground and if I'm not careful I could just slip away off into nowhere over the edge of a cliff. During a good race adrenaline masks the hurt in my thighs, the searing in my lungs. Not even the whack of a tree limb against my shoulder registers. No pain at all, not until a few moments later when the race is over and and the adrenaline wears off.

Within a minute or so of sprinting, my deep breaths can hardly supply the muscles of my legs and arms and back with enough oxygen. I must race down this mountain, through boulder fields, jump over long-fallen logs, and drop off small cliffs, on the edge of blacking out.

I launch myself off a berm and land in a bed of rocks twenty feet down the trail, upright and on course, still pedaling. During those few seconds when I am airborne, I ease up a bit, relax for a deep breath, and appreciate my delicate grip on life.

Skintight and colorful, my form-fitting Kevlar and Lycra outfit makes me feel like a comic book superhero: my mission; to prove that girls love dirt! by reaching the pinnacle of the podium while battling the evil forces of brake drag and off-camber turns! Every time I hop on my mountain bike I am confident that I am making a small contribution toward making the world a better place, albeit indirectly.

All the high-tech gear I wear inhibits free movement and restricts my ability to breathe. But the safety pads are so necessary, in case I slide out in a gravel-filled turn or misjudge the landing at the base of a ten-foot drop-off, or worse. Protecting my eyes are goggles that allow me to discern the invisible lines that I have scraped into this mountainside during the week's practice. Lines that I have carved deeper each night in my sleep. Ruts in the hard-packed dirt or sloppy mud that I must stick to like a train to its rails if I hope to win. I've drawn a map of this course during this week's practice, on and off braking points, turn to turn, drop off to jump, and noted where to change gears. I study the lines of this map at night and play them over and over in my head like a favorite Django Reinhardt guitar riff so that on race day I can hit every note. Focusing on these lines that wink in and out of the blinding sun and through the black shade of trees and into the floating fog of trail dust, at forty miles an hour I race down this mountain trail that can break bones and ruin careers. I'm transported back to my mother's kitchen table, to the sound of her voice saying, "You are making a mistake trying to do this."

My heart is beating almost two hundred times a minute, trying to clear out the lactic acid, but the fascia surrounding the swollen muscles of my forearms prevents the blood from exiting through the venous system back into my lungs to renew the cycle. As my arms lock up, the circulatory system breaks down. My forearms seize, my fingers claw up. The bike begins to feel like a powerful jackhammer, only I'm supposed to use this wildly-bucking tool to draw a delicate line down the mountainside. Sometimes when this happens my body just shuts down and then it only takes a small rock or divet on the trail to throw me off course. That's how a lot of crashes during a race occur, because of a little bobble.

Sure I risk crashing. And sometimes I do, pretty badly. But I do not allow the fear of failure to prevent me from trying. In the beginning friends and family told me that I was crazy. But I have learned that the limiting factors of my potential lie within my own head. True, I have banged my helmet-clad bucket a couple of times. But the rewards of being a gravity goddess are greater than being able to buy a home in the Bay Area, another home on the Central Coast, and a fifty-foot sailboat.

I see ahead the finish line, and as I shoot across it my gut clues me in to how well I have done. I brake hard and slide-turn into a skidding stop so that I can look over my shoulder to see my time on the leader board.

At the end of a race it's easy to pass out. Often I drop nearly three-thousand feet in elevation in as many minutes without any sort of decompression chamber. My shoes are mechanically attached to the pedals and there have been races that I have cleared cleanly the whole way, no crashes, no dabs, not a foot touching the dirt once, only to end up beyond the finish line too weak and too dizzy to disengage my foot from the pedal. Slowly I lean over sideways and fall to the ground in front of the assembled crowds, and media, and my competitors, like a burned up Wily E. Coyote on one of his zany *Road Runner* rocket-powered contraptions.

That's what I want. To have the best finish I need to be lifeless, devoid of any soul, empty of any energy. I want it all spent on the mountain. I may have had a good run, but I have no idea how the other racers are doing. Would I be the fastest down the mountain? Was today someone else's race of their life? Would someone else be the goddess?

My team manager will help me remove my helmet because my gloved fingers are too unresponsive still to do it myself. And then my manager will either slap me on the back or ask me if I am injured anywhere. A water bottle will appear from somewhere and be stuffed into my hand. If needed a warm wet towel will wipe most of the race from my face while we all wait to see who the winner will be.

Sometimes an official will notify me with a coy whisper or a firm clipboard in the small of my back that I have been selected for the testing for performance-enhancing drugs, and the official will walk beside me as I make my way either to the luxuriously appointed VIP lounge or to the hastily put together and grimy first-aid station where I can provide a urine sample in semiprivacy.

And it's my job, especially after the race standing on top of the podium, to smile and look professional. It's this part of the dream job that affords me that luxury of riding my bike in the woods on sunny midafternoons in vacation destinations all over the world during the week. It's what I have been doing now for almost ten years. It's what led me from a precarious state of mind to where I am now: Preparing for another race season. Imagining tomorrow morning's race.

PART I

Thesis/Question:
How Does A Mild-
Mannered Research
Scientist Transform
into a Gravity
Goddess?

Chapter 1

Background and Fundamentals

As a young girl I was a bit of a sloucher. As a matter of fact I slouched right up until I discovered mountain biking wouldn't let me.

I should also mention that I probably shouldn't be racing a bike at my age. Not to mention that I have no particular talent for mountain biking. I shouldn't be a pro. Shouldn't even be able to ride a bike like I do. As a kid I never owned or raced a BMX bike. I never built a plywood ramp in the driveway from which to launch summerlong jumps. Prior to turning pro at age twenty-eight, I had never been a college or pro anything. Experts in the sport consider me too tall for downhilling. I am not really a sprinter, and have no special sense of balance, as anyone who has seen me dance can tell you.

Further, my father doesn't own a bike company and my brothers didn't hand down my love for the sport of mountain biking. I had to find mountain biking all by myself. And once I did, my whole life changed.

I didn't even own a brand new, genuine, mountain bike until I was twenty-seven years old, an age when many of the pro racers I compete against are considering retirement. Racing a mountain bike at this level has been a sheer act of will—and some good luck.

But from childhood I wanted to be the best at something—to be recognized for my ability in some way. Vanity, I concede, and also a sin in Catholicism, but compelling nonetheless.

When I made the commitment to become a professional mountain biker, I was like most "near" thirty-year-olds. Tied to a career path as a research scientist, I was already under pressure from my parents to settle down and marry someone, anyone (except the guy I was living with, Marc), and confronted with the cynicism of my college friends and coworkers for falling in love with mountain biking.

Back then my friends were living out their dreams: opening a vegetarian restaurant, finishing up a doctoral program, teaching their kids to ice skate.

Back then I didn't have a dream. I was merely playing it safe.

• • •

When I was little girl I imagined myself a famous musician someday. I studied classical piano for twelve years at the Peabody Institute in Baltimore where I grew up. My parents hoped that I would play in an orchestra someday, the New York Philharmonic or the Boston Pops, perhaps. I did too. I was blessed with perfect pitch—the ability to discern any note as it stands alone. I diligently worked at my musical studies to the point where on the piano, and later on the guitar and the saxophone, I could play any piece without prior practice as long as I could see the sheet music. That's called sight-reading.

I could look at the scribbled notations on a page and translate them into sound as easily as reading a newspaper out loud. You'd be surprised at how many famous musicians can't read the little scribbles. But my musical performances were merely proficient, hardly profound, technically accurate. My fingers could ramp up the pace of a tune like they were winning a race, but a race to nowhere without an element of soul.

Many musicians play instruments because that is the most articulate expression that they can muster. Despite my gift of perfect pitch, I couldn't write or compose music, or even play the piano extemporaneously. I could never play the freestyle jazz solos that I so much admired. I was well into college when I admitted that shortcoming to myself. It hurt. When asked I used to tell people that I was a musician. And then, after so many years of hard work, I felt like I no longer could.

In college I was a better-than-average student and would have been even better, I suppose, if I wasn't nearly great at drinking games. Nevertheless I threw myself into studies. I really did crack the books. But it was rote work that gave me no sense of fulfillment.

Doing something athletic, I had a better sense of self. On a skateboard, even into my twenties, I was mistaken for a boy when I rode the half pipe in Ocean City. The first running race I ever entered was the Boston Marathon. I caved and rock climbed and scuba dived. Raced sailboats with rich old men. Hang glided. Did karate for quite a while; making it to the not very advanced stage of green belt.

When I was much younger I wore all the usual uniforms: soccer, field hockey, and basketball. My mother, bless her soul, really tried to get me excited about figure skating and tennis and synchronized swimming. I think she really just liked the outfits. But those organized sports didn't get my adrenal glands to work overtime. When I was older I could drink heady microbrews for free most nights while playing pool, because I was good enough to control the table, and a free beer was the cost of admission for a game. Though I always won, it never crossed my mind to wake up early the next morning and practice my caroms or whatever real pool pros do.

But at none of these activities did I ever reach a level of

excellence. I was good without really trying. Oddly enough, that can be debilitating. I had been good, not great, at a lot of things. I was slouching through life.

So how did I discover mountain biking and what would becoming a pro do for me? Why did I want to jump off a normal career path, hop onto a mountain bike, and risk embarrassing myself?

I am still finding out. This might sound Hemingwayesque but I want to know, truly, that I have done as best I could at this one thing: racing a bicycle. It's creepy to admit that Ayn Rand would agree that cycling itself is pure and simple, racing even more so. It's more an exercise in will power than a feat of strength. For my efforts I realize that I now laugh more easily, sleep more contentedly, and enjoy a simpler state of being. I intend to race a few more years and hope to win a championship, but regardless, after my career ends I will always ride a bike and know I was the best I could be.

If I was suddenly cast down from a mountain bike and had to confess that life as a professional mountain biker wasn't going to work out, I could resume a career in science with the dedication that pursuit demands. Perhaps even return to music. I might marry and start a family and not feel cheated or sad during rainy afternoons when the kids were gone. That later in life, when it became difficult to climb stairs or to work in the garden, I would be able to withstand rocking in my chair comforted by the knowledge that I had risked failure in order to win. That, if anytime after I suffered doubts about anything, I still would know who I was. If I hadn't pursued this goal so relentlessly, I'm not sure I could say the same thing.

My first race of this 2002 season, my ninth year earning money by pedaling a bike through the woods, will be tomorrow morning. I'll be competing against racers like Anne Caroline Chausson, the perennial world champion; Missy Giove, mountain biking's original gravity goddess; and young guns like Tara Llanes and Kathy Pruitt, all world champions themselves.

The day before the race, I'd stood shivering on an observation tower doing a TV interview. I would rather have been someplace warm and getting a massage in preparation for the next day, but duty called. I was asked to assess my chances.

"The main competitor, definitely for the women, is Anne Caroline Chausson. She has been racing mountain bikes, and other bikes, since she was a little girl. She has incredible talent and she's got a great head on her shoulders. Knows how to race. And can be dominant. Everybody else is striving to beat that girl. And, actually I got to do it last year. You know, I tried really hard and I came here early and dialed the course in."

The truth is I had won that race because I had been willing to throw myself into a rock pile that was the finish line right in front of the TV cameras.

"Basically she is forcing all of us to improve in greater increments than we might have if she didn't exist. So, you know, I'm glad she's here."

And I was. I was really glad that Anne Caroline had come all the way from her home in France to kick everybody's butt once again. That not only was she showing me how to be a better racer, she was also compelling me to be a better racer. When I entered my first mountain bike race, a small amateur race, I never thought that in a few years I would be lining up next to world champions. Back then I didn't even know what downhilling was. I just knew that I liked riding my bike in the woods. I liked that more than anything else. So it is an honor just to line up next to her to race. And it is a great satisfaction for me to be racing against her for Team Luna.

The team is such a feel-good program. Gary Erickson, the owner and CEO of Clif Bar, came up with the idea of an all-women's professional mountain-bike team not only as a way to market his company's already successful new nutrition bar, the Luna Bar, but also as a way to create a foundation on which women could compete in professional sports at a world-class level. Gary also conceived this women's professional mountain bike team, in conjunction with the Breast Cancer Fund, as a way to make a difference in every young girl's life.

As happy as I am to be racing against world champions on such a cool race program with such a lofty mission statement, I am still always gratified to have discovered the world of mountain biking in the first place. Racing as a pro has just been an added bonus. Riding, I think, the best downhill bike ever produced, the Santa Cruz V-10, outfitted with all the best high-tech, practically James Bond stuff, is a dream come true. Through a very round about way the sport of mountain biking has transformed me from a nerdy science geek—into a nerdy bike geek—into a Luna Chick. And along the way I've morphed into a gravity goddess as much by accident as hard work.

And also because I was willing to suffer a little more to go a little bit faster.

After they were through with me, the interviewers wanted to speak to my boyfriend, Marc. I had no objections at all to stepping out of the limelight, out of the cold wind and off my feet, and dipping deeper into my thermos of hot cocoa, into the swirling aromas of warm retrospection. I wandered off to the edge of the tower's windswept platform and stared at the colored circles strewn across the sky by the setting sun. As Marc's thick Boston accent recounted for interviewer Spence and the Outdoor Life Network's viewing audience how I had made it this far on a mountain bike, I couldn't help but think that a basic axiom of Euclidian geometry needed revision; that the shortest point between two points can sometimes be a circle.

How did a mountain bike make this happen?

Chapter 2

Stage 1—I Was Just Riding Along . . . When a Mountain-Biking Bug Bit Me

In 1989 I had just submitted my master's thesis on bivalves—oysters and clams, benthics, muddy filter feeders—the bottom dwellers of the waters. For a long time I struggled to come up with a sexy title for it until I hit upon: The Induction of HSP-70 in Crassostrea Virginica Infected with Perkinsis Marinus. (Really grabs you doesn't it?) I was working part time in a pathology lab at the University of Maryland's Baltimore campus and earning some extra cash as a cocktail waitress on weekend nights, which required that I make a quick change from a sterile white lab coat into a black miniskirt, hose, and sleeveless tux top. Large gilded letters, Water Street Exchange Ltd., crowning oversize mahogany doors failed to hide that it was a yuppie fern bar sandwiched in between two of Baltimore's oldest brokerage houses; Legg Mason and Alex Brown & Sons. Stockbrokers and traders, yellow power ties on their chests like badges of Reaganomics, crowded in during happy hour to make time with other guys' secretaries, and to outdo one another in a contest of single-malt hopscotch.

A Friday night's tips were enough to cover my month's share of the rent for the skinny row house I was sharing on Federal

Hill while I avoided thinking about what I should do next with my life. Federal Hill consisted of a few square blocks of "historic" brick houses squatting together side by side around a bit of green park, which sat on a lump that overlooked Baltimore's Inner Harbor. The new aquarium had just opened up on the water's edge and exposed brick, hardwood floors, and track lighting were creeping up the hill from the new hotels nearby. My place was cheap because it had recently been condemned. There was a lot of talk at the time of a new baseball park across the way in the old Camden train yards. I skateboarded back and forth on summer nights from home to the Water Street Exchange, and after last call all over Baltimore when the city was still and the streets were slick and quiet. With baggy clothes and hair tucked inside a baseball cap, I passed for a boy.

I was twenty-four and in between things. The battered upright piano in my bedroom provided some comfort but also was the source of some unease, like a framed picture of a first boyfriend or the worn leather and faded glory of a high school yearbook. I was either going to be finished with graduate school or commit to another few years on some campus for a doctorate. I was going to work things out with my adored, however long-suffering boyfriend, Chuck, or sever that first love relationship loop as clean, and final, as possible. Not easy after five years of on-and-off romancing. I had to decide whether to accede to my family's wish that I meet some nice young man with a promising future and settle down to one of Baltimore's suburban ring communities, or to strike out on my own, somehow.

I was ripe for suggestions.

There was this bartender at Water Street who had been pestering me for weeks the way that boys will. Nothing really remarkable about him. He seemed like a pleasant diversion. He was from Boston and had a thick accent, but since I had cousins from Massachusetts, I didn't think his way of speech was exotic or sexy or anything. While I waited for him to make up my drink orders, I'd watch him move behind the bar grabbing bottles and slamming glasses around and talking nonstop to three customers at once. He was shorter than I—but then again, many boys are—stocky and funny looking with a thick neck, barrel chest, and large forearms. But there were those pretty, intelligent hazel eyes between long almost girlish eyelashes. A handsome all-around frat-boy face. He had wide shoulders, but tiny little soft hands and little stubby feet. Not really fat. I mean he didn't have a belly or anything but still he must have weighed about two hundred pounds and was a wink shy of five-foot-nine inches. He had thick muscled legs, the left even more so than the right, from standing in place all night pivoting around the axis of that left leg. Not really my type except perhaps for one curious thing.

He was funny, although he rarely smiled himself.

His name was Marc Fitzgerald. And after weeks he wore me down. He confessed that he was on the rebound from a serious relationship, but I agreed to go out with him on a date anyway. I never really liked the rebounds.

He was very early, double parked, and standing on my stoop when I got home from karate. Not a good sign. And there was no real music in his car. A cassette player missing a knob was bolted into the dashboard, but he had only two tapes. I held them in my hands on my lap, Miles Davis's *Sketches of Spain* and ACDC's *Back in Black*. Music can tell you a lot about a person. As he drove like an asshole through Baltimore's few large streets on the way to the Bel Loc Diner I tried to figure out if he was a musical minimalist; if he had enjoyed and studied the whole canon of western music and pared that great body of work down to its most simple elements, jazz, the quintessential American art form, and rock and roll. In this case the rock and roll was even more rebellious than the norm since ACDC was

Australian, conjuring up isolation, an edge of criminality, and a Mad Max worldview. I looked at his profile trying to determine in which light I should view him. Making a left from the right-hand lane across three lanes of traffic he broke the silence.

"They were in the glove box," he said, "when I bought the cahhr. We can listen to one first and then the othah. Or, if you like one more than the othah we could keep listening to that one." His expression was blank. Was he joking?

Looking back now nothing worth remembering happened except that on the way home at the end of the night, we played a game where we each named a different kind of tree. It was one of those car games that kids play in the back seat on the way to the beach. This game lasted nearly two hours as we careened in circles around Baltimore screeching his baloney skin tires and stalling out his transmission. He made me laugh because some of his trees were culled from literature and philosophy. He gave them such peculiar names, like the Tree of the Knowledge of Good and Evil, the Bao Bao, and Yum Yum Trees. The Lorax Tree. And he made me mad because he cheated using a whole bunch of Latin arboreal terms, which I think he made up. But his face showed no clue.

Still he didn't recognize any real live trees that I indicated through the window like maple and birch and red oak.

He was a city boy, he admitted, and felt comforted by the warmth of burning dumpsters, the glimmer of broken glass, the peal of car alarms, and the din of delivery trucks. I didn't see it becoming serious for me. A month or two later, he moved back to Boston because Baltimore didn't have good late-night Chinese.

We kept in touch on the phone though. He wrote me strange letters. He visited a few times. One weekend he drove all the way down to Maryland to compete in a triathlon. I watched him splash into the cold water of a murky lake. I watched him hop onto a skinny-tire bike. I watched him slide off the bike's slim saddle and run down a country road. Watching was boring. Afterward he made me laugh about how tightly he was dueling during the whole race with a pregnancy pod of third-trimester triathletes. We drank some beer on the beach and another guy I was dating almost beat him up. Marc didn't seem to mind one way or the other. A few weeks later Marc called and asked if I wanted to do one leg of a shorter triathlon here in town with him. We'd do a relay. Most guys invited me to a club or a concert. No one had really asked me to compete in a race before.

I said sure. But I didn't have a road bike and really couldn't swim straight. No problem, he said. I could either do the run or I could borrow his bike. Whichever I preferred.

The night before this triathlon Marc rang the bell of my parents' house at the end of a cul de sac beyond the suburbs of Baltimore in Glen Arm, to meet my mom and dad, Dorothy and Al. During dinner, we all sat in a circle around the kitchen table and he told them about himself. How he had been a swimmer from when he was a little kid up through college. Persistent tendinitis in his shoulder forced him out of the sport. How for years, having trained as much as ten times a week up to five hours a day, he had developed an unusual diet. Marc ate as much as he wanted whenever he wanted, expecting all the calories to be burned off in the pool. After college, unwilling or unable to alter his diet, he began to run. After lots of ten-kilometer races and a few Boston Marathons (which he never finished because his neighborhood buddies would hand him a cold beer at the top of Heart Break Hill and throw him off his pace), Marc got into triathlons. It was either that or get into larger pants, he joked. He knew that he was just a Super Bowl party away from looking like those guys in the Lite beer commercials. As we reduced the mounds of my mom's expertly homemade crab cakes to crumbs,

Marc explained to my parents what the race was all about and how they could help, if they wanted to, by shuttling us in the car between each leg. My parents didn't have very much to say.

After some Boston cream pie, my mother's gastronomic tribute to Marc's heritage, I flipped a coin to determine whether I'd do the bike or the run part. Across the table my father sat stiff in his chair, one button at the throat of his collared shirt revealing the gulping swallows of his apprehension. While the coin was in the air, the starched cuffs of his shirtsleeves lay flat on the table, the soft pink tips of his bony fingers froze, his dessert largely untouched. Aware all the time that the coin's fall was inevitable, unless he reached out to snatch it. My father is not the type of man who reaches out and "snatches" any spinning object without proper eye protection and industry-standard safety gloves. Dad is an engineer after all. But my mother, I half believed, could, out of sheer will power, freeze a tossed coin in midair with a slight twitch in the mauve line of her lower lip.

In the air I called out, "Heads!" If I'd known that I was about to set in motion a series of events that would eventually result in twin love affairs—with a conveyance and a man—I might have given my choice more thought. The scientist in me would say that it didn't matter—genetics is destiny and all that. Somehow on the molecular level the universe was conspiring to get me on a bike and together with this man. Very romantic stuff.

Marc would swim 1.5 kilometers, then I would cycle for twenty-five, and then he would finish the race with a ten kilometer run.

"It'll be fun," he said. "Salty food and beer are much more rewarding after a good sweat."

I was anxious.

My parents were ambivalent.

Mom and Dad are loving and caring; their five children are their universe. And yet, we kids were encouraged to say

"Mother" and "Father," when referring to them, the extra syllable a veneer of formality that marked the boundaries of our
household. We Strebs as a family seemed satisfied with hand-
shakes amongst ourselves, rather than hugs and kisses. And we
didn't talk much about love or sad mushy things as much as silly
happy things. The love was there, but very subtle in that German
kind of way. So ambivalence was the strongest response Mom
and Dad could call upon to express their concern and worry
about this news, this bike race. They wanted me to be happy,
but they did not want me to enter this race, even less so with this
boy. I knew that. But for them to say so in clear terms would be
confrontational. Confrontations lead to conflagrations and in
our house the conversations were never more heated than a tepid
cup of chamomile tea.

Marc helped me wash the dishes. Afterward we retreated
down to the basement to the guestroom where he was bunking,
and he showed me his bike. It was a Cannondale. He made a big
deal out of it because it was aluminum and "made in America."
It had skinny tires and little mechanical clips on the pedals for
special shoes. There were the normal road-bike-style drop bars,
and attached to them were aero bars with pads on which you
rested your elbows and extended your forearms way out in
front. On the far end of the aero bars was another set of gear
shifters and another brake lever which, when pulled, simultane-
ously squeezed both the front and rear brakes equally. The saddle was narrow and skinny and hard and there was a water
bottle cage behind it for aerodynamic efficiency. I climbed on the
bike while Marc held it steady and pointed out all the equipment
to me while explaining in limited terms, "That's not important.
You don't need to know what that does, just don't touch that.
You gotta keep this like that." Then he looked up at me, "See,
it's simple." I can't say I agreed with him, but if he could race on
it I was sure I could too.

I didn't own a pair of the special shoes that clipped in, so Marc switched the pedals over to the more traditional cage style. I would race in my running shoes. Marc raised the seat height and adjusted the handlebars because I am so much taller than he is and he is so much wider than me. Just get a good night's sleep and relax he told me. "It'll be fun. Don't really worry about the racing part. There are pros here. Just enjoy it and if you like it we'll do more. It can be addictive."

That night in my old bedroom, surrounded by my grade school artwork pinned to the walls, I didn't fall asleep until it was almost morning. But I have always been like that: reluctant to end each day, laying in bed with the covers pulled to my chin, staring at the lids of my closed eyes, quelling the riot of dreams.

I am the only girl in the family. My four brothers, John, Dave, Mark, and Chris, had made sure that I knew how to throw a football and tackle too. My oldest brother, John, had been into bicycle road-racing years earlier, before he became a surf bum and moved to California. He had epoxied together a super-light aluminum bike frame that still sits in my parents' garage with all the other now-too-small and broken sports equipment. My parents had encouraged all my brothers to be athletic, and me as well, to a point. It was just different for a girl, they believed. Only my brother Mark understood why I didn't agree.

The morning of the triathlon my parents had a lot to worry about. They worried about all the cars on the road. They were afraid I was going to fall and get hurt. My mother suggested that I switch the racing saddle for the wide sheepskin-covered one, the kind with metal springs under each cheek, that was on the old Schwinn Cruiser bike that my father rode on the boardwalk down at Ocean Beach. She was concerned that the racing saddle was not designed with female anatomy in mind. But they were both more concerned with my new friend, Marc.

He was not exactly the kind of boy that they hoped I would bring home for dinner. He drove a French car. That was enough to stiffly raise my father's eyebrow. Dad was a meticulous engineer and a high ranking official with the Department of Energy. I know he didn't think much of French automotive prowess. Marc was managing and bartending in a funky neighborhood landmark in Boston, and although he was considering going to law school, my parents would have been more approving if he were graduating from a law school. And I found out later what had kept my parents awake that night. A sticker affixed to the bumper of his car, "Dukakis for President."

My parents drove us to the lake where the swim began and there we picked up our numbers and little wrist bracelets that, as a relay team, we would have to wear in lieu of carrying a baton. Nearly a thousand competitors joined us. The plan was for my parents to wait until Marc finished the swim and I took off on the bike, and then they would drive him to the city where my bike part ended and where Marc would begin his run to the end of the race. It is a universal dad thing to be obsessed with driving routes and timetables and meeting schedules. But Marc assured him that, no matter how deliberately my Dad drove our wood-sided Chevy wagon, they would still get into Baltimore ahead of me and in time to continue the race without delay.

Watching the swim from the shore, I did not understand how Marc could swim so fast with those tiny hands and feet. All the pros were of course out of the water much sooner, but he was in the middle of the pack and there were hundreds strung out after him many minutes behind.

With my newly purchased space alien bike helmet overhanging my head, I twitched beside the bike in the transition area waiting for him. We lost a lot of time during the exchange, since we never really practiced that part. As we fiddled with the wrist bracelets I asked him for any last minute advice. "Just make circles. Circles," he said. And as I pedaled off I knew that he meant my pedal strokes were to be in circles. Not up and down, but circles with equal speed and force and energy all the way around. An even split between the left leg and the right since one leg can only spin as fast as the other. Circles are what I thought about as I headed out on course.

Out on the road the strain of the circles became a constant. The smooth sweep from the top of the circle rounding the bottom and back to the top, while maintaining an equal effort to the opposite leg in synchronicity filled my universe. There was no room for anything else. It didn't take long out on the road to erase concerns from my mind about finishing up school. About Chuck, my boyfriend, who I was struggling to leave behind. Wiped away were worries about what my parents thought of Marc, and dismissed were my own thoughts about what he might mean to me.

The universe around me shrank to the steady squeeze of pain in my thighs, so that after a while there was nothing else but labored breaths and pain and the rewarding drip of sweat caressing my cheek, and the circles of hurt.

I learned later that Marc had watched me ride off and then jogged over to the outdoor shower area to get the pond scum off his body. My parents stood in their weekend uniforms of suburban powder-blue and beige slacks like sentinels in the parking lot waiting for him. The wagon was all warmed up and the grease-penciled map beside the driver's seat. "Shouldn't we be moving along?" my father asked politely. His door was already open. My father is tall, and seems even more so, because he maintains such good posture, like those red-coated guards at Buckingham Palace.

"You can relax, Mr. Streb. We have plenty of time. This is Marla's first bike race. All the pro men and pro women will come in before her, and then most of the other men before she shows up. I just hope that she has fun and doesn't get too discouraged at the sound of all the disc wheels whizzing past her."

I just made circles. I don't remember passing anybody or being passed. It was all I could do to balance my elbows on those annoying pads and shift gears. Even though I only had to move a small lever with one thumb in order to switch gears, every time I did so, my pedal cadence fell apart and the bike swerved from left to right and the other riders near me yelled, "Hold your line!" After a while I just shifted into the biggest gear, kept it there, and pedaled as hard as I could. It didn't seem to be a long time at all. My legs were burning and my neck was cramping up a bit, but I never slowed down. I kept the pain inside. I never let anybody racing near me see for a second that I was hurting.

I guess I am a lot like my father that way. We both keep our feelings, hopes, and fears deep inside. Dad contains it all by choosing his words carefully, ever guarded against letting a "Whoopee!" or a "#@%$&!!!" escape his lips. I always thought Dad moved so deliberately, like he was wrapped in an invisible suit of armor, because any mistake he made would open up a chink. My father rarely played sports with us when we were kids. He did campaign for a few summers with my older brother John on what must have been the most strategically navigated Laser sailboat on Chesapeake Bay. The closest the rest of us kids got to racing that nineteen-foot sailboat was spreading out the sails on the driveway and washing out the wrinkles. My grandmother had told us that Dad had a "condition." That as a child he contracted whooping cough or scarlet fever or something, and as a consequence developed a heart murmur. So my dad was always on guard against getting too excited, or riled up, or finding himself in situations that he couldn't control. That's why he was drawn to engineering, I suspect. Attention to detail, anticipating contingencies, double checking figures, strength to weight ratios, all to ensure against nasty surprises. His influence on me explains why I chose to study science.

Dealing with me must have been, and probably still is, a trial for my father. I am sure that morning he wanted me to race well, but carefully.

When I realized I was nearing the end of the bike race I really turned it on. As I whizzed into Baltimore's Inner Harbor I could see all the race banners and the crowds standing thicker on the sidewalks. My front tire traced the chalk lines drawn on the black pavement, and the few riders that were ahead of me, into the transition area. Since relay racers have a high number assignment I had to ride to the far part of the empty bike lot to our allocated spot in order to hand off the bracelet to Marc. I raced to our spot and hung the bike up on the rack and disengaged my huge, Darth Vader-inspired, helmet.

Marc was nowhere to be seen. I started to worry. More and more bikes were coming in now and filling the empty racks around me and the runners were taking off. Finally, I saw Marc climbing over the orange tape fence into the transition area. He was unwrapping a Snickers Bar. "Hurry, Marc! Over here, hurry!" I yelled. Stuffing the whole bar into his mouth he ran over and we passed the bracelet.

"Hey Marla, are you sure you did the whole ride? Did you stay on course the whole time?" he asked in between swallows of nougat-covered peanut.

"I don't know. Just hurry. We're losing!"

"Well, I didn't know we were supposed to win," he said, spraying peanuts and flecks of milk chocolate in between great mouthfuls of air as he took off running as fast as he could on those little feet of his.

I found my parents in the crowd. "I had to wait forever. Where was Marc? Did you guys just get here?" I asked. They looked me over from head to toe for cuts and bruises, and my mother insisted that I put on some sweatpants since the running shorts I had on were kind of revealing. Together we all walked toward the finish line to watch the pros sprint by and to wait for Marc.

"No. We made it here in good time," my father said. "We took the six-ninety-five instead of Wheeler Road, and then went down Light Street and up that way and parked close to the Fish Market. That way we only had to walk . . ."

My mom interceded. "No dear," she brushed my sweaty bangs from my shiny brow. "We were early but Marc wandered off to find an energy bar. Something about replenishing his 'electric light levels,' he said."

I noticed that the bike lot was just now almost half full and those that were still streaming in were riding much slower than I had.

Marc finished the run in the middle of the pack. We hugged. Awkwardly.

Now that our race was over I didn't know how to feel. It was fun to race, but we hadn't won. My participation in it seemed disconnected. Maybe that was the nature of doing a relay. I didn't really feel like I had done anything. I understood that there were professionals in the race and others for whom this sport was a full-time obsession, but still I thought that we could have finished better. I didn't really see the point of racing if you didn't try to do your best.

Marc seemed pleased anyway, his barrel chest expanding larger with each whistling breath. He said it should be enough reward to have competed. My parents were beaming more, I surmised, because it was over than because we had done well, and yet my mom suggested we wait for the official finish results so we could see our split times on each leg and compare ourselves to the rest of the field. Mom had been the captain of her college basketball team. She still plays tennis, engaging in a twenty-year-long grudge match with a lady from the club. I suppose she instilled in me more than a little competitiveness. But Marc said that the organizers would mail the finish results info out in a week and we'd be better off to leave now if we wanted to beat the traffic crush. During the drive home he asked me again if I had missed part of the course or if I took a short cut.

I didn't know if I had, so I just shrugged.

Then he shrugged.

That was my first bike race and didn't think much of it.

Marc returned to Boston.

I was still waitressing at night and working in the lab during the day. Still preparing to defend my master's thesis. One of my professors was on sabbatical so there would be a delay. At least for another semester. The waiting was unbearable. Almost too much to endure. Beer helped.

One weekend during a visit to my mom and dad, I fished out from the basement my dad's Schwinn Cruiser. Summers of boardwalk action in Ocean City and winters of inaction in the basement at home had frozen the chain and rusted the wheels. But it still worked. Pretty much. I pumped some air into the huge yellow tires and hosed it down with a can of WD-40.

I intended to ride just up to the corner candy store, Sander's. But because this was a suburb near Maryland's famous horse country, amid rolling farmland whose cash crop this summer seemed to be new housing subdivisions, the corner was actually a few miles away. By the time I had pedaled to the candy store's doorstep I had forgotten why I had dug out this old beat-up bike in the first place. My sweet tooth had subsided. I pedaled right past Sander's and on down the treelined winding road.

As a young girl I had first explored these winding country roads amid farmers' fields full of croaking frogs and stalks of corn rising above my outstretched hand. But this morning was the first time since that triathlon with Marc that I had been on a

Checking out my time. Check out that wacky helmet! (*Author*)

bike. There were a lot more houses now, in fields where, when I was a girl, I used to hunt for arrowheads with my best friend, Lori. Though it was midday cars zoomed each way, unlike my memory of the trickle tide of dads driving to work in the morning and then returning in the evening. My grown-up legs tried their best to make wobbly circles on that beat-up bike. I had no particular destination in mind, I concentrated on the few feet of road just ahead of me, enjoying how the canopy of leaves above me created a green-spackled tunnel.

With nothing to do but think, I saw how appropriate it was that I was out here just riding, meandering. I felt like I was just riding out this entire phase of my life, graduate school. Just waiting for it to end. I really didn't know what I wanted to do next. Where I wanted to go. I was enjoying myself, but wasn't feeling particularly satisfied. Nothing seemed to fire my passion. I felt empty. That admission was frightening. Riding these roads, I realized I couldn't count on the world to wait for me while I figured all these things out. So I pedaled to fill my legs with pain. Pain was something real.

And the next day, I rode again. This time twice as long. And on Monday morning as I drove back to Baltimore, to my legally condemned apartment, and to my lab job, it was comforting to know that my dad's cruiser was stuffed into the trunk of my car. It felt rewarding to know that the next day, on Tuesday morning, I would ride to the campus. I had at least that to look forward to.

In retrospect I realize that I was trying to tell myself something, but I wasn't ready to hear what I had to say just yet. Not even when I came up with an even more outlandish idea.

Marc had just finished his law school entrance exams and had sent me a letter from Boston moaning that he wouldn't know for a couple of months whether or not his scores would be high enough to be accepted to his chosen schools.

I put the letter on top of my piano.

After a week or so Marc called and, after some catching up and small talk, I asked him if he wanted to take a bike trip. My question surprised us both.

"To Europe? You mean ride all over?" Marc asked.

During my six years of postsecondary school education I had satisfied my quota of trips to the usual destinations: Bahamas, Jamaica, Puerto Rico, etc. Islands of rum and blended ice and late-night discos. I couldn't remember one trip from another. All my photos looked the same. Hedonism hadn't been all that satisfying. Might as well give athletic ascetism a try.

"Yeah. And we'll camp and stay in youth hostels and check out all the small towns and villages that most Americans can't because they never want to hike too far from the tourist trains."

"For how long?" he asked.

"That really depends on how cheaply we can get by once we get there. We'll make a big circle ride. On bikes we'll be able to explore Paris and Madrid and Berlin. Cover miles and miles of streets and plazas and museums and places where great things happen in an afternoon. And then do it again if we want since we won't be stuck with some tour group." I knew that would really interest Marc. He was always going off about history and assassinations and politics and stuff like that. He was amusing to listen to since he was almost a caricature of the Massachusetts liberal.

"Well, would you like to go?" I asked again.

My invitation hadn't really come out of the blue. I needed a change. I wanted another perspective on this life. I had always assumed that when I graduated from Mount Saint Mary's College there would be a flash of insight; just as the dean flipped the tassel onto the other side of my mortar board the world would be rendered in vibrant blue colors and chords. The schematics that underlie each shape and tone would be revealed. There'd be the scale and units of measurement to help make sense of it all. Parallel lines would converge in the distance to an event on the horizon. That never happened and that's one of the reasons that I went on to graduate school.

Another reason was I've always been fascinated with the

ocean so a master's degree in marine biology seemed logical. But during my master's program still no blueprint to the world was revealed to me. I hadn't felt as though I had undergone any sort of transformation. I could tell that there would be no epiphany on the morning I was awarded my master's degree. I was nearly twenty-five, and already worried about turning thirty. However an easy way to change perspective is to move your vantage point. And since I wasn't sure what location would give me the best insight, a trip would be necessary. I'd have to take a long trip. One without a clear destination. Cover a lot of ground and try to find what I was looking for.

"Sure . . . but when? I'm waiting for these cruel test results."

"Me too. I'm stuck waiting too. Let's stick it out in Europe. I'd much rather kill time in some cool cafe on the Left Bank then in some pub in Fells Point." Not really a lie. I mean we would visit cafes, but not to kill time. I hoped that in some jazzy little bistro there would be a long blistering drum solo, and then a clash of cymbals and then . . . it would all make sense.

"Listen, let's not worry about school for a few months," I said. "We're both working little dead-end jobs. Let's take a bike trip across Europe and we'll camp at night and eat French bread and drink cheap wine. And see Venice and Amsterdam, and ride the Alps and along the Mediterranean coast. It'll be an adventure. But you'll have to help me convince my parents that it will be safe and we won't get hurt or into trouble."

During my freshman year of college my brother Mark, with whom I was closest and shared the most profound personality traits, went to North Africa as a Peace Corps volunteer. His great humanitarian venture ended when he was killed by a drunk driver. The loss of his life dragged my family from its "Father Knows Best" suburban fairy tale into the real world of pain and disillusionment and unmet expectations. From then on my parents struggled to protect us from harm. I just wanted Mark back.

Away at Mount Saint Mary's College I had no one to share Mark's loss with, and no experience with which to endure it on my own, so I "acted out." Mark was the closest brother to me in age. That's the simple reason why we were so close in other ways. I remember as a young girl, tall and skinny, buck teeth, whispy thin hair that seemed to float loose from my ponytail of its own volition, the wonderful words Mark yelled the second he came home from his school each day, "Hey, I'm home! Where's Marla?"

Mark was an excellent student and a talented musician. He wasn't really a varsity-letter type of athlete, but instead was very athletic in a rangy, wiry, sort of way. He was indefatigueable during our long hikes in the woods by the reservoir, and he was a fearless diver from the cliffs into that cold blue reservoir water. Mark made a gift to all of us with his loud, unaffected, easy laugh. I can't say with honesty that Mark was a good-looking guy. He possessed all the Streb family attributes out of proportion, as though he were a type of uber-Streb. The dominant feature of his face was his craggy Streb nose, but enhanced with numerous bumps and curves from breaking it so many times while aggressively skateboarding on his homemade plywood ramp. On that ramp, with Mark's encouragement, I tore a hole in the knee of my first pair of "big girl pants." You know, pants with a zipper and belt loops instead of the little-kid elastic waistband. I loved those pants but Mark was so excited with my skateboarding that I didn't mind tearing them. I can remember Mark's hair, thin like mine, waving all over his head, unsettled and churning with energy, like a storm at sea as he ran alongside me riding on his skateboard.

During his high school and college years at the University of Delaware and Tulane, his skin remained acned and blemished, and yet his eyes were so bright, his smile so energetic, that he radiated a kind of beauty. His ability to dismantle lawnmowers, CB radios, and anything else composed of set screws, circuitry, and split springs, warmed my father's engineering heart. That he was able to mostly reassemble everything brought even more joy to my mom's neat and tidy heart.

At an early age Mark had figured out all on his own that one person can make a difference in the world. The way to do that was a little bit at a time with your own hands. The inclusion of his scrawny little sister into his world of possibility and promise made it really difficult for me to keep that outlook when he was taken away. I was so devastated by his passing that I couldn't cry at his funeral. While I was away at college, those tears remained bottled up inside me. Unable to cry, I smashed a few dorm windows, broke a couple of bookcases, drank until I blacked out so that many times I only became aware of what I had done the night before when I was sitting in the dean's office the next morning. My mom did her best to keep me from getting kicked out. Her biweekly persuasive presence in the dean's office, and the diligence with which I maintained a high grade-point average, kept me from expulsion.

Even after I was graduated, after I had my own apartment in Fells Point and was doing well in my master's program, I still was tiptoeing on the edge around the hole in my life created my Mark's absence. The assurances I made to my parents and their insurance policies covering me were binds that were beginning to restrict and chafe.

I was now at the same stage of life as my brother Mark was when he decided to go into the Peace Corps. He had known what he wanted and how to get there. And I didn't. My parents were worried. They didn't want to lose another child.

I had to find a way to loosen things up. To put some distance between myself and my brother's death; between myself and my parent's concerns. This European bike adventure did sound like

My brother Mark. The "uber-Streb" and my main inspiration. (*Author*)

great fun when I listened to myself. And it really wasn't a whole lot of money. Airfare was the costliest, and then a youth hostel membership, a tent, and sleeping bag.

I told Marc what I could afford for this trip, budgeted out of my waitressing tips. Marc said my biggest expense would be buying a bike, but a bike would be forever, and I would always use it, and he knew a bike messenger who could get me a deal. And besides, he had a bunch of credit cards he intended to max out, he said, and planned to repay when he finished his independent documentary film, *Great Naps of the Early Twentieth Century*. I didn't know which part of that was truthful. But he agreed to go. That was good because I knew that my parents wouldn't get a good night's sleep the whole time I was gone if I went alone. They would feel even better if I were making the trip with a Catholic girls' group, but Marc would have to do.

I was still seeing Chuck more off than on, and every now and then a Seth, Rob, or Ken as well. None of it was serious. Not even really casual. More like fruitless. It was common knowledge in my circle that I was more "flirt than fun." Since I was looking for something, I thought I had better exhaustively rule out that it was a man; I believe in the scientific method and its rigorous testing methodologies. Disappearing for a few months on a bike trip through Europe would make it easier for a clean break with all of them.

Because I was smiling for dollars at Water Street still, and perhaps drinking a little too much, this trip would be a fresh start and maybe a healthy one too. I needed a physical activity since postcollege there would be no more organized sports like soccer and rugby. Maybe afterward, if I liked spending that much time on a bike, I could get into triathlons. I didn't think it would be too difficult during the trip to fend off Marc. I had a green belt. And I knew that we would be camping and that meant no makeup and few showers, and those conditions usually put a damper on developments like that. I'd just have to make it clear to him that I wasn't interested in that kind of a relationship with him. Maybe he'd fall for some Swedish dish. Anyway the trip would be good for him too, because he confessed that he also had been drinking too much and then staggering around his empty apartment with his old girlfriend's underpants on his head. He didn't have cable TV at his place, he explained. Didn't believe it was good for you.

Our plane tickets were from Boston to Amsterdam, round trip and open ended. That meant we would begin and end our cycling odyssey in Amsterdam and we hoped our money would last about two months. It was obvious, especially to my parents, that I had more money and managed it better than Marc. Another reason why my parents' weren't too keen on this adventure with him. But I promised to call and write home often. I even hinted that when I got back it was on to a doctoral program for me. When the wine was all gone and after we had helped load the dinnerware into the dishwasher and said the chorus of good nights, and after Marc slunk down to his bunk in my parents' basement, I had one last round of hushed negotiations with my mother.

Dad was never involved in these types of conversations.

"No. It is not sexual."

"You are an adult, Marla. But don't pretend that we, your parents, were born yesterday. A couple of months in one tent. With a boy?"

"Nothing is going to happen. I promise."

Technically I was still a virgin, as far as my parents wanted to believe, since I wasn't married to a board certified pediatrician with a large private practice who was from a nice Catholic family. And I really didn't fool around a whole lot, but the thought of any little bit was too much for my parents.

"It doesn't sound right. You don't know this boy very well."

My parents were asking that I not strain their credulity. Leave them with a veil of plausible denial that they could hide their faces behind when at the bridge table with their friends.

"Mom, you've seen Seth in a tee shirt right?" Seth was one of my latest exhausting avenues of exploration. He was the guy who always wanted to beat Marc up. Seth belonged on the cover of *Men's Fitness*. "And you know how much Chuck looks like Bruce Willis, right? Well, believe me when I say Marc and I are just good friends. He's not my type."

"Why do you want to spend all this time with that boy then? Alone and far away from, well . . . your family?"

"He makes me laugh," I said. "And, he's pretty safe." Any aspect of safety regardless of context appealed to my mother. I assured her that I would be a good girl.

• • •

We slept on the plane to Schisspol Airport, then waved in a new morning on a train to Amsterdam, and then assembled our bikes right in the train station's great concourse. Loaded wide with all our gear stuffed into bags and bundles strapped front and rear, we pedaled off to one of Amsterdam's coffeehouses where we immediately bought a small brick of hashish.

In college I smoked as little pot as any elected politician, and Marc none at all he said. But we were here in Amsterdam where it was legal and culturally accepted. Now I'm not advocating casual, or for that matter, intensely serious drug use. Nonetheless I have always felt more comfortable in a roomful of Dead Heads than in a room of judgmental, close-minded, holy roller Absolutists. And an hour at the Bulldog Cafe hash house did turn the city into a swirl of colors and a stew of smells as we rode from end to end on our first day. New money, new words, new sounds, strange smells of foods, and jet lag were all jumbled together.

I found myself in one of the world's greatest cycling cities. Amsterdam is a temple to alternative transportation, and riding a bike through it was like pedaling among the pews of a great cathedral, and all the pedestrians were looking at me as though I were as holy and as respected as a bishop. Cyclists there are more than equal to car commuters, and that is a very empowering feeling. Amsterdam is an amalgam of geographic freakishness and astute civic planning. It was laid out centuries before the SUV and other modern forms of transportation, and yet seems to be doing fine. The city is very flat; its only hills are the mild slopes of the hundreds of bridges that crisscross the miles of canals. Large and small ferries laden with commuters, tourists, school kids, and tons of heavy freight ripple each canal. In winter months when some canals are frozen solid thousands put skates on their feet and glide to and from work and play. Along the smooth flat canal banks are bicycle freeways that continue right onto the grid of streets, which themselves are shared with a heavily used light-rail system. I saw hundreds of ugly yellow beat-up bikes that kids and office workers and old ladies were riding around on. These yellow bikes were free for the public to use and share as needed. If someone was walking along the sidewalk and came upon a yellow bike leaning up against a phone booth, they would hop on and ride the rest of the way home and leave it in front of the step of their neat five-story walk-up apartment for someone else to use to get to the cinema or dinner.

We could zip from one part of town to any other quickly and with ease as long as we kept our wide eyes open to all the goings on. Nothing like Baltimore on whose streets cyclists are like sitting ducks and whose only commuter rail system is a dead end, beginning and ending in no particular place. In Baltimore, public bike racks are a gallows of ancient padlocked front wheels and cannibalized frames, a buffet for thieving bike vultures.

On the edge of Amsterdam's red-light district we window shopped some of its strange wares before finding a hostel and calling it a night. The hostel was populated with college kids, rowdy soccer hooligans, skiers, hikers, and cyclists from all over the continent and the world. All united by a desire to take a needed shower, enjoy a hot meal, practice their language skills on one another and grab a good night's sleep.

During breakfast at this hostel I quickly learned the joys of plain yogurt, not the flavored fruity dessert types I was used to on the shelves of Safeway or Vons back home. And I tried coffee served in bowls with no handles on the sides, warming my fingers as I breathed exotic blends. I was used to Folgers. There were no Starbucks in Baltimore back when George W.'s father was president. I met a couple of Australian girls who had begun their backpacking odyssey six months earlier, and they explained how to wash clothes in the sink scrubbing with just a bar of soap and how to slip a clean skirt right over some hiking shorts when an impromptu dinner invitation was offered, and the ease with which one can dispense with all types of underwear while on holiday.

Eager to start the next morning, Marc and I loaded our gear onto our bikes and pedaled off riding side by side chattering over each other's words toward a small town chosen for no particular reason other than we had heard of the cheese called Gouda, for which it was named. What came first, the cheese or the town?

We were eager to tell each other about all our new discoveries like ten-second timer lights in the hostel hallways that took twelve seconds to scamper through. That American electric shavers wouldn't fit European outlets, but did fit their trash barrels. That one of the most popular songs among fellow travelers was Vanilla Ice's, "Ice Ice Baby." I kept thinking of a Steve Martin joke about the French. He said, "It's like they have a different word for everything." Windmills and canals and dikes and beautiful tulips showed the way while on the other side of the world the Gulf War was just brewing and, at the time, I didn't care.

The hash must have affected Marc a whole lot more than me because he began to talk a blue streak about how we were actually riding below sea level, and the significance of the windmills as they related to drainage, and what a Dutch oven was. The day slipped by and I slipped away. I was just learning how twitchy this new bike of mine was. The bags up front weren't as large as the ones in the rear, but still their weight exaggerated every twitch of the handlebars. The aluminum frame was a bone tingling conduit for every pebble and crack on the street. These were the skinniest tires I had ever ridden, and I was terrified of flatting. We had agreed to only bring two patch kits each with us for the whole trip. But it was pretty cool to know that everything I needed for the next couple of months I carried by myself. Hours later at the edge of a cow pasture we pitched our tent and gorged on a round of cheese the size of a softball and some thick bread, and drank cool white wine from the bottle. The further into the countryside we rode, the more Marc struggled to keep up with me.

A pattern developed. Marc would rise at the crack of dawn. Outside the tent he would engage in noisy activity until I crawled out of my sleeping bag quietly cursing all morning people in general, Marc in particular, since he was the only morning person around. I'd slip into one of my two pairs of tight Lycra riding shorts, a tee shirt and fleece, and then try to brush my teeth and scrub my face with what water remained in my water bottle from the night before. Then we'd break down our little campsite at the edge of a farmer's field, load up, and ride off to a cafe for our morning treat: dark-roasted coffee and warm-from-the-oven bread and jam. At a small table in the morning sun we would choose a destination and a route. As the day's ride would begin we'd experiment, again, with an artifice of the local culture called a hash pipe, marveling at its quality of craftsmanship and economy of design, passing it back and forth as we pedaled out.

When he'd hacked his last bout of coughing, Marc would surge to the front for a bit, but then the roadway would narrow and I would scoot ahead. Or there would be a tiny rise. We were still in Holland after all, flat as a pancake. But no matter. I'd pull ahead and Marc would drift behind, and we'd not meet up again until hours later.

After a week or so Marc couldn't convincingly make the case that he was still suffering from jet lag.

"It's lack of protein. I have way more muscle mass than you," he reasoned.

So along with our morning coffee and hashish, Marc added to his portion a slice of cheese and an egg, more often an omelette.

"You see, a bigger engine requires more fuel." He'd slap at his wheezing chest with both hands. "You can coast along on fumes 'cause you're not putting out much energy."

But even after tanking up on additional fuel he still would trail off after a bit and I'd have the cobblestone road or the riverside ribbon of asphalt all to myself. After about an hour alone I no longer looked back for him. He'd catch up, I thought.

The countryside rolled before me. My legs made circles, my lungs filled, and my eyes watered in the crisp air as I coasted over old bridges, alongside fieldstone walls, and through clouds of fresh hay smell. Past fruit orchids and bright-green fields dotted with snowy sheep and shiny-coated cows. Leathery-faced old men were on their road bikes, jaunty little velo caps on their heads, sometimes a cigarette dangling from their mouths. They waved and smiled and then they flexed their knotted calves and sinewy thighs and steamed away despite my efforts to hang on. The small cars that shared the road never were a concern. Nobody blasted their horn or edged me off the road into the dirt.

I wasn't racing or anything. I just felt good on the bike. Maybe the morning hash did round minutes off the hours. It was a warm September, and there were apples to pluck from trees beside the road and I could ride forever. I guess some people are unable to appreciate the solitude that a bike ride bestows. Playing the piano for so many hours as a kid, and studying science for many hours more as an adult, had given me a taste of solitude in abundance. Now on a bike alone, I had the wind and sun and the story of every village that I rolled past as companions. I fell into a rhythm: It was just me and the bike. I was counting about eighty pedal strokes each minute. And my heart was beating at the top and bottom of the circle that my right leg was scribing. Two beats for each whole circle. I could up the tempo as I pleased simply by pedaling faster. Ribbons of green tree limbs and snatches of blue sky peeking through, and the inky-black pavement and flashing white paint of the road's dotted line. The whoosh as my helmet sliced through the air diminished the chirps of birds, and the mooing of cows. A white noise, an empty rush of sound, like a seashell cupped to your ear was all that I could hear and then after a while even that disappeared into the silence of an empty concert hall. I put my head down and worked harder, more steady, with greater effort. My field of vision began to shrink to a cone-shaped wedge from a point directly below the rolling edge of my skinny front tire, flaring out at an acute angle for ten or fifteen feet. Beyond this limited geometric boundary my peripheral vision was obscured by my own physical exertions.

Small villages grew and receded along the way, and people waved, smiling now that the ugly American tourist season was over. They probably thought I was Canadian.

As the sun traversed across the sky the hash's mellow miasma wore off and was replaced by a steady intravenous drip of endorphin. My leg muscles were luxuriously warm and pliant. I was aware of each fiber, it seemed, as it stretched and twined from my hip flexors to my toes. Each deep breath that I took was another puff of energy, another drop of endorphin, the body's natural narcotic. For hours no thoughts at all but this private symphony, in this gallery of colors. No radio waves re-peating jingles, no cable TV beating images into my head. Just circles and chasing thoughts from their conclusions.

In a town square as I sat that afternoon, exhausted and exhil-arated, in front of a medieval fountain writing in my dog-eared journal, Marc rode up.

"I'm carrying the tent, the cooking gear, all the bike tools, and all this other junk. That's what it is. Not that any of it is heavy. I mean I can handle the weight, no problem. It's the wind. My bags front and back are crammed fulla stuff and you only got those skinny little rear bags so you're not fighting the wind as much. See?" His words snuck in between his breaths and his blinks were a semaphore of punctuation.

So, I started to carry the tent and the lantern.

And other things.

One night sitting cross-legged in front of our camp fire in Germany's Black Forest with Marc roasting albino-white sau-sages on sticks and me blowing through my pocket harmonica and us both drinking from tall thick-glassed bottles of beer, Marc explained:

"It's all genetic. I'm a sprinter. At least I was when I was swimming in school. Fast twitch muscle fibers. Explosive power. So in the mornings when I start out I just end up going too fast. Probably 'cause of my sprinting tendencies, and then I fade later on."

I stopped blowing and smiled, "Oh. So do you want to start out slower tomorrow? Tomorrow we could make it to Lake Ti-tisee."

"No not slower. We'll never make it in time to find a good spot to camp. Going slow is really not the thing." He was mak-ing gestures with his hands. I think he thought that was an effec-tive communication tool. "Ya see, every morning when we start out, I been going first and you been riding behind. And that means that I'm doing all the work, fighting the wind, setting the pace, and you're just sitting in tight behind me not working as hard, so when I start to flag an' you pass me, you're really fresh, like ya haven't even been riding or anything, and that's why once you get in front, I can't keep up with . . ." But it seemed to me that his hand gestures were making him breathe even harder.

"Sorry. I wasn't laughing. It's the beer," I explained. "It's really strong and I'm not used to it. So what do you want to do? Do you want me to carry some of your clothes and the . . ."

"No, no. We'll take turns. In front. I'll go first and then you go. And we'll switch every couple of minutes or so. Whenever the leader gets tired. It's called a peloton and that's how the Tour de France guys go so fast. Don't worry. I'll lead the attack on all the hills and even though we'll be making better time it won't be too hard for you."

"Okay. Sounds good to me."

"Good. That way we'll get to Titisee even sooner and we can explore all around there. Maybe we'll stay at the lake for a couple days, d'y'think?"

"Sure. The *Let's Go* book says that it's real beautiful and there's a famous beer hall in the town."

With that settled we stared into the fire at yellow-orange flames that leapt to lick the dripping fat from his roasting sausages.

"Fire's nice, huh?"

"Yes. Nice and toasty."

"Hey. Do you want a massage?" his ravenous lips smacked from across the flickering flames of our fire. Over its flickering and ever dancing circle of midnight light, his eyes licked the salt from my limbs.

"Umm. . . . That's okay. I'm gonna down this beer and go to bed. Thanks anyway. Finish your hefeweisen. Good night."

The next morning we did take turns riding to Titisee, but it

Taking a brief break from making circles in Belgium. (*Author*)

didn't work really well. I was done swimming and my hair was dry when Marc showed up. It was getting dark and it was too cold he said to jump in, so he washed with handfuls of water and fistfuls of soap at the lake's edge. We went to a beer hall and got quite drunk with some college kids and sang songs. Marc knew enough German to make everybody laugh when he told stories about how much chocolate he had eaten in Brussels.

In the morning when we woke up it was raining. Inside the tent cross-legged we breakfasted on bread and cheese and drank from our water bottles. Marc read out loud from a collection of Gabriel García Márquez shorts. We carried that paperback, along with the *Let's Go* bible and one other, some Hemingway shorts. I thumbed through our crease-torn maps. It rained all day. In the afternoon we stashed our bikes inside our tent and hiked through the rain into town and strolled under the high-ceilinged corridors of some museums. That night we slept cold and wet again in our tent, so bone chillingly cold that I woke up in the night to find Marc with my fingerless cycling gloves on his stocking feet, and in the morning we decided to take a shortcut and hop on a train to Switzerland.

"That's a couple hundred miles away and this weather probably won't make it over the Alps." Marc reasoned. "When we get to Geneva we'll ride through flowery meadows under blue skies. And besides, I've never had real Swiss chocolate before."

At the train station we bought a loaf of bread and some cheese and a bottle of Jaegermeister. I'd read somewhere that this particular German liquor contained wormwood, like absinthe now illegal in the United States, which drove Poe crazy and fueled the jazz of New Orleans. We sat in a freight car with our bikes hanging beside a few others, and shared the bottle with two Australian hikers and an American college exchange student as the Moselle River Valley chugged past the train's window.

The next thing I remember, I was standing alone, in the dark, on a train platform. Yellow light buzzed from the train station's flourescent lamps throwing illuminated hoops onto the dark cement platform. Two fingers of my right hand were cut, though the blood was almost dried. I held my hands out into the shower of light. One was clean and deep, the other more of a scratchy scrape. Marc was gone and I had our two bikes with me. I didn't know where I was or how I had gotten there or what happened to Marc. I experienced the eerie sensation that I was back in Baltimore feeling the effects of another grief-driven act out.

After vomiting over the side of the train platform, I felt much better. I sat down on the cold cement and dangled my legs over its edge and began to remember telling Marc how much I wished this bike trip would last.

"All this is going to end in a few weeks. As great as it is. I'll have to go back to school and finish up and then start more school all over again. Or get a real job in a lab somewhere. In a hospital. I hate that smell of alcohol and bleach. And I'll have to drive my car to work everyday 'cause I have to look nice since I am a girl. Girls can't ride bikes to work. You are so lucky. Nobody cares what boys wear. Boys could wear the same shoes every day for a week and no one would say anything, but we can't wear the same skirt and top twice in the same year. And it's the other women who enforce that rule on us. I hate that. I want it simple. Like on this bike trip. Just a few things. That's all you need. Your legs supply the rest. I wish there was a way my legs could supply the money too. Just a little money to keep riding like this. Maybe we could get jobs as bike tour guides on those eco tours. A little bike job, so I could see how the rest of the world lives. The houses here are all small, except for the castles. And the cars are small and the people eat dinner at home, or at the corner cafe in the evenings, not in their car during their commute. I wonder if it's like this in Asia. Or do people in Tokyo live like we do back home, working all the time and driving and buying things that aren't needed. I wish I could go there, to Japan, and ride my bike around and find out. . . . That would cost so much money though. The plane fare alone. But people are so friendly when you are on a bike. I guess that's because everybody remembers having a bike as a kid and that makes them soft, and they ask you questions and they open up. Maybe it's because you pay a toll in sweat as you ride through their neighborhoods that they respect you. Rather than just rolling through in a double decker air-conditioned diesel bus. When you are lost on a bike people want to feed you and find where you've been and for how long. Like that farmer who let us shower in his house. And I'm glad I cut my hair real short. Everything seems different."

My head was beginning to pound now but I remembered Marc saying we could do it, see the world on bikes, but we'd need a sailboat.

"Just a small one," he said. "We'd be able to sail to Japan and India and Africa and leave the boat someplace for big long bike trips. The boat would be our hostel that we could shower and cook in it and store our bike junk. We'd probably have to work half the year, like you said, in a bike shop or as bike tour guides, but it'd be easy. There are rich Americans all over the world who are too ignorant to learn the language of the land that they are living in and they would need our help. Just shopping and buying stuff and getting their cars fixed or watching their kids. The world's littered with Hiltons and Holiday Inns, and I could bartend in any one of them during the American tourist season, and we could save our money and sail the rest of the year to someplace far away and see the country and the people on our bikes. And the boat wouldn't cost that much. The wind is free and we'd just fill it up with one-hundred-pound sacks of potatoes and rice, and I'd catch fish. And then we'd be able to get to China to ride our bikes the length of the Great Wall. Wouldn't that be something?"

That Jaegermeister stuff was also something. I "woke up" a little more while I was brushing my teeth. Over and over again in a small bathroom. I was smiling at myself in the mirror. The bathroom was in a train station. I had been on a moving train the last I knew. With Marc. Where did he go?

I must have blacked out for hours. I realized now I was thirsty. I could drink a river. I locked Marc's bike to a light pole and scribbled on the back of one our maps that I'd meet him in Zurich, Switzerland, in the morning at the train station. Just to be thorough I listed a few other alternate meeting places, some of which, it turned out, existed on no map ever drawn, and added some other dates in no relation to anything logical. I dropped the key to his bike lock into his water bottle. He'd find it there. I stuck the map into a zippered pocket of his pannier. I patted the pocket with satisfaction. That seemed like a good idea. Its conception exhausted me. I wobbled off on my bike to find a water fountain and a warm bench away from the yellow lights in the train station to sleep on. In the morning I was dreaming of a tea kettle whistling when I woke with a cricked neck and cracked lips. When I returned to the light pole Marc's bike was gone. He had left no note for me.

I hopped on the next train and hoped to see him in Switzerland, his face smeared with chocolate and waiting for me at the first train station. In Zurich, I didn't find him despite riding around the station a few times. We'd always planned to use a hostel nearby in a town called Fallenden as a base so I headed out there.

"He's already over the Swiss chocolate by now and deep into the cultural experience of Swiss ice cream," I said to myself as I climbed out of town and into the green hills. The ride was only a few hours.

He hadn't checked into the hostel yet, so I did. There was a piano in the corner of a sunny room that overlooked a high valley. I breakfasted on muesli and fresh yogurt and felt much better. I was the only one in a small room in one of the eaves, and I washed some of my clothes in a sink and laid them out on my bunk to dry. The surrounding peaks were white capped and dusty footpaths disappeared into their distance, probably leading to the source of those constantly jangling cowbells. Along with Poles and Swedes and other Americans, again, there were Australians staying in the hostel and two of them asked me if I wanted to join them in an afternoon hike. I locked my bike out front by the heavy wooden door so that Marc would easily spot it when he showed up and hiked with the two Mel Gibsons for the summit.

Marc hadn't arrived by the time we returned, but I wasn't worried. All along Marc had told me how much he hoped to be in Munich for the Octoberfest. And how this year, 1990, the two Germanies—East and West—would be reunified on October 15. A moment in history. He was always talking like that, *moments in history*, and he'd whistle through his teeth with gravitas. The fifteenth was only a couple of days away and Switzerland was a small country, so we might chance upon each other here, anyway more certainly than in Munich, I thought. I'll stick around here and see if he shows. We'd been on the road together for a while now, and I felt that I needed some breathing room. Marc was funny and he could tell a good story, but he never would have wanted to go on that hike for instance. And maybe the Aussies wouldn't have asked me because they thought we were a couple. Marc hadn't tried to kiss me or anything, but it was becoming difficult to head off those awkward opportunities. Maybe this time apart would cool things down. Before falling asleep that night I resolved that I had to leave the hostel in the morning no matter what because the two Aussies were driving me crazy. Many Australians take vacations every three years or so that last six months or more called "walkabouts" and they tramp around all over in real short shorts and tight tee shirts into every nook and cranny, and these two guys had just come from France and were jaded because, for the last three weeks, they had been deprived of bitter beer.

As I toured the country the Swiss cyclists asked me how many races I had seen Greg LeMond, an American, in. He had raced in that summer's Tour de France and won, again. A major accomplishment for anyone, especially an American. I was embarrassed to say I hadn't seen him race at all. I'd watched some

Baltimore Orioles' games, and a couple of Redskins' games but never a bike race, except that one triathlon that Marc did. But in Europe cycling was a big-time sport and thousands of fans lined the roads for races and LeMond's poster was in the windows of every town's bike shop, and on the walls of many cafes and bistros. Bike racing in Europe is a common man's sport. Traditionally it is a sport of the working classes. Every farmer's son or factory apprentice wants to grow up to race in the great tours. To be a professional cyclist in Europe is to be the hero of your town, sometimes your country, like a Cal Ripken Jr., or Johnny Unitas. The Swiss usually are comfortable in two or three languages and as I rode through the country many wanted to know how my trip was going and where I was headed next.

They told me of their cycling trips to Italy and Portugal and even across America. Moms and dads tour on bikes with their kids. And I thought I was being so adventurous! Yes, since Amsterdam I'd seen skinny-tire racing bikes, but now I began to see also cruiser bikes that moms ride to pick up their green groceries or bread. That businessmen in suits ride, rolling up one of their pant legs to keep the greasy chain from soiling the cuff, and pedal off to work in the bank or office. The Swiss army even has a bike division! Army guys prepared to defend Switzerland's hills and valleys on bicycles! If it's one thing the Swiss are famous for it is their efficiency, and they believe that bicycles are a cost-effective way to move troops and equipment over large distances and over difficult terrain quickly day or night, independent of fossil fuels. (The Swiss also haven't fought a war since popes decreed the world flat, but the point is made.) Imagine Rambo on a bike! What American would pay seven dollars for a ticket to see a movie like that? It is not unusual, although expensive, for a European to own two or more bikes. I was asked if I had ridden in places back home that I hadn't even heard of like

Marin, Crested Butte, and Durango. Those were places for mountain biking they told me. A reverence in their voices.

I was making my way toward Bavaria, toward Munich and staying for a night at a hostel near the border. I was writing in my journal by the fireplace when one of the cooks at the hostel sat down beside me. He was French. He asked me how my trip was going. His name was Martin he told me and he was working at the hostel because it was so close to the trails that he rode his bike on. He was cute. Big brown eyes and olive skin. It looked like he had never used a razor blade. That Gallic nose that gave his vowels that nasalistic styling. Skinny, all hip bones and shoulder blades. Martin wanted to practice his English on me, and with his legs comfortably crossed as he sat next to me, told me his plans to go to America next summer. I couldn't give him that much information on how to get a job in a bike shop in America or what Colorado was like. He wanted to race mountain bikes in America. He wanted to be a pro. But he asked me anyway if I wanted to join him in the morning for a ride up one of the hiking trails. Martin said I could borrow one of his training mountain bikes. We agreed to meet right after breakfast. He had some more work to finish in the kitchen but wished me a good night's sleep.

My first Frenchman. That's what kept me awake for a long time. And then some crazy dreams about my old college friends running me around the lab at UMBC. They were holding flaming pages of my thesis as they chased after me. I was running slowly.

In the morning after a half liter of coffee and some toast with a chocolate creme spread called Nutella smeared thick on it, Martin showed me the bike I was to use. It was the first real mountain bike I had ever seen. It was French and looked like an old Schwinn beach cruiser except that it was shiny and had all new Italian parts. My Cannondale had all Japanese parts on it, and Martin didn't think much of them. He liked the frame though. Aluminum. The bike he loaned me was steel. It was heavy and the tires ballooned up so much that I didn't think they would roll.

"We'll go easy. You stay wid me the whole time and I'll go slow. When we get to the top, zen we'll rest a bit before we descend the mountain."

The ride would take about two hours he said. It was steep from the start, but without the panniers I had gotten used to lugging, the going wasn't too bad. I had hiked up similar trails where you needed a walking stick or had to reach out with your hand for balance sometimes. I dug in. I just kept on going. Making one slow painful circle after the other, each revolution pushing me another foot up the hill zigzagging from side to side as much as the narrow trail would allow when the mountain became really steep. The pedals keeping a steady metronomic beat: left right, left right, one two, one two. I tried to stand up on my pedals like I normally do while riding on the road but my rear wheel just slid out from under me and I fell.

"*Non!* You must seet in the saddle in the climbing. For the tire to bite into the dirt. *Seet!*" Martin warned.

Sometimes I was riding so slowly that the bike was almost perfectly still. I was simply balancing. Then the front tire would come up against a small rock no larger than an Easter egg and I'd be stopped and then I'd tip over. The beat lost, I'd have to climb back on and start all over again. After a few minutes Martin was way ahead, which infuriated me, and I couldn't see how he got over such obstacles. I pushed the bike a lot. I wanted to keep him in sight. Such a simple object to occupy one's time. Keep the bobbing Frenchman's helmet in sight. That's all. Not as complicated as monitoring parasite levels in the tissue of oysters from the Chesapeake. Not as confusing as choosing which boy to go to the movies with. Not as upsetting as acknowledging my parent's desire for me to be safe, while trying to exercise my own yearning to live my own life. I didn't have to think about where Marc was and if we were ever going to meet up again. I wasn't concerned about the phone call to my mom telling her that I was now alone and still planned on staying another few weeks, and then trying to enjoy myself knowing all the time that there would have to be a price paid upon my return for that freedom. Just keep my eyes on the Frenchman. Keeping time with my feet: one two, one two. I was fully within that moment, reducing life to its simplest essence. I don't want to get too Zen, but one of the great lessons I learned was how to focus, how to stay within myself and my experience. Now. Not then. Not when. But Now.

My breaths weren't drawing much air, and I started sweating, and after a while I didn't know how much longer I could maintain the tempo. I looked up the trail and Martin was closer now. I put my head down and the sweat dripped off my brow into my eyes, stinging, but not as painful as the burning fibers of my thighs and the ache in the small of my back—but still I wanted to catch Martin. I hadn't really liked the way he said he'd go slow for me. I was much taller than he, and now I resented the way he had stared at my boobs when we were talking. I pressed the grips on my bars forcing some traction into my tires. One two, one two, the slow pedal strokes were measured out. In syncopation my heartbeats fluttered like a humming bird's wings. I began counting. I'll just do ten more pedal strokes and then if it's too much pain I'll quit. I got to ten and then started over. And over again, refusing to quit. After a while it was too taxing to mouth the numbers, especially the number seven's extra syllable. I just cajoled myself up the trail. When I reached the top I saw Martin sitting on a stone bench at the edge of a tiny hotel's gravel parking lot. It wasn't the top. Behind the hotel the mountain went on and on up into the sky. Martin was a little out of breath.

"Do you want to stop for a while?"

"No. I'm okay."

"Don't you want to rest?"

"Just need to fill up my water bottles. That's all." Walking to the hotel's burbling water fountain felt worse than riding. I was dizzy and my back hurt more now that I was standing up. At least on the bike there was progress for my pains. "I'll be ready in just a sec."

Martin wolfed down two bananas—very expensive in Switzerland—and took a long pull from his water bottle before getting back on the trail. He was off like a shot once more, but this time it didn't take nearly as long to get him back in sight. It seemed the longer the ride lasted the stronger I became. I was trying so hard. Unnecessarily hard actually but I didn't realize it then. What was killing me was a lack of technical skill. The many times that I had to put a foot down on a switchback stole my momentum. Each water bar or rut that threw my front wheel robbed me of another twenty or thirty seconds while I picked up my bike, looked around, and climbed back on. My heart rate was maxing out because I was so much more off the bike than on it. Nevertheless near the top I was riding right behind Martin.

"You see. I went slow for you. To make it easy so you like it," he said as he stopped at a small ledge where the dirt trail turned to slate, a black ribbon in the snow against the sky. "We turn around here. This is it."

On the way down he was out of sight by the first turn. I fell on the first turn. I was going fast, relishing the hard-earned speed, when the turn appeared out of nowhere right beneath my wheel. A combination of too much brake and awkward body English threw me to the ground, but at least on the mountain side of the trail and not the valley side of the trail . . . way down below. I could never establish a rhythm. It was go, then go too fast, and then stop too late. But I felt great. This was something I had no idea was possible. If you looked up the mountain from the hostel this zigzaggy trail looked too difficult for goats to climb. And here I was, riding a bike on it!

By the time I arrived back at the hostel, Martin had already washed up his bike, now gleaming as it leaned against a low stone wall. He was sitting beside it, a pile of fresh banana skins on the ground beside him. Thick blue arteries snaked their twisted way down his forearms. His brown hair had sweaty blonde streaks in it and his uneven white teeth gleamed as he smiled at me. He was barefoot and his large splayed toes were dug into the cool green grass. His helmet and shoes and socks were in a neat pile on the stone wall. I was a mess. I dropped my loaner bike down and plopped down in the grass beside it.

The handlebars were no longer straight, having been twisted in one of my turns. I had straightened them so many times that I just left them as they were. I had scrapes on both shins and the pinky of my left hand was bruised purple. Dried snot striped across my tee shirt. A smile split my face.

Martin cleaned up the mountain bike he had lent me while I showered in the hostel and changed into my little black skirt and a short-waisted top. Over a bottle of sweet Reisling on the stone veranda of the hostel that overlooked rolling green dairy fields and the snow-capped mountains brilliant in the slanting afternoon sun, we sat side by side on large wicker chairs, my bare legs stretched out and crossed at the ankle resting on his knee. I sat gingerly in the chair because my butt was bruised from one of my crashes. It was a strange-looking bruise. There was a splotch of deep red in the middle, then circled around that were rings of black, blue, and ugly yellow. It looked more like a bug bite than any bruise I'd seen before. Martin told me all about how he had always wanted to be a bike racer. To race in the big tours. But he wanted to win races right away. He didn't want to "work" for a team leader. He didn't want to wait three or four or five years for his turn to try for a win. That's why he was going to Colorado. To race mountain bikes, because in that kind of racing there were no teams, no team leaders, and no workers. Not like on the road. In mountain biking whoever was the fastest, the strongest, won, because everybody raced on their own. There was no help from anybody.

He was a nice guy. There was something about him I really liked but I decided Martin wasn't my type. I don't know why. The bruise on my butt was killing me and I wanted to stand up and walk around a bit. Standing on my tiptoes I stretched and felt dizzy. Martin continued talking about racing as a pro. I think it was the accent on the second syllable of his name. Or his strange love for bananas. I just couldn't get over that. I knew then that in the morning I'd be leaving early. But that mountain-bike ride had been pretty cool. He was right about that.

On the morning of October 15, the day of the German Re-unification, I had ridden to the outskirts of Munich and then hopped on a train to get to the heart of the city. After I had disembarked and unloaded my bike, I rolled to one of the information kiosks on the train station platform. Streams of boisterously singing, beer-drinking Germans were filing past me on their way to the beer gardens. The confluence of two great rivers. Thousands of people, East and West Germany, would once again become one country after having been so long divided following World War II. Marc and I had always planned to be here in Munich on this day. But where? Where would I find Marc? At one of the dozen beer gardens? Each held about three thousand drunk *lederhausen*-clad patriots and half again as many besotted tourists. Marc could very well be waiting for me at a prominent landmark, in his mind, like a marble statue of some guy on a horse in front of a public building where an important document was signed a hundred years ago.

At the kiosk, Scotch-taped over the "You Are Here" map of the city, fluttered a sheet of paper. It caught my eye. I reached up and pulled it from the glass. On it was written in messy hand-drawn letters, "MARLA!!! DO NOT MOVE!" And below that in smaller letters, "I am staying at a Munich hostel. Actually, there is no room in any of them so I've been sleeping in a park. But stay right here! I come by every hour. I'll find you!"

How smart. My little friend.

I looked around. Where was he? Was he hiding?

But I had to go to the bathroom. So I locked my bike to one of the kiosk's legs and made my way to one of the station's *badenzimmers*. Scotch-taped to the door marked *Die Damen,* was a sheet of paper. On it was written in those cute hand-drawn letters, "MARLA!!! DO NOT MOVE!" And below that in his familiar scribble . . . "I am staying . . ." It was a copy. He'd photocopied the same note.

The train station was jammed with people, more unloading every minute. I milled about for an hour looking for his face in the crowd, then decided to head outside for some fresh air. Across the wide street was a newspaper stand and a few cafe tables. I hadn't eaten any breakfast and one of those giant pretzels smelled good. I leaned my bike against the wrought iron of one of the cafe chairs in which sat a very fat man with a little feather on his green felt cap, and I glanced at the metal wastebasket that stood on the sidewalk beside him. To it was Scotch-taped a sheet of paper. On it was written the endearing and thoughtful letters, "MARLA!!! DO NOT MOVE!"

Laughing I looked up and down the swarming street and saw that on all the streetlight poles there were sheets of paper. And at all the crosswalks. I was just finishing my pretzel and still had mustard on my face when Marc rode up. Just like in some corny movie, our eyes locked on each other's and we both smiled, felt a little awkward, embraced, and then our lips met, mine mustard flavored and Marc's tasting of beer and salt. That was our first kiss.

"I was afraid you were going to start looking for me," he said laughing, "and we'd never find each other in this madness!"

"So how many signs did you put up?"

"Thousands. I got here about three days ago and after one whole day riding around looking for you, I figured out that was useless. So I went to the library and ran off a whole bunch of copies and taped them up at the train station, at all the hostels, the American Express office, the Hof Brauhaus. Anyplace I thought you might show up."

"I planned on finding you the adventurous way," I said, "but yours was a pretty good idea anyway."

Marc signaled for the white-aproned waiter. "*Zwei beer, bitte,*" he yelled over the riot. Then resumed. "Not really. Then I went to a beer garden and had a beer and figured I would just check the station entrance and signs in an hour. But these Germans are so damned efficient and orderly and clean, that at most places my signs were already removed and thrown away." He reached into one of the bags on his bike—"As soon as I put 'em up they take 'em down!"—and pulled out a thick sheaf of papers each with my name at the top.

We ordered more beer and then celebrated our reunification as well as Germany's.

I wanted to tell Marc all about my first mountain bike ride. How I had ridden so high up on a trail that there was snow that I could reach out and touch. I wanted to tell him about the rocks and the mud and riding back down and how fast I went and how many times I crashed. How much fun it was even though the climbing almost killed me. How I was just about to catch Martin when I ran out of mountain. I wanted to tell Marc that Martin was going to Colorado to race mountain bikes. But I didn't. I was so happy to see Marc, I didn't want to get him all riled up and bent out of shape about Martin.

But I was surprised at how glad I was to see him. Maybe I'd even tell him someday. So for the next few days we celebrated our reunion, and then we rode on to Austria. Then through the Alps to Italy. Along the Mediterranean to Marseilles, where we each were tattooed on the soft part of the back of our earlobes. Marc's tattoo was of an ice-cream cone and mine remains a secret. Along the coast to Gibraltar. A week in Morocco, then to Madrid and Paris. The last bit of Catholic in me expected to travel to Damascus so that I could be knocked off my bike like St. Paul, but no such luck. My conversion experience, my epiphany, would have to wait. Eventually we made our way to Amsterdam and then, to home, to what would be for me a different world.

Chapter 3

Stage 2—Fight or Flight Response

After our bike trip Marc returned to Boston. To bartending and the wait list of law schools that he couldn't afford to attend anyway, he said.

I returned to my row house in Federal Hill. Soon after, I successfully defended my thesis with the help of beta blockers my father gave me. Beta blockers were little pills that took the edge off of nervousness. My father took one before he gave presentations or speeches. I was still nervous but I was able to mumble answers to all my examiner's questions and earn my master's degree.

The piece of paper that I had worked two years for hadn't changed Baltimore. My bevy of boy toys hadn't loosened their grip while I was away, and everything else was the same except for me. My friends all wanted to go to the Fish Market on Sunday to giggle at guys, shoot some oysters, and drink a few beers. My parents still wanted to know what I was going to do with my life.

The bike trip had changed everything. The deep-tissue bruise that I got the day I was mountain biking was now completely gone. Physically, it was as though I had never gone on that mountain bike ride at all. But the effects of the rest of that trip were obvious. I now drank my morning coffee from a bowl rather than a mug. I gave away my television and most of my clothes. American Wonder Bread on which I had grown up was only good now for the rat traps behind my piano. The world was much bigger than Baltimore, the self-proclaimed City That Reads. Though there was a job, scientifically shucking oysters, waiting for me at UMBC in the research lab, I never returned to it after coming home from my European adventure.

Instead I got a job as a bike messenger. Somehow I knew it would feel better pounding away on my dad's old single-speed cruiser with no rear brake through Baltimore's small downtown than it ever would in the lab or on my piano. I really loved being a bike messenger outside in the wind and rain and sun. No dress code. I got to ride sidewalks and go the wrong way down one-way streets, justified by the fact that I was making up for the time I spent being lost. Just trying to do my job, officer. I fortified myself with the healthy mixed cocktail of adrenaline and endorphins. The only downside to messengering was the uselessness of my newly inked master's degree, and the relentless repayment schedule of my student loans that had secured it. The only other negatives of being a bike messenger were the low pay and lack of benefits. And that I was hit by two cars and one truck.

My parents thought I was crazy riding a beat-up old bike delivering packages to offices where real work was being done. Was this a creative way of looking for a real job? Was I also handing out resumes? Was I meeting any nice lawyers? After a day's work of hard riding while downing a cold beer in Sisson's or in the 8 by 10 Club, my friends who had real jobs rolled their eyes when it was my turn to recount how my day had been. How large the potholes were and how close the corners were that I cut. I knew it felt right riding a bike but after a few months I couldn't justify it. Not even to a bartender. I had to admit I wasn't making the best use of my master's degree. I should either find a doctorate program or get a real job. I rode as a messenger for about six months. Then one day I dented the passenger door of the chief of police's limo, which resulted in a phone call to my employer and my dismissal the next morning.

All moves are desperate in a way. You simply tend to ponder longer those of a chess game, than those of life's game. I had to make a move. New York was too big. California too far for my parents' sake. To bide time for my next indecisive move, I took a part-time job waitressing at night at one of the nicer restaurants in the new hotels.

A few weeks later in the restaurant at one of my tables there was a sweet old lady. She called me dear. She spoke more with me during dinner than with her husband, who was refusing to wear his hearing aid. Coming from North Carolina, she thought very highly of Duke University and its town Durham, extolling that it was such a charming city. And it was only a six-hour drive away. After cleaning the ketchup bottles at the restaurant that night, I rode my bike home and snatched a couple of the resumes that I had made up a few weeks earlier and still hadn't done anything with, and jumped into my car still in my waitress uniform. Baltimore was definitely too small. I drove through the night, sleeping a few hours in a Virginian rest area beside an idling eighteen wheeler, and the sun was just rising as I neared Durham, North Carolina. My parents had a condo in Kiawah, South Carolina, near Charleston. They couldn't object to the distance. It wasn't that far away. Durham wasn't a threatening city by any means; a small college town.

I ate breakfast in a little place called Biscuitville, and that's what I ordered with lots of thick syrup, but passing on the Southern staple of sausage-based gravy. Choking on my mug of canned coffee I thumbed through the local paper. Cheap housing was available. This area was booming according to the newspaper. Glaxo, the drug company, had expanded in the Triangle Research Park. Whatever that was. Jesse Helms, whoever he was, had been re-elected. The Durham Bulls, Kevin Costner's baseball team, had won once again the other night. Christian Laetner and Bobby Hurley, cute newspaper photos I had to admit, would be returning as starters for Duke's Blue Devils basketball team. This could work out.

My parents would get used to the idea that I was on my own and capable of living on my own with no danger. Not like what happened to Mark. My parents were never crazy about his wish to join the Peace Corps. The Peace Corps was such a sixties thing and they had hoped that Reagan's second term would never end. They craved that security. My bike trip to Europe hadn't broken their safety hold on me. They had momentarily relaxed their grip only to tighten it harder upon my return. They were acting out of love, but still I wanted to escape from the little world of Baltimore.

In the Biscuitville bathroom I washed my face removing what remained of my waitress red lips and blue eyeliner and applied scientist-muted lip gloss and only mascara. I added a scrunchie to my still-short hair. I'd rent a small house and live alone. The fratlike row house in Federal Hill was getting stale. Besides, the owner had just sent me an eviction notice because the new ballpark at nearby Camden Yards was going to make him a millionaire. The black skirt and white blouse would do, but I stuck my waitress name tag in my small purse and changed my pumps to flats. The leather of one toe was a little scuffed so I repaired it with a black Magic Marker.

This was the best way to resolve my Seth/Chuck/Ken dilemma, I rationalized. I would be using my degree. A real job, not the soap opera of UMBC and its revolving retinue of Ph.D. candiDATES. The earrings were a little large but better that than none at all. In the backseat of my car I rummaged around in my pile of fun clothes and found a black suit jacket. It belonged to Seth, and it was huge, but on me it looked like I was wearing the corporate shoulder pads that were all the rage then. It was only a two-minute drive to Duke and a fifteen-minute interview. The cytogenetics department seemed like a decent place. The work itself was going to be so easy to learn. Less than twenty-four hours after I left I was back in Baltimore, and made it to work that night only having to rub off one day's makeup and rub on that night's.

It was only a few weeks later that I got the phone call from Duke. I had almost forgotten what I had set in motion, and I could have simply turned the job offer down. But I didn't.

Where Durham's shady streets turned seedy on the edge of the college district I found a small house. I signed a lease for one year. At $310 a month my rent was more than twice what I was paying in Baltimore. I moved my stuff in. Paying that much money was proof of how serious I was about this career move. Each morning I pinned to my white lab coat the laminated card that identified me as an employee. I parked my car in the employee lot. On the dashboard I placed my Duke University parking pass. The first couple of weeks passed quickly and were occupied with learning the lab's techniques and protocols. I immersed myself in the work. At the end of the day I wore my lab coat as I walked to my car. Sometimes I wore it while I picked up a quart of nonfat milk at Krogers. I hung that white lab coat on a peg on the back of the door at my little house. I draped my little purse on the handlebar of my Cruiser, which partially blocked the entrance hall, and then I collapsed on the couch and reached for the remote control.

The bike trip had taken care of some things. That fling of a vacation, and my mad desire to become a bike messenger, had really made me focus on what I was supposed to do: get a good lab job. Bikes were for kids. Maybe on the weekends for adults. Maybe.

The first two or three weekends I drove home to Baltimore to pick up the odd sweater and stack of music tapes, and to drop off loving assurances with my parents that everything was okay. I retrieved my brother Mark's saxophone from a corner of his room and sat up late nights in my house in Durham teaching myself to play, imagining that Mark and I were sharing each bluesy note. I rescued a kitten from the animal shelter.

I usually ate dinner, a salad, alone in front of the TV. Once in a while I ate out. But I didn't feel comfortable at a table by myself. Sometimes instead of eating I drove out into the dark country and parked so I could play Mark's saxophone. Most nights I went to bed early.

The lab was a factory line in a research hospital that was funded by tobacco dollars. My job was to analyze amniotic fluids searching for chromosomal abnormalities in preborns checking for various birth defects. If a woman six months pregnant with a hacking cough wearing a Joe Camel leather jacket showed indications of an underweight fetus, the diagnosis was lack of proper vitamins. In the hospital emergency room middle-aged men with stained-brown teeth sat wheezing, waiting for their diagnosis and passing the time flicking Bic lighters with yellowed fingertips. These men were asked by the admitting nurses if they ever worked in a coal mine, never how much they smoked. At Duke University Hospital there was no lung cancer, no cigarette-related pathologies.

For a couple of months I was able to deceive myself that this move was the right tonic. And then a disquieting murmur set in. For the first time in my life I was living in a house without a piano to lean on. I found myself sneaking into Durham's only Catholic church on the edge of town to reel through its small piano and limited sheet music. It was hard to ignore that it was never properly tuned. Days morphed into weeks, and then one evening after work, I realized I was hungry but didn't want my salad. I drove around and around Durham and then back to

Chapel Hill looking for what I thought I wanted. Not pizza. Didn't want Chinese. The barbecue stuff smelled flavorful and smoky, but I knew I didn't feel up to gnawing on some sinew. I went to bed hungry that night. The next couple of days were similar. I didn't want to read my morning newspaper. The morning disc jockey seemed more annoying than usual.

Saturday afternoon I was playing the sax in a corner of the living room and then I realized I wasn't playing. The sax sat in my lap. I was watching the TV. The TV was always on. Always. I hardly watched TV. And now I knew all the programs and was on my way to becoming a Trekkie.

This was crazy. Why wasn't I outside? Why was I trying so hard to just think about work, and work only? Why was I watching TV at all? I put away my sax and grabbed my cruiser and wheeled it out the door. I rode to the edge of town into the pine woods along the Haw River, muddy and cold, splashing the other noises in my head away and bathing me in the drumming beats of warm endorphin washes. I slept well that night, and on Sunday I woke up early and went for another bike ride.

I promised myself that I would leave my car parked as much as possible. On my skinny-tire bike I commuted to the lab and explored my new town's diners and music clubs.

The darkness settled quickly these October nights. I rode my bike home down streets lined with maples and oaks. Lit by streetlamps the reddish and yellow leaves glowed like jack-o-lanterns. Cool evening breezes rustled the fallen leaves along the curb. Past the ivy of the university. Past the small shuttered downtown. Red-brick ballooned and large windowed, four stories tall, blocks long, connected with one another high above the street by wooden arteries, faded white letters so large that they could be read only from a distance, the hulks of the tallest buildings silently exhaled a rich and stimulating melange of coffee and compost. The scent trailed me home past the minor-league baseball field and blew through the blinds of my open window. It wafted across my bed and lulled me asleep, only to wake me in the middle of the night with a start and the realization that the smell was death. Death in the air, through the window, the smell of curing tobacco as the leaves hung in the buildings whose chipped and faded letters spelled Liggett Meyers, R. J. Reynolds, and Bull Durham.

Every morning I woke with an unearned exhaustion. One Saturday I wrote a long rambling letter to Marc, then I went back to bed. He called midweek and said he'd be coming down for a visit.

I took a personal day from the lab that Friday and was sitting on the stoop of my little house. A large bowl of coffee warmed my hands beneath the weak winter sun when I saw his car pass by for the first time. It was a different car, not the French one. This was an old brown Datsun hatchback, which Marc upgraded in conversation to a Nissan because, years after his model was produced, the manufacturer changed names. Mark said he didn't want to add to the confusion. I watched him circle past my house two more times. His window was rolled up so he couldn't hear my yells. I finally got on my bike and caught him at the corner stop sign.

Through the open window I could tell that he was punchy from the all-night drive and stank of highway fast food and spilled beer. His face was a little fuller than I remembered. But I didn't care. I had missed him. "Do you want to take a nap?"

"Yeah, but not until we've painted this little town beige," he said. "Where do I park?"

"Anywhere on this street. What do you mean, beige?"

"From your letter it doesn't deserve to be red."

• • •

Monday morning in front of the lab we sat in his idling Datsun–Nissan. "That was so much fun," I said. "You'll be okay driving back home? You hardly slept the whole gluttonous weekend." Marc had seen enough of Durham while circling my block that he said we had to go to a real town. We tried to be spontaneous and drive to New Orleans, but after twelve hours in the car we decided Atlanta was good enough.

"I'll sleep through New Jersey."

"Will you come down and visit again?"

"I'll do even better than that. Everything in Boston is tanking right now. The bar I'm working in is right across the street from the Boston Garden, the Bruins don't look like they're going to win many this season. I don't think this bar will make it. Already the owners are carting cases of Absolut and boxes of steak out the back door. I'll move in with you. Split the rent."

"You will?"

"Yeah. You'd be doing me a favor. Boston is not a city to be looking for work in right now. I could get a job in any college town. As long as there are lots of underage kids there is work for a bartender."

"Isn't Boston a college town?"

"Yeah. Yeah, but the letter you sent me wasn't from Boston. Marla, you don't belong here. Don't you see that?"

"What are you talking about? I've got a good job. A better one than you've got. I have a nice little place and a kitten."

"Your cat ran away, Marla, 'cause you're sleeping all the time."

I guess I did tell him that I hadn't seen Little Glove in a couple of weeks. "But it doesn't make any sense. If I don't belong here what good does your moving in with me do?"

"I'm gonna help you figure out where you do belong."

"Why do you want to do that?"

"Because if you can figure out where you belong and what you're supposed to do with yourself, maybe you can help me find out what I'm supposed to be doing."

Marc went back to Boston and packed up.

A few days later, for a hundred dollars, I bought a Specialized StumpJumper mountain style bike from one of the guys in the lab. Top of the line with big knobby tires and flat pedals with clips. It came with those straight handlebars with the shifters that sat on top. It was more at home in the mud and rocks than on Durham's leafy, lined streets. To make it my own I painted candy-cane stripes on its frame, red and green.

Marc arrived a week later with a couple more bikes, some books, some really heavy stainless steel and copper pots and pans, an impressive set of chef's knives, and his own bed. That was conditional. I had told him that he had to bring that along.

We rode our skinny-tire bikes on still-dark mornings through the rolling country outside of town. We rode our fat-tire bikes over fallen logs and down the winter creek beds under the long afternoon shadows. Mark bartended four nights a week and I drank seven. I totaled my car. No injuries, but I was lucky I didn't get arrested.

"Listen," he said to me. "You work in a hospital. Go see a doctor."

"A doctor?"

"Yes. Just to make sure there really isn't anything . . . you know, serious. About why you're behaving this way."

Marc was scaring me. He was supposed to be here to help me out not to frighten me with serious things. But since I did work at the medical center, I knew it would be crazy not to take advantage of its resources. I usually worked right through lunch, picking up a couple extra hours of overtime each week. I waited a couple of days and then during lunch I visited a specialist, gave blood and urine samples, filled out forms, and sat for X rays.

When I came from work Marc was putting the finishing touches on the ugliest sitting bench I had ever seen. It had kept him occupied while I wrestled with the doctor's diagnosis on my own. Marc was quite proud of his work. "Didn't even use a napkin drawing," he beamed as he shimmed one of its shortened legs with part of the Sunday paper. I hadn't called my parents. There was no piano in this little ramshackle house on which I could bang some keys. It was a raw winter afternoon. I felt all alone. The trees were bare. The sun about ready to set and the wind was whipping dead leaves across the wooden porch of my little house. I plunked down on Marc's listing pinewood bench and started to cry.

Marc had never seen me cry. Few people have. He just held me and let me bawl. He stroked my hair until night fell and my tears didn't. "Okay, okay, okay," he kept whispering.

My tears ran dry and the snot was spat out. And I told him essentially what the doctor had told me.

"You're telling me that you either have brain cancer or AIDS, is that it? And this is what the doctor told you?" he asked quietly. "Marla, you can't keep all this stuff wrapped up inside. That's not good. It's okay to cry."

I nodded, and sniffled and cried some more.

"Okay. The brain cancer first," Marc said thoughtfully. "Did he show it to you on the X ray? You know. A lump, a splotch, a scribbled Post-It note that says with an arrow pointing, 'Cancer here.'"

"Nope. He said the X rays were inconclusive. I'd have to schedule an MRI."

"So why does he think you have brain cancer?"

"Not all the tests are back yet, but my blood is all messed up. Elevated levels of some white blood cells. Low levels of some hormones. Anemia. Restless sleep. Lethargy. And he said that my depression is symptomatic also."

Marc stroked my hair and didn't speak for a long time. "Marla did you tell him that you're pretty much a vegetarian?"

"No."

"Did you tell him that you eat only a bagel for breakfast, skip lunch, and then go for a two-hour bike ride in the evening, and then hardly eat any dinner and then get drunk before passing out?"

"No." Embarrassed. Was that an accurate description?

"Did you tell him that you haven't had your period in at least two years? What is it called?"

"Amenorrhea. No."

"Did you tell him that you hate your job, you don't fit in this town, and can't get a full night's sleep because you want to lie in bed all day?"

"No."

"And there wasn't anything on the X rays?" I shook my head. "Now, Marla. Did you tell him about Seth? About you and Seth."

Seth was a student I met at UMBC while I was teaching some classes on human anatomy and physiology. Seth was quite an anatomical specimen. Very impressive. He was older, in his mid-thirties, and rippling with muscles. A Continuing Ed student, Seth had been in prison for ten years for dealing drugs and attempted manslaughter. He told me it was in self-defense. He was a former drug user, but had been clean ever since he went into treatment in prison. Seth was trying to turn his life around. He'd come from a very wealthy family in Utah and had just really messed up when he was young. Like I was almost doing. I'd been attracted to him physically of course. But also to the motorcycle-riding "bad boy" part.

"Well, yes. I had to. Seth was the last guy I was with."

Marc stood up and then pulled me up from his rickety bench. "Marla, first things first. We are going out to eat."

"I'm not hungry. I'm telling you that I'm gonna die and you want to eat!" I was very upset.

"Marla, you're not going to die. Not from brain cancer anyway. We are going to eat the best steak in the Golden Triangle.

The thickest juiciest lump of meat we can get in any one of these three shit-hole towns around here."

He dragged me into his car. We picked up some beer and tequila, and with the yellow pages on his lap, drove to all the steak houses in Durham, Raleigh, and Chapel Hill. "He can't be a redneck. He is my doctor. He works in a hospital," I argued as we drank and he drove searching for the perfect blend of affordable price, soft leather booths, and huge portions.

"That guy's a redneck," Mark frothed. "I'm a liberal, and don't believe in perpetuating stereotypes, of course, but I do believe that there are numerous segments of the population that hold cultural norms and societal values outside the mainstream that warrant their own nomenclature . . . so, I can call that asshole a redneck!"

"But . . ."

"No buts. You are going to eat steak. And tomorrow I'm gonna cook you steak and eggs for breakfast. And at lunch you're gonna eat a hamburger. And tomorrow night we are going to barbecue half a cow right on the front porch," Marc laughed, as he pulled hard into the parking lot of the Black Angus. "It's not Ruth's Chris, but it'll do."

"Do what?" I asked while passing him the tequila.

"Make you menstruate. Give you a period. Menses. The way you are supposed to. And that'll take care of your anemia, and your messed-up blood levels. Going without periods is a lazy and dangerous way of practicing birth control. If that redneck's brother probably wasn't the best lawyer in this incestuous shithole town you should sue his ass and hang his medical degree on the back of our toilet!" We had thrown the cap to the bottle of tequila out the window, so Marc propped the half-full bottle against the emergency brake handle. "Come on, let's eat! And don't fill up on the salad!"

He seemed so confident. The lump in my throat was diminishing. And he had been driving so dangerously that I was more concerned about my immediate future than my long-term prognosis. Marc was a city boy. He knew things. He knew that we could drink while driving around in Durham as much as we wanted as long as we were white. He knew that we could walk up and down the aisles of the Kroger's drugstore emptying the whip creams of nitrous oxide and laughing maniacally as long as there was at least one black man in the store trying to buy groceries. Marc had a goatee and short hair and he knew that meant he was a fag here in Durham. Marc knew a lot about how people can be mean to one another.

As I chewed my bloody, rare filet mignon Marc explained how unlikely it was that I had AIDS. "This asshole thinks you got AIDS not because of the high white blood cells, but because you are twenty-five years old. You got lovely breasts. Very lovely. And long legs and you aren't married. All the girls around here got three kids by the time they are your age. You got short hair and you are athletic so he thinks you might be a dyke. And you're from Maryland and that's practically a Yankee state and that's where he thinks dykes come from. And when you say you are not a dyke, he really doesn't believe you. Or he just wants to get off a little while you tell 'im about your sex life. And the form right in front of 'im has some boxes to check off . . . 'Ever have sexual relations with a known homosexual, with a Haitian, with an IV-drug user, and with anyone who was in prison . . . ' And there you go. Seth was a drug dealer and in prison. A couple of checked boxes and you've got AIDS. No real doctor is gonna tell you you got AIDS until you've already had pneumonia and your skin is breaking out and he's eliminated every other possibility with batteries of tests first. AIDS is not the first kind of thing that comes to mind."

I was just finishing my steak, hoping to save some room for the salad.

"First of all you said Seth was in prison for ten years. He got out in what? '89? That means he was last using drugs in '79. And Seth is a big guy. I mean, of course I could kick his ass if I was into that sort of macho crap."

I didn't think so but Marc was on a roll so I let him continue.

"But he didn't seem like the kind of guy that would be taking it up the . . . well, you know, pooper, in prison. And you said he was busted on federal charges and came from a rich family. That means he was probably in a country club where bad shit don't happen.

"And he's from Utah . . . not exactly the sodomy and needle swapping hotbed of the West, right? Right?"

"Yes." It felt good to say yes even though I couldn't dismiss the mental picture of Seth squashing Marc like a bug with the open palm of one of his broad hands, so I said it louder, *"Yes."*

"Good. Marla you're not sick. You're not going to die. You're just a little confused. That's all. You just have to figure out what you want to do. And this," both hands swinging out like he was tossing a pizza, "obviously isn't it. Figure it out and then find a way to do it."

Marc poured some more wine into our glasses and ordered dessert for the both of us.

"You know what we need? We need a program. What's today's date?"

I don't remember now exactly what the date was but it was toward the end of January. But I do remember his response.

"Great. That gives us plenty of time to train for the Boston Marathon. We are gonna run and eat and train for the Boston Marathon. And all that is gonna make you feel better, and that will take care of the depression, and when we finish the race we'll pack up and blow this town. We'll ride our bikes across the country, right to Mexico and keep on going if you want!"

I did. "You mean that? Another big bike trip?"

Marc nodded his head vigorously, "For as long as you want."

My cycle did resume. I didn't rely completely on the caveman diet that Marc prescribed. I started to take some vitamin and iron supplements with every dry bagel. My energy levels soared and my attitude did improve. I moderated my alcohol a bit, and I stopped lamenting my situation in Durham, and instead Marc and I plotted our escape from it during our training runs for the marathon. Marc had this rule that we should run only every other day. That was so we wouldn't get sick of the routine or develop little nagging injuries like shin splints or hamstring pulls. Sounded wimpy to me but it was one of his rules. The running jolted my body out of its doldrums and provided a new daily rhythm.

We rode our bikes on our off days, and during these long country-road rides Marc confessed that he had looked over the race results from that triathlon relay we'd done back in Baltimore and assumed that there had been a mistake; my split time on the road ride was fast enough to be competitive in the women's pro class. And in Europe there was nothing he could do to keep up with me. He tried everything, he said. So during these "off day" training rides would I please go easy on him?

We rode our fat-tire bikes in the woods a lot too, and during those rides Marc was so far back that we couldn't even talk to each other. I rode for hours by myself. Sometimes I thought of Martin. Not of him really, but what he had said. About mountain-bike racing. I wondered if he had made it to Colorado. If he was racing now.

As the date of the Boston Marathon neared we sold Marc's car and gave away a lot of stuff and buried the rest in a time capsule whose general location escapes me now. I bought a 1971 VW bus, the kind with a stove and pop-up roof and a pernicious oil leak. The plan was to drive up to Boston and do the marathon and then keep on going. Just load up the bus with our bikes and sleeping bags and see America. All our belongings stashed on the top in big Tupperware with the word *Socks* painted on the side to deter thieves. We had decided that we had to bring our own hostel, the VW bus, with us since the American people wouldn't be so warm to the idea of us pitching a tent in their cul de sac.

Marc was nearly broke, his normal state of being. I wanted to head toward California eventually, San Diego, finally. My brother John and his wife Elaina were already living there, and I had visited a couple of times and liked it. I also knew that being near my brother would ease my parents' anxiety. Marc's plan was simpler. I'd drop him off when he found a place that he liked. He said he also was trying to figure out what to do, and he said he would recognize it when he saw it.

I'd never gone back to see that doctor. I never went to see anybody else at Duke about a second opinion either. Mortality was so scary that I just put it out of my mind. In denial I drove the bus to Boston, Marc sitting beside me, his mouth nonstop. Denial is a very powerful tool, and I used it to finish that marathon in a little over four hours. Finishing was an accomplishment but it wasn't transformational. I never really experienced that runner's high so often talked about. I think it was because I went so slow for Marc. Although despite my promise of restraint I did outsprint him to the finish line. I thought the marathon was an imbalance of adrenaline and endorphin. Not enough rush for too much hurt. The race, like Boston itself, seemed colorless and mute. The following day we went on a short bike ride through the Fells, a local patch of woods and rocks hemmed in by the hum of highway, to avoid stiffening up, and then we headed back to Durham. After we picked up our few belongings, I pinned a U.S. road map to the ceiling of the bus and we drove away.

• • •

Monochromatic fish in the world's largest fresh water aquarium alongside the Mississippi River in Chattanooga. Nashville,
Elvis's house in Memphis, Vicksburg, Smoky Mountains. Twilight zone in a closed-to-the-public Dolly World. Midnight encounter with a tobacco chewing, pickup-truck driving, overall
wearing, gun rack displaying, Lower Arkansas crystal meth
cook. Me trying to hold up my shorts with one hand while looking for something useful to grab with the other. Marc scrambling outside the VW bus swinging a frying pan and both of us
thinking of *Deliverance* and regretting the choice of this particular campsite. Past Arkansas prison farms, through the flats of the
Mississippi Delta, free pool, and seventy-five-cent beer in Baton
Rouge. Jazz and late nights in the French Quarter of New Orleans. Tequila and Memphis blues on a brilliantly bright afternoon in a dark and damp Beale Street saloon. Replacing a
master cylinder all by ourselves with the helpful guidance of a
cross-eyed, overall wearing, man-child. Meals of candy bars and
canned beans from 7 Elevens, Quik-Stops, and Gas-N-Sips.
Reading out loud Kerouac, Twain, Thompson, Miller, and Stein-
beck. Hundreds of thousands of bats swarming out of caves at
dusk. Alligators in bayou country during a morning trail ride
snapping at our feet. The grassy knoll in Dallas. Hole in the
walls in Sante Fe. A mountain lion at sunset. Mac 'n' cheese.
Fifty-mile bike rides across deserts and through small towns and
along nowhere roads. Sometimes, thinking maybe that I might
really be sick. In the Painted Desert on the side of the road
spraying polka dots on the white elephant of our bus and re-
naming her Vidalia. Huge bottles of four-dollar mescal. Taking
a slug and then savoring a sip of cheap *cerveza,* and then lick-
ing coarse salt out of each other's belly buttons, and then suck-
ing the sugary syrup of cactus candy from each other's necks
while sitting on the steps of a closed barbershop in a Mexican
border town on a sunny afternoon. Swimming and sunning

and unsuccessfully trying to catch flying fish in the gulf waters with a jerry-rigged cast net fashioned from Vidalia's rear window screen. Riding single track at dusk along Austin's Colorado River. Marc fast talking our way into the back door of a nameless little club on Austin's Sixth Street, the town famous as the setting for *Slackers*, beating a twenty-dollar cover charge and finding ourselves in a cramped shadowy vestibule just off the stage with no place to go but straight, right across the stage over wires and cables and in front of blue and red lights dodging long-haired rastas and skittish sound men and jumping off the stage right into the first row of a swaying and neck craning crowd of five hundred.

We acted so cool and self-assured that the bouncers and the band and the crowd thought we were in the band and we not realizing, until we saw him onstage a few minutes later, that the dirty little man whom we almost tripped over on our way through the back door was Yellow Man, the headlining albino, partially paralyzed, reggae near-legend. I had touched him.

WalMarts looming on the edges of dusty little towns like life-sucking vampires. Hiding Vidalia behind a medical supply store, loading up the mountain bikes with panniers and gear and peanut-butter-and-jelly sandwiches and riding up the trail from Durango to the pass and over the mountain camping for the night in an expensive-to-live-in "deserted" town, Ouray, and then coasting down to Telluride for the Blues Festival. Back in Durango drinking coffee in the same cafe where other people were getting paid to ride their mountain bikes in the woods. Mountain bikes hanging from the walls of fancy restaurants in that cowboy town like trophies. Thinking maybe Martin was riding a nice bike like that somewhere. Playing the sax late at night under a desert sky, the notes rising and falling like twinkling stars. Not knowing the day or date for long stretches. Checking the oil and then adding a quart anyway like it is a religion; no questions only solemnity and a sense of awe that this little engine designed before World War II and manufactured when I still had my baby teeth was still pushing me along. Long rambling discussions about anything that pops into Marc's mind. Me not saying much except to egg him on into a foamy liberal lather. Camping in strip mall parking lots. Camping at state parks. Camping on the side of the road, the breeze of passing eighteen wheelers almost capsizing us. Catching stares from children and glares from their mothers because, early on in this trip, Marc lost a bet that he could eat fifty oatmeal cookies in an hour, so I shaved his head with razor blades and dull scissors; so for a long while he was brightly bald except for his chin whiskers. So different were we from many of those we met that we began to feel persecuted. Paranoid even. Then running from an imagined secret police bureau that we, from Burroughs, referred to as InterZone. Homeric battles at night with mosquitoes. Reading *The New York Times* now and then to see what's happening in the world from which we had withdrawn. Avoiding tourist traps. Despairing that the only safe place for Marc's malodorous sneakers at night was wrapped in a plastic bag on Vidalia's roof. Writing letters and postcards that were never mailed. Trying not to get on each other's nerves and always remembering to "play nice." Regretting only a few times that I was so tipsy in Memphis, not from the tequila or Arkansas ragweed on which we coughed inside the jazz club near the open window . . . but from the huge draughts that Marc was pouring from behind a bar that was not being used by the club staff, so that I lost my hip bag with all my ID, and a notebook that was heavy with self-important ink. Lightning storms that played for hours on the far shore of a wide lake and not a drop of rain. Both ends of a rainbow. Rolling Stones. Morissey. Red Hots. Bob Marley. Talking Heads. Elvis. Buddy Guy. Lots of the Dead. Color-coded pins on the map, a National Geographic Club map, the kind you see on the wall of second grade classrooms taped to Vidalia's plywood ceiling. Blue for good music. Black for campsites. Green for great rides on our bikes. Red for the vistas where I gave in to Marc's relentless pursuit. In the middle of it all running into Chuck, my old long-suffering boyfriend, who was sitting nauseous on a bench here on a corporate team-building exercise and me just feeling free and not much else. Living to ride our bikes like we did in Europe. Only now and then aware of the ATM machine's increasingly bad news. Borrowing an abandoned canoe from the roof of a station wagon. Feeling that Chuck had become just the name and face of a guy I used to know. I wondered if someday I would feel that way about Marc. Walking out on a bullfight in Mexico. Coming to a signless crossroad and flipping a coin to see if we turn left or right. Driving forty-five miles an hour, top cruising speed, while everybody else zooms past. Agreeing that there wasn't much country left, and we couldn't go on spending on gas and not working, Marc thinking he had discovered something back in Durango and going back to look for it. Marc saying he'd find a way to get an old sailboat.

"People give away wooden ones in the back of magazines. They just want young people to fix 'em up and take care of them," he assured me.

I dropped Marc off at a bus station in Las Vegas with his bike and panniers and fifty dollars that I hid in his water bottle. He was tanned, and I had been trimming his chin. That and all the riding we'd done during this road trip on such a limited budget had slimmed him down a bit. I realized he was handsome in a different way than before.

"We'll get one," he promised, "and we'll sail away with our bikes and continue this trip. You save up what you can in San Diego, and I'll figure out what I can do and in a year we'll have a boat."

I will miss him, I realized, and cried to myself as I drove, my mountain bike strapped on its rack to Vidalia's front grill, on westward through the desert to the sea by myself.

And as the tears dried in the hot night air I put this last adventure behind me. Staring out the windshield I resigned myself to finding a job and a place to live, and starting life over even as the headwinds crazily spun the wheels of my StumpJumper.

Chapter 4

Stage 3—False Remission

I wanted to do this. Find a place for my life in San Diego. I am going to stop all this goofing around. Get serious. Get a real job and go back to school. I didn't want to be a burden to my brother John. He had garaged his surfboard and built up a promising career as a real estate appraiser. Bought a nice house, hired a couple of employees. He is a sink-or-swim kind of guy and he knew that if I could carve out a new life for myself in California, I would. If I couldn't he wouldn't be able to help me anyway. So after some awkward hugs and a shower I steered free of his place in Pacific Beach. I had to tell a little white lie to my new sister-in-law, Elaina, telling her that I was staying with some friends and not sleeping in Vidalia. Otherwise she would have insisted that I use their guest room.

During these first few September nights I camped in Vidalia, shuttling among parking places in the tonier sections of La Jolla.

On my StumpJumper, the newspaper's classifieds folded over my handlebar, I circled all around San Diego discovering my new home, my fresh start. Exploring is always good. The canyons green and brown with scrub, and the trails that connected the city's neighborhoods, a highway for bikes separate from street traffic. It wasn't Amsterdam, but the sun felt good. In short order I found an address on a dead end with a curvy pool in the backyard and a big kitchen and four bedrooms. The house's surfing, college-student residents must have thought I was a strange hippie chick, but two of them were single guys so it wasn't that difficult to talk my way in. I had worked a lot of overtime in Durham and still had some savings so I was able to give them the first and last month's rent in cash. I squeezed Vidalia up against the house and moved my stuff in right in through my bedroom window.

Too bad. There was no room for a piano.

Now I needed to get a job.

I had a real address and a phone number that I could put on the top of a resume, so I rode in shorts and a bikini top over to a Kinkos in Pacific Beach and conjured up what went below that. My name was easy, but the address had actually been hard. I mean I had driven all the way across the country, left everything behind me, old boyfriends, boxes of clothes, my tape collection, and even death, so that I could type my name in the center an inch from the top of a blank page, above *24 Colima Street, La Jolla, CA.* The template I had chosen from the booklet *How to Write an Effective Resume,* dictated that below that, a column on the left side should be headed Objective and a short sentence with a strong verb and one direct object should follow. But what objective? It is daunting to stare at a blank page, to fill it in with what you want to be and all that you have done. To recount your life in such a way that it has a purpose, an aim, that can be articulated in one sentence with a strong verb and no extraneous adjectives.

The plastic swell of the chair was uncomfortable but I sat there for a long time. The back of my bare thighs sweated a warm pool on its molded contours. I stared at the computer screen. I squirmed some more.

What was my objective?

If I told the truth—that I really didn't know but I would be willing to try hard to find out—I'd never get the job. Any job. So I left that sentence blank and moved on to the next column heading entitled Experience.

That sentence, also with strong verbs void of adverbs and florid adjectives and all nouns in their proper cases, was managable only if I knew what my objective would be. Do I write that my experience was that people who were the smartest, most charismatic, the best liked by their friends in high school, those with the most hope and promise for a future, like my brother Mark, would never be given that chance? Do I write that I was a Gen-X Mary Tyler Moore, and I was going to try to make it on my own? That white people can shoplift more successfully than brown? That I was sure I didn't want a life with a two car garage, a two-hour commute, and two-time marriage, but didn't know what else? That I knew I really liked riding my bike? No. I couldn't write any of those things as part of my experience and hope to get a job. So I left that one blank too and moved down to the next column, which were the dates and locations of my Past Employment. I typed in:

1991
Duke University Hospital
Durham, North Carolina
    Cytogeneticist in a diagnostic clinic screening for
neonatal abnormalities. Special skills included
working with chromosomal band patterns and blah,
blah, blah.

1990
University of Maryland
Towson, Maryland

Research Assistant in a government-funded study
measuring the effects of parasite levels on the ecology
of Chesapeake Bay. Special skills included developing
protocols and methodology for detecting toxicity at
the molecular level, blah, blah, blah.

1986–89
University of Maryland
Baltimore Campus, Maryland
Research Assistant in the Pathology Department
blah, de, la, la.

There was now a half page to go. I had to fill most of it with
Education. It was easy to fluff that stuff out. About the main
thing I learned in college was the ability to write more words
than needed to convey a simple idea.

For References I omitted any names from Duke and instead
typed in the names of the doctors whom I had worked under at
UMBC and the name of my advisor in grad school.

The rest of the page was filled with liberal use of spacing, the
creative use of fonts, and the immodest use of letter sizing.

The two nettlesome sentences needed at the top of the page
for Objective and Experience were still blank. I fidgeted in my
chair until it was dark. Finally, I saved it to a five-inch floppy
and logged off. I rode home and threw on a black sweatshirt
that was in the dryer and belonged to one of my housemates and
hopped back on my bike. I had a plan.

Most academic jobs are posted on bulletin boards in hallways that janitors sweep at night with wide brooms and graduate students litter during the day with their ambitions. By the
time these jobs are advertised in a Sunday newspaper the positions are filled by a recent transfer student, a cousin of a
coworker, a friend of a friend already working in the lab, etc. I

cycled along the ocean's edge, along the bluffs of Torrey Pines to the University of San Diego's campus bookstore, then in front to the racks of student newspapers and posted flyers of "keggers" and campus guides. There I grabbed a map of the university. There were a number of research institutes marked on the map. One of the most famous was the Scripps Institute of Oceanography. That's where I wanted to work.

I had always imagined swimming in a warm salty pool with sleek and smiling dolphins, and that I someday would be the one to discover that they had wanted to talk all along, but only to me, and we'd sing their secret dolphin songs to one another and I'd be famous. That was part of another plan. I'd worked that one out in college during a cold winter lecture on the economics of pre-Revolutionary America.

The implementation of this more current plan to get any job was deliberate. At each cluster of research buildings I pushed open the doors with the knobby tires of my front wheel and and coasted over to the bulletin boards and tore down each posted job listing, and stuffed them into my sweatshirt. I pilfered the whole complex of buildings in a matter of minutes and pedaled like crazy to the nearest Kinkos in the university town center, and popped in my floppy.

I typed in each job listing and its requirements, exactly as they appeared, as my objective and my experience. Whatever they wanted me to be, I'd be. Whatever they wanted me to do, I'd already done.

I know it wasn't very creative, but it was efficient. Honest? Not really.

I then printed fifty different resumes and paper clipped each job posting to each resume, so I would know which was which, and then raced back to the university. It was quite late by now and flung far from the rowdy dorms so the halls of the research institutes were quiet. I opened all the office doors that were left unlocked and smiled my way into those that weren't, courtesy of the sweeping custodial staff, and laid my resumes on the desktops of each scientist who had posted a position needing to be filled. Smugly I rode home under the moon and along the sandy bluffs, the stars twinkling on the ocean all the way to Colima Street.

Dr. Fox called one afternoon a couple days later and asked me into his office for an interview. That night I fired up Vidalia and let her idle for a while so I could be reasonably sure that she could get me to Dr. Howard Fox's office in the morning. Just in case, I stuffed my StumpJumper into the back. I wore my best interview outfit. Light blue blouse with a little color at the collar. My hair pulled back in a scrunchie and some lip gloss and eyeliner. Flat shoes, hose, and a black skirt that was maybe a tad too short for a roomful of recently-graduated-from-school science club members. Perfect.

"Our area of research is in a branch of neuropharmacology studying the SIV virus," Dr. Fox started out after a brief walk through his lab. There were a couple of alcove offices spilling esoteric journals and illuminating the waxy linoleum floor with the glow of their cathode-ray computer screens. In the big room three or four benches were laid out with glistening equipment, dials and knobs, and boxy machines that made beeping noises. Some grad students hovered around a stainless-steel storage unit of test tubes, petri dishes, and latex gloves, and some postgrads tittered behind a giant stainless-steel refrigerator. The walls were posted with hazardous material warnings and the too-small windows at shoulder height were obscured by a jungle of wild green plants that streamed their tendrils to the floor and across as if they were trying to escape from some mad experiment. Same as any other lab except that these people sported suntans. "Are you familiar with the techniques associated with enzyme-linked blah blah homida homidas?"

"I'm familiar with the relevant literature . . ." I began to answer. Familiar is such a great word. It is a key word that opens a door to a whole world of exaggerations, hyperboles, and embellishments.

"Good, good. And have have you ever done DNA polymerase chain reactions?"

"Reactions? Oh yes, quite substantial reactions," I answered. I'd read in a surf magazine that Kari Muller invented the process where a small fragment of DNA can be extracted and teased into self-replicating so that it can be identified, studied, and manipulated in various ways. He had first conceived of this groundbreaking process after taking a hit of acid, then driving home late one night. He had won the Nobel Prize for his discovery. He was now a millionaire and liked to surf at Swami's, a break up the coast nearby. I'd had a big reaction when I found that out.

"Good. Good. And do you have any objections, personally, emotionally that is, to dealing with animals in your research? In addition to the *Norweginus rattus albinus* this lab performs cerebral dissections on macaques as well. Have you dissected any primates in any of your other lab positions?" he asked, and then waited for my response.

Macaques are like the little monkeys that the Italian organ grinders in New York used a long time ago to solicit tips from the amused crowds who thought the little furry creatures were so cute and childlike. I thought they were too. But I wanted the job. Even though this lab wasn't in the marine biology department at the Oceanographic Institute it was pretty close. They shared the same parking lot and food commissary. And once I was in, it would be easy to make friends and network and hop into another lab. That's what I hoped to do, transfer over to the

Oceanographic Institute to the dolphins. I didn't think there was anything wrong with padding a resume a little bit. I hadn't lied about where and the dates that I had worked before. I just tailored the objectives and experience to a more targeted audience, that's all. But as far as slicing open the brains of little monkeys, I didn't know what to think. I certainly hadn't done it before. Fruit flies and worms were really not a problem. I'd sliced up lots of oysters and clams for science while earning my master's degree, but it was hard to get emotionally attached to them. Oysters and clams were hard to get anthropomorphic about, but even white lab rats had eyes that looked at you, and little pink twitching noses that seemed to be sniffing at their fates. I didn't feel great dissecting the pink tailed, white furred, never-once-been-outside-in-their-lives rats. But they were still rats and I'd had enough dealings with rats in my row house in Baltimore to justify snuffing them for science. But baby monkeys with tiny little hands that clenched your fingers and eyes that blinked at you?

I needed the job. I knew that my mother was getting reports from my brother John, and that she would start to worry soon if I didn't call home shortly with the good news that I was somewhere at the university, had enrolled in a doctorate program, was dating a geneticist, and that I was considering registering as a Republican.

"Certainly, I've performed a number of dissections on primates in the past." The number I had in mind was zero.

"Good. Good. If I were to hire you for this position when do you think you would want to start?"

Dizzy with accomplishment, I walked to Vidalia. Maybe I was somewhat dizzy thinking about those little monkeys too. The drone of cars wafted across the parking lot as I swung open Vidalia's door. The day was getting on and the traffic was building up. I decided to leave her where she was and ride home. It was only about a ten-mile ride if I stuck to the streets. A little longer if I rode trails. I'd told Dr. Fox that I could begin work the following Monday. There would be time to ride back and drive Vidalia home over the weekend. I crawled into the back of the bus and closed the door and quickly changed into some riding clothes. A *number* of dissections, what was I thinking? How could I have said that? How did those words come out? Riding along the red banks of the bluffs I acknowledged and then put away how I had said such a thing. Under palm trees, the ocean waves crashing below me, the hum of car traffic now far behind me, I rationalized that a *number* of dissections could really mean just a few. Actually none at all. I rode past where the hang gliders leap from the high bluffs out into the thermals over the white waves. Zero *was* a number. Invented in India a long time ago. Zero was as much a *number* as one. A zero number of monkey dissections was equal to a thousand number of monkey dissections I argued to myself, as long as I meant any *number* in principle. That was the important thing, the principle. One two, one two, I pedaled circles and the *numbers* increased stringing out zeros until I wasn't thinking about numbers anymore. Or monkeys. I was just making circles.

In San Diego I had settled down. I sent Marc a postcard of its beaches telling him how much I was liking it. How much I had enjoyed the trip with him. How we should keep in touch.

My housemates welcomed me with eight ball in the game room and a belly flop contest in the pool. My parents, although concerned, weren't too worried about me. Brother John was keeping an eye on me. I tried to keep it as simple as I could. That's very hard for an American, especially in southern California, a desert of iced frappucinos, off-road trucks, convertibles, propane space heaters on margarita-cocktail decks, as many siliconed breasts as widescreen TVs. There was a buffet of boys and surfers and navy sailors and struggling actors and retired real estate executives. They were just too much with their music concerts, their afternoon sails, their bonfire beach parties and their first wives and stepchildren and their pregnant girl-friends. I kept a small closet for girl clothes and an old wooden dresser for play clothes that Terence, one of my housemates, had found on a sidewalk on trash day. I bought a skinny single-size mattress and box spring and drove them home on Vidalia's roof, tied with a string, then laid them directly on the wooden floor without a frame. Beside them, a reading lamp sat on cardboard that used to box up a twelve pack of Corona beer. I hung a green plant in the window to catch the sun, and from my bed I could look out and see Vidalia's simple polka dots parked a few feet away.

In addition to Terence, a computer freak and road-bike geek who afforded those habits by working at a hospital downtown, there also lived Ari, who was still in school in a premed program and worked nights at a liquor store on the beach, and Roger and his girlfriend, Gina, the "mom" and "dad" of the house who shared the biggest room out back by the pool. The yard was full of surf stuff and bike parts and the diningroom table was strewn with textbooks and technical journals, and water bongs. Roger, just finishing up his degree, was legally blind and out of neces-sity, a neatnik. Roger was polite when he discovered where I had temporarily misplaced some of my mountain bike's head set bearings on the hallway floor. I think everybody was pleased when Roger and Gina lucked into a housing opportunity closer to the beach. They most of all. Some nights when I came home late I slept in Vidalia rather than make noise. I didn't want to empty out the house of all my roommates.

I was the oldest in the house by at least five years. In relative terms that was a statistically significant generational gap. I tried not to think about that too much. For me living in San Diego was as mindlessly fun as college had been. I exhausted myself not thinking about much at all.

Work was okay. A few weeks after I had been hired I over-heard Dr. Fox on the phone to his wife, who also led a research team in another building, "She doesn't know anything! Glenn has to show her how to do everything twice and then go over all her work after she is done."

I froze in my lab coat. It was one thing to talk your way into a job. It was entirely another to prove that you were up for it. That night I shut off the lights in the lab. The next day I turned them on. On Saturday afternoons when Dr. Fox popped in for a moment to check on a minor detail in his office he found me in the lab working. I was meticulous in my lab journals. I smiled all day long. I organized and inventoried the lab's entire stock of frozen cell lines. I stuck it out and by the new year learned enough about running gel sets and working under sterile conditions using the autoclave and hood, and setting up polymerase and enzyme linked immunosorbant assays, that I could sneak out while my experiments were running. The whole lab did. Most of the guys like Glenn, one of my new boyfriends, surfed the breaks at the foot of the bluffs on which the Institute sat. Troy played Hacky Sack. Deepack played a computer modeling game about building an entire futuristic city. I rode my bike. Dr. Fox encour-aged such behavior. He thought the breaks focused concentra-tion and he was right, except in my case they diffused it.

It was the little monkeys.

They kept me awake at night too. The alarm would ring and I'd lay in bed exhausted but too afraid of losing my job to do anything but get up and crawl into a sports bra and a pair of bike shorts and hop on my bike. The ride was about ten miles, longer if anybody passed me because then I had to chase them down even if they were headed far out of my way. Rather than be late for work, I started my commute earlier and earlier. I du-eled each morning with roadie packs and solitary triathletes on the roads, and on the dirt with anybody with whom I shared the trails. All of this energy was spent trying to purchase peace of mind from those little innocent wide-eyed monkeys.

Part of my job was to inject them with various strains of SIV; the simian equivalent of HIV, and then monitor the pathology of the virus and eventually dissect them. Because I was new, I wasn't faced with these grim prospects for the first few months. Then, I was. One. Then another. Then as the weeks passed into months, dozens of them.

What had to be done, I did, but I organized it in such a way that immediately after each step in the process there was a window in which I could hop on my bike and ride for an hour. I pounded away the shame and remorse into the trails that I rode. The pangs of guilt were displaced slowly by the narcotic drips of endorphins that mountain biking provided. I would come back to the lab sweaty and dusty, sometimes soaked and muddy, and throw my starched white lab coat on right over my filth and scrub clean my hands to my elbows with lava soap and disinfectant and acetone and do again what I had to do until it was time to ride home. And during the ride home I would try to wash away all that I had done. This was AIDS research! I should be proud of what I was doing. And I was, except for the nagging detail of the little monkeys. During my ride home my lungs would fill with sea air and my legs would burn with acid and my mind's scientific rationalizations would be wiped away by a concert of pain, the symphony of serotonin, the serenade of dopamine.

When I got home I'd chug a cold beer in the shower as I listened to the evening's potential diversions as they played on the answering machine: nine ball with Troy, music at the Casbah with Glenn, a Woody Allen film with Andrew, the new one: a sailor. Without thinking much about it I subsisted only on dry bagels and small salads. Bikinis, short shorts, and cropped tops were everywhere and I had to fit in. Maybe it was my competitive nature, but I wanted to have the flattest stomach on my stretch of the beach. A girl's self-image in the So Cal surf culture can take a real pounding. I wanted to keep hearing the rewarding ring of the boy phone. My weekends were stuffed with surf trips to Mexico, volleyball on the beach, or if the phone hadn't provided exciting enough offers, Vidalia would struggle to the foothills of mountains so that I could climb high on my bike to the top.

Russ and Norm were two of the guys I met during the Wednesday evening Cantina Bike Shop rides. Riding with guys was so much more convenient than riding with girls. First of all there were no girls. Just a few really. Even though cycling is one of the most popular pastimes in America, despite almost every kid whining for a new birthday bike, there are hardly any organized school programs for biking. There are certainly no mountain biking Title IX programs to nurture schoolgirls into women cyclists. Instead, school officials and cops and parents too, shoo kids from riding their bikes or skateboards on public streets. Only ball parks are built, not enough BMX tracks or skateparks. If boys are discouraged from bike riding or skateboading, girls are practically forbidden! The argument about health and safety is a canard. How are kids more healthy being driven to school, rather than riding or skating? That kids, if they have to ride at all, must by law wear helmets doesn't make any sense. Don't more kids get injured each year riding in the backseats of SUVs? Why are they not compelled to wear helmets as auto passengers? Whenever I saw a girl on a trail she was always with her own harem of guys, hardly ever a girl riding alone or even less likely riding with a group of girls. I didn't know why, nor was I concerned. I didn't really care. Guys were out there doing what I wanted to do so I jumped in with them. And mountain bike guys like Russ and Norm treated me like one of their own as long as I could hang with them. Or at least within a respectable distance.

We three got together a lot to ride and afterward to drink beer. They showed me how to "true" or align a wheel with a spoke wrench and how to fix a busted chain and lots of other things. They were both big guys but very strong riders. They were both tall and tanned and long haired with sun-bleached streaks. Russell maintained a bit of belly from the hours he put in at the La Jolla Brewery. I would have tried to cast a spell on him if he hadn't lived with a longtime girlfriend who was pretty cool and even tolerated Norm riding wheelies on the grass of her front yard. Norm and Russ rode all the canyons around the beaches like they were keeping score of a private grudge game in their own backyard. After every ride they fought over who had been the stronger, who had cleared that "tricky section" better and who had waited longer for the other at the Brewery to show up. I secretly nicknamed them the "Erosion Brothers."

Russell had a fancy, shiny, Yeti Arc. Norm had a bike I'd never heard of before, a Boulder, but it was supposed to be pretty good. Anyway, both their bikes were looking better than my StumpJumper. Even though I didn't have a cool bike and even though I was just a girl they asked me to join them on a weekend of riding in the desert. I anticipated it all week long, but regardless went to a coworker's wedding the night before. I woke in Vidalia early that morning to Norm pounding the sheet metal of her door as loud as the pounding in my head.

The sun was just rising as I followed in Vidalia, dry mouthed and fumbling with empty water bottles, behind Norm's pickup out to the desert. When I parked behind Norm's pickup I looked worse than when he had woken me. They were laughing at me. I wobbled in the desert sand and blinked in its harsh light. Russ pulled open the tab of a beer can and I threw up as he drank it right in front of me. But I was here and I wanted to ride and all hangovers pass, I told myself.

So we rode. I wanted to show them. But the desert is not a place for vanity. It is too unforgiving when not shown the respect it deserves.

Hung over, dehydrated, no breakfast, too many layers of clothing for the afternoon sun, I was soon in big trouble. The ride was an out and back, the turning point a shrub or rock that held some significance for the two of them, but none for me. I was off the back from the start and on the return leg was drifting further and further behind. My sweating had stopped hours ago. I hoped that they were making the same turns that I was making. I felt light-headed and my elbows and knees were floating way up in the air as though they were being manipulated by piano strings, and my bike bounced all over the desert single track. I was a wooden puppet with an inane and pained Howdy Doody smile. Russ and Norm were probably back at the parking lot, drinking cool springwater, munching on watermelons smeared with peanut butter, I fantasized. How far did I have to ride to find Vidalia? I didn't know. The narrow single track I was riding was ribboned with tire marks. I had stopped a couple of times to discard a sweatshirt and to pull some sticker bushes from my Farmer John tires. Maybe I got turned around and these tracks could just as easily lead out deeper into the desert rather than back to the parking lot.

Which way was I going?

The horizon was a range of distant mountains and the sky a cloudless blue. The sun hovered almost directly overhead. I couldn't see any power transmission lines overhead or hear any highway noise from any direction. There was a passenger jet high in the sky but its contrail was trailing from Las Vegas, or was it from Los Angeles or Phoenix? How could I tell? I had a spare tube and a pump. An air pump. Not a water pump. Not a pump that I could stick into the dirt and gush cold blue sweet water in a rainbow arc. I was wearing a big old Bell helmet that did help to keep the sun from beating directly down onto my boiling brain, but through which no cooling air could circulate. My bare arms were burning up. Dirt smudges are not an effective form of SPF. My socks were heavy with a muddy mixture of sweat and dust. Was it faster to walk? Objects in view took on trails as I my head bobbed up and down. The trails stretched into mild hallucinations. To think that I was okay with dying out here on my mountain bike was calming in a way. I could pick my spot. Any spot.

How about that comfortable-seeming rock over there? How many people can choose when and where they will die? My brother certainly didn't. Mark was a sleeping passenger in the front seat of a bus crossing the Saharan desert when a drunk driver plowed his truck through the windshield. What had Mark been dreaming about? Anytime I wanted I could stop pedaling and get off my bike. I could write something in the sand. I dreamed about finding a sharp stick and a wide expanse of smooth white sand. I imagined stringing pebbles and fossils and bits of stones into words arranged on a large flat rock. I could make a petroglyph carving into the soft sandstone of a boulder with one of my quick-release skewers. The tools and the process of writing some profound last words grew incredibly complicated, but it didn't change the realization that I had nothing to say. Just my name and date of birth. No other accomplishments that I was proud of enough to immortalize on my own tragic epitaph.

For myself, I had to do something. If I could ride out of here, that is. Or things would be done for me, or to me, before I had a chance to satisfy myself. Death is a funny thing. When I was in college, rather than crying, after Mark's death, I partied harder.

Kathleen, one of the popular girls who knew how to dress

and act around boys, had lost her own brother a year earlier. When I returned to school after Mark's funeral Kathleen sort of adopted me. She protected me from myself. She told me that the following year we would be roommates, and we remained so for the next three years until we graduated. We grew so close that the two of us were often mistaken for sisters. The saddest part of moving on was saying good-bye to good friends, and to special friends like Kathleen.

During a trip to Jamaica a few years later, our hospitality van was hijacked on its way from the airport. At three in the morning we were all robbed at gunpoint in a sugarcane field. My girlfriend Lori was shot in the hand and the driver was killed. I thought we would all die and had hours to think about it while kneeling in the sugarcane until the sun rose on a new morning. It was a big deal and made *USA Today* headlines. After we were rescued the survivors were flown immediately to Washington Dulles airport and met by their loved ones. I was the only one who wanted to stay as a guest of the Jamaican Bureau of Tourism. Having escaped the voodoo of death I felt like I could scuba to the island's deepest depths, crawl into the darkest caves, disco in the dodgiest clubs with impunity. And I did.

And now I knew I could leave my bike on the trail and walk into the desert cactus never to be found. Just like hopping on a small boat and sailing away and leaving all this behind like Marc was always talking about. Disappear and what was the difference? But fading away in slow anonymity wasn't a fantasy that truly appealed to my vain sense of self. There was some riding I had to do.

So I kept on pedaling, and whether it was severe dehydration or heat stroke, the desert began to sing to me. I felt like I had super powers of single tracking. If ever there was a mountain bike race where you had to stick splinters up your fingernails at each lap I'd win. If ever there was a contest to see who could ride the longest on a saddle made out of carpet tacks, I'd win. I just kept making circles in the desert. Whichever way I rode it was always single track and never an access road. Delirious, I kept on pedaling, and when I did make it to the spot where we had parked our cars, Norm and Russ took me off my bike and sat me down in Vidalia's shade and streamed water bottle after water bottle of cool water into me. There were no peanut butter-smothered watermelons, only plasticy-tasting energy bars, oatmeal and apple flavored, but I chewed their elastic granules into a viscous bolus and swallowed them down.

That was the morning ride.

We sat around our little campfire that night, the boys drinking beer and me sticking to water as Russ and Norm teased me.

"Marla, I can't believe you hung in there like that. Especially after the way you looked this morning. We thought you were gonna die out there. Didn't we Norm?" Russ was shaking his head, blonde floppy strands of hair, good naturedly, like a yellow lab.

"Yeah, we thought we'd have to mail some Hallmark cards to the family, and we were fighting over who was gonna be stuck driving your bus back to the beach." Norm's long frame was sprawled out on the sand against the night sky, a very effective windbreak. I was cold, as usual. So I hunkered down closer to the fire grateful for Norm's long limbs every time a gust of wind flickered the fire's flames.

"But you rode much better this evening, much smarter too," Russ said. He was the sensitive type. We all had gone on a short moonlit night ride after devouring our campfire chicken, scorched potatoes, and corn on the cob. "You even took along a water bottle," he reminded me making me feel better. Russ has kind eyes.

I deserved all the ribbing. The experience was an eye opener. Especially the morning ride. I went slower and paced myself

Me with the "Erosion Brothers," from left to right: Russ, Norm, and John. (*Author*)

more during the second ride. I drank a lot more water too. The evening ride wasn't that hard. These guys were so cool I felt lucky just to be riding and hanging out with them. From all the years of being the only girl in science class or working in a lab I was used to hanging out with guys. But these guys were real mountain bikers.

"There's a race next weekend at Camp Pendleton. You should go if you think your bus can make it. Me and Russ are going."

"A race, huh?"

"Yeah, you should do it. Enter the beginner class," advised

Russell. "I bet you'll have fun. We're racing expert," he said with a raised eyebrow that imparted the gravity of his commitment to the sport.

"Yeah, I'm going," said Norm, "but I'm not wearing those faggoty-ass shorts that you wear," he cracked, throwing a plastic bottle of springwater at Russell.

"Cut it out!"

"Make me."

I climbed into Vidalia to sleep. Their voices were a lullaby.

"I'll throw the rest of the beer into the fire."

"I don't care."

It took a while but I started to drift off.

"You'll care tomorrow when you don't have any after the ride."

"No I won't. I'll buy some on the way home and you'll have to ride in Marla's bus and she goes slow and I won't give you any of my beer."

My last waking thought was that I am hanging out with real mountain bikers.

Chapter 5

Stage 4—How I Was Initated into a Tribe of Mountain-Bike Racers

For one week I was gloriously obsessed with the idea of this race. I was an automaton at work, which was the best way to experiment with the monkeys, all my thoughts focused on the upcoming race. Didn't drink for the whole week except for the Wednesday pitcher-n-pool night at the Tiki Hut, after the Cantina evening ride.

I had planned to drive the sixty miles to Camp Pendleton and practice the course and then camp that night and be fresh Sunday morning for my beginner class cross-country race. When Vidalia didn't start, I had to switch to Plan B. Every owner of a 1971 camper bus should have a Plan B.

I fished the touring rack for my bike out of the closet and stuffed the panniers with a tent and sleeping bag and camping stuff. I could ride to Pendleton in a couple of hours, and there really wasn't much difference in terms of comfort between sleeping in Vidalia and in my tent, and besides I'd get a good workout.

Recently I had bought my first *Mountain Bike* magazine and on its glossy pages I saw pictures of John Tomac, my new hero, wearing plain black socks. That's what I wore now as I pedaled furiously hopping from one group of weekend, pot-bellied road riders to the next, my panniers bulging wide with a camp stove and boxed spaghetti. Arriving hours later at the still-empty parking lot, I found a spot a little bit away from all the expected action to pitch my tent.

I peeked out of my tent early the next morning and saw that a gypsy/carnival camp had sprung up all around me. I crawled out of my tent into this strange world and fumbled getting on my bike, burdened with a full bladder. I rode through the parking lot past pods of black skin-tight shorts looking for a Porta-John or convenient row of secluded bushes. I dodged the jutting horns of bar ends, a new invention that stuck out from the ends of the handlebar at a perpendicular angle designed to give the rider a stronger purchase while climbing up hills. I wheeled among milling groups of testosterone-bathed boys bouncing up and down pogo style on their Rock Shox front forks. Some guys had their bikes clamped into work stands and were adjusting their stems and seat posts and gel-filled saddles. Manufacturers' logos screamed for attention from hot pink and Day-Glo orange jerseys on the chests of buffed and tanned cyclists. A war of dark wraparound sunglasses was waged under egg-shaped helmets, it seemed, as each rider tried his best to mimic an Imperial Storm Trooper, even to the deep aspirations punctuating their speech. I couldn't find Norm and Russ through the thin film of clay dust raised by the thousands of fat tires warming up for the race. At the promoter's tent I signed up for a one-day NORBA (National Off-Road Bike Association) beginner's license, and finally squeezed into an overfilled Porta-John.

Anybody can enter a NORBA race by purchasing a one-day license for about ten bucks and then whatever the entry fee might be. No more than twenty or so for the beginner class. The one-day license gives you a taste of racing and protects the race promoter from getting sued if you get hurt. If mountain biking was really dangerous there would be no insurance coverage at all, so rest assured that ninety-nine percent of injuries are ego damage.

I had a couple of hours to kill so back at Camp Marla I chewed a cold bagel smeared with mostly fat-free peanut butter and then got on course to do a lap. Mostly I practiced this one tricky section where I had to roll down a loose rocky ribbon of dirt into a dry creek bed of toaster-sized stones and then snake up the bramble and stump-strewn other side. The first few times I fell as I headed down into the creek bed. Carrying too much speed, I hit the brakes and locked up my front wheel, which threw my rear wheel and me with it into the air, performing a painful "endo."

I had forgotten what I believed to be the cardinal rule of mountain biking. No brakes.

So the next few times I didn't use the brakes at all. I just let the bike carry me down the slope in a controlled free fall. That's something that kids learn to do almost instinctively. Like throw a Frisbee or dribble a basketball. Those lessons learned at an early age are very difficult to absorb when you are older. When your bones aren't as soft and your musculature not as flexible and scabs, bruises, and scrapes are much more of a concern.

Trying to do something for the first time at an older age is not impossible. Maybe just a little harder. And sometimes being a little older works in your favor. How many fifteen-year-olds do you see running marathons or swimming the English Channel? It's not that they don't have the strength or the endurance; they don't have the mindset. They lack concentration and focus. It would be more likely for a septuagenarian to run a marathon than for a seventeen-year-old to bounce a tennis ball against a curb for four hours; the teenager would quit out of boredom.

So I was trying to focus on how to get through this creek bed even if it took me all morning. I was doing okay just letting go and then bouncing down into the rock-strewn creek bed letting my unchecked speed carry me right up the other side until I slammed into one rock too hard and front flatted.

"Damn!" I had one spare tube with me and I was saving that in case I flatted during the race. I finally found the two tiny holes, which were side by side like the puncture marks of a snake bite, and was pressing the patch, making sure the smelly glue was oozing out all sides evenly when, "Hey you aren't gonna race on that are you?" said a voice from nowhere.

"Well, yeah," I said aloud squinting up into the sun. Who was talking to me?

"Don't you have a new tube?" the voice intoned, just a hint of reprobation.

"Yeah. Right here." I reached into the bag under my saddle. I held up to the voice the inner tube still in its cardboard box. "I bought it yesterday, but if I use it now and I get a flat during the race, it'll take me forever to fix it," I said, blinking out of the shadows into the sun. Back then I wore the goofiest Styrofoam helmet and under that a baseball hat. My ponytail stuck out the back of the hat through the hole made by the adjusting strap. And sticking out the front of my bike helmet was the sweat-stained bill of the baseball hat, which flopped down and blocked my view all the time and was supposed to keep the sun out of my eyes. I twisted the bill of my hat and strained to see the figure that owned that voice.

Standing over the gleaming unpainted aluminum top tube of his bike the figure reached around to the back of his tight sleeveless jersey and pulled out a tube folded neatly with a rubber band. That was a good place for a pocket, in the back of a shirt, I thought. I was wearing a tee shirt twisted with tie-dyed colors. It was too big and the sleeves were rolled to my skinny shoulders, but it didn't ride up my back when I was hunched over with effort pedaling my bike. Maybe because I was standing down in the creek bed, and he was up high on its bank, that I was aware of his authority. Maybe because the morning sun's sharp angle delineated his features: tall, angular, purposeful. His form-fitting shorts and top rippled with potential energy and his shirt was emblazoned with a giant logo in the middle of his chest. A superhero.

"Here, take this," he said, and tossed down to me a tube. His voice was reassuringly deep. His words were measured in between the deep bellows of his chest.

So great was his goodwill toward me that I felt like I could not meet his gaze so I fixed on his calves, which were at eye level. Smoothly shaved skin wrapped his gastronemus and tibealis beautifulness tightly, so that the veins and knotted ligaments and twisting tendons stood out like a choice cut of meat in vacuum-packed plastic wrap. I reached into my saddlebag and pulled out the five dollar bill that I secreted there along with a tube of red lipstick for emergencies.

"Thanks a lot."

I tried to hand him my emergency money. It was a little extra and he probably wouldn't have change but I didn't mind paying a small premium for the convenience and security of racing on a fresh tube. I should ask him something else. What is his name? Hi! My name is Marla. Are you racing today? That's dumb. Of course he's racing today. Should I ask him if it's okay if I ride the course with him? Would he wait for me to fix my flat? Would I slow him down?

"That's okay," he said, smiling. "But, I'm all," he said, making an elaborate facial gesture whose total meaning was lost to me because his features were hidden behind his wraparound Oakley sunglasses, "fully sponsored. I got like mega tubes at home so, no worries."

"Sponsored?" I asked. I had been wondering why everybody had corporate names on their chests and corporate stickers on the windows of their cars. Oakley, Onza, Specialized, Yeti, and others even more obscure to me than those. How does he do that? Could he tell me how to do that? Is there a secret password you leave on a bike company's answering machine and then you get a new bike shipped next day priority?

"I'm all," he said, this time a vigorous pantomime of Christmas morning present opening, "the UPS boxes every week with like, tubes and tires and stuff." Then he smiled. He smiled right at me. "But, gotta keep my heart rate up. Good luck." And then he clipped into his little pedals and grabbed onto his cowhorn bar ends and scooted off down the trail disappearing into the dust.

Wow that's pretty cool, I thought, as I put my wheel back on. My first pro. You'd probably have to be pretty good to be sponsored, I thought. How good? Could I ever be that good? I wondered as I climbed back on my bike and rode upstream. I needed some riding room to develop enough speed to roll up the bank and out onto the other side, but I was in the wrong gear, and almost at the top lost all my speed and began to lean over to the right in slow motion, and couldn't get my sneaker out of its old-style metal cage fast enough, so I fell over again.

I learned a lot during that practice lap.

The race itself was a personal challenge. All the different groups assorted according to their respective colored number plates lined up one behind the other, all of us racing our own races for varying numbers of laps.

During the race I had no idea how I was doing as guys were passing me on both the left and right, but I imagined that there were girls right behind me and if I eased up the slightest bit they too, would whiz by me. Noisy flashes and images of sounds filled my head even as my legs began to cramp. I passed a couple of girls, even some guys, but I was really surprised to learn after the race that I had won my class, beginners, by many minutes. I climbed to the top of the podium, and had my picture taken.

When I was given my ribboned medal my knees were weaker than at any time on the course. I had raced hard and tried my best, and it had hurt, but I had never let up. I had won and it felt great! For all my neophyte fumblings and prerace foibles, I had done okay. More than okay. But it would take a while before I could make sense of it all.

I wanted to wear my medal all around the parking lot as I looked for Norm and Russ. But I knew that would be dorky. I couldn't find them and I really didn't know too many other guys. I wanted to thank my hero pro who had given me the tube, but I couldn't find him either. So I packed up my stuff and loaded up my bike for the ride back to La Jolla.

It was just getting dark back at the house and we all celebrated with a couple of beers, my housemates happy for me. "Hurry up and shower," Ari implored me. "We're waiting for you so we can all go to Coasters. It's two-for-one night!"

"I'm not going to Coasters. I have to get up early and train."

"What are you talking about? You love Coasters!" Terence objected.

"I don't love Coasters. I just go there. There's another race next weekend in Alpine and I have to get ready for it."

Too weak to resist their chanting "Coasters! Coasters! Coasters!" it was very late when I got home as it was so many times then. I called Marc despite the hour to tell him the good news about my race. I told him about pro riders, about how cool it would be to ride full time.

Marc told me that I could compete with and beat anyone in Durango. Though drunk, I still had to discount what a guy says when he wants to get with you, even if he was a thousand miles away.

"I'm telling you, you are faster than a lot of these pros. Not right now, but after a few more races you can be. Here in Durango when you're buying milk at City Market you get ride re-

On top of the podium at a California amateur series race. (*Author*)

ports about everybody . . . how Travis and Daryl were dropping
Bob Roll, by how much Julie gapped Ruthie on the climb to Pur-
gatory. In the coffee shop you hear what crazy new stuff Her-
bold has been testing. How many different bikes the UPS guy

dropped off at Tomac's house. Mountain-bike racing is what this town is all about."

"Well, this was only my first race, and it's only for fun. I'm really busy at the lab."

"Working in a lab you might as well be in Durham or even Baltimore. Didn't you get anything out of our trips? You should try to become a pro. A pro mountain-bike racer, and if it doesn't work out who cares? At least you tried. And then you can stick your head into an electron microscope satisfied that you failed. A great big failure can be as important to a person as any run of the mill victory. Look what Gallipoli did to Churchill. Changed everything."

Marc loses me sometimes when he talks about history, but I had to admit he was pretty much an authority on failure. And besides, being a pro sounded cool, but I wasn't sure how I felt about having to wear all those logos. Wouldn't that make me a sell-out? Wouldn't I be trading what I love most about mountain biking—the freedom, the sense of empowerment and rebellion from following the unconventional path—if I had to wear a uniform? Like if I was working at McDonald's? I was getting sleepy and didn't want to talk about biking anymore.

"What are you doing? What are you doing in Durango anyway? What are you up to?"

"I don't really want to tell you too much about it. This isn't a secure line. But I can tell you this much . . . down in the basement I am growing our forty-foot sailboat."

• • •

The next weekend I chalked up another win in the beginner class and immediately considered myself to be a "sport" rider—the next level up. I was now a mountain-bike racer obsessed with mountain-bike racing. I threw myself into racing and began a training journal into which I have made an entry every day now for almost a decade.

In it I chronicled my waking heart rate and my daily weight and my caloric intake and the intensity and duration of the day's training. Over that summer my long and smooth cocktail waitress legs began to morph into sharply defined, purposely built, black and blue, dermabraised, athlete's limbs. I sought out new friends. People who interested me because they stressed their lactic threshold, knew great single-track trails in southern California and were willing to show a girl the ropes. On a date, in the passenger seat en route to the movies, I'd keep one eye out the window focused on the suburban San Diego canyons that we zoomed past, scouting for single-track trails that I hadn't seen before, while my date might drone on about boring stuff like an upcoming IPO at the genetic lab he was working in. In my lab while pimpling petri dishes with pipettes, I daydreamed in increments. My professed goal was to be good enough to win a race as an "expert" level racer. Only on long training rides did I dream of being a top pro. We all do stuff like that. Like sing real loud in the shower with your eyes closed, just you and Mick Jagger. Or while you're driving your car and weaving through traffic, you imagine that you're in a contest to see who the best driver is. Doesn't everyone think that? That's mostly what television feeds on—our desire to be something or someone other than our mundane selves. Pure escapism as we slay vampires while still trying to pass trigonometry, balance our work in an emergency room with a complicated love life, become America's next pop sensation. Television is so you don't have to think up dreams for yourself.

For my part I began to dream of pro racing. Racing in a category below your level is called "sandbagging" and sandbaggers were the scourge of Russ and Norm's post–training ride La Jolla Brew Pub cool-down sessions. For fear of being labeled a "sandbagger," I moved up to the expert class within a few months.

I stopped winning. A slew of near wins, flat tires, and bonks interrupted my dream. Embarrassed but not broken, I simply refused to respond in a negative way. I gritted my teeth and put my head down and steeled myself to try harder and train longer. During my commute rides I transformed every encounter with another cyclist into an imagined drag race with the local hot shot, Jeanette Denison. She was sponsored. She won expert races. I wanted what she had. The big showdown would be in a few months at the Cactus Cup, the NORBA race season opener. All the big factory teams and the top pros would be there, and if I beat Jennette Denison I might get sponsored. Sponsorship meant that I probably wouldn't have to pay the thirty dollar entry fee at all these races I've been doing. Maybe even get some tires and brake pads for free. What could be better?

I did well enough at my local races to get on what's called a "farm team" of one of the bike manufacturers. The deal worked like this: I buy a bike at full retail price with a Rock Shox front fork and the fancy Shimano components, and if I raced well enough as an expert during the upcoming season, the bike company would reimburse me for my race-entry fees and give me, as well as the few hundred others on the farm team, a shot at making their pro team. They gave me a shirt I had to wear at the races. During the season at the races a team mechanic would give me a tune up . . . lube the chain, straighten out my hopping wheel, basically make sure that my bike was in decent enough shape to finish a race. Maybe I could score some slightly-used tires from some of the real pros. Or brake pads. Or shifter cables. It seemed like a pretty fair compromise.

Wearing their shirt was better than not racing at all.

Turning pro was still too ambitious to really attempt, so I focused on being a top expert and getting my money back for this two-thousand-dollar bike. I have never bought a new car so I had no experience making seventy-two monthly car payments just to win the title of ownership, but I did plan on realizing this dream in monthly installment payments of sweat and bruises and stiff joints so black and blue I looked like I was in a car wreck.

The day I bought my bike at a local shop I was so excited that I wheeled it into my bedroom and telephoned Marc and described every bit of its details to him, and how at the end of the year it could be mine for free.

Over the winter months he'd been leaving me dozens of encouraging messages on the answering machine and mailing me other encouragements like *Mountain Bike* magazine with my photograph pasted over the shoulders of Julie Furtado, the current national champion, and my typed name snipped and pasted over Julie's name wherever it appeared in an article describing her most recent race win. In these propaganda packages Marc also placed advertisements made with Magic Marker and glue for imaginary mountain bike products with my name on them. I would race so well and be so famous that someday I would have my own bike company called Streb Cycles whose bikes would all be polka dotted like my VW bus. And I would have my own energy bars called MarlaBars made of red licorice, Now and Laters, Gummy Bears, and a coating of Red Hots. Marc had a lot of time on his hands because he had sliced one of his hands open in an accident at the restaurant he was cooking in, and was sitting around all day during the Colorado snow season receiving worker's compensation while the severed nerves and tendons healed. He filled my head with weird racing ambitions, so I was surprised and a little hurt when he asked me, "Did you get that in writing from that farm team that they would give you your money back if you won enough races?"

And then, two months before the Cactus Cup, during a smaller race, I took a big fall. I went over the handlebars. A mountain-bike rite of passage: the broken collarbone.

When I got home from the hospital my housemates set me up in my room with a pitcher of iced water, a stack of magazines, and my favorite Grateful Dead tape in the boom box. Then they abandoned me and went about their own lives throwing the Frisbee and playing Hacky Sack by the pool, taunting me with the gleeful sounds of their full range of motions. I called Marc. I was so upset. Now I was probably going to miss the Cactus Cup and my big showdown with Jeannette Denison who wasn't even aware of our epic rivalry, and I was never going to be able to get my money back for that bike, which cost more than any car I had ever bought, and I was going to have to give up being a mountain biker and return to the sterile world of science.

"It's not fair! I was trying so hard, and the doctor says it won't heal for six weeks."

"Marla, this seems bad. It does. But tell me. What was the worst day you ever had in high school?"

"But I'm talking about mountain biking and I don't want to relive . . ."

"Humor me. I know this sucks, but what was the worst thing that ever happened to you in high school? Didn't some jerk stand you up at the prom or something?"

"Well, in high school I was tall and skinny. My boobs didn't come in until my junior year of college. I was a nerd and I didn't have any sisters to show me how to wear clothes and what to do with my hair and stuff, but I had this huge crush on this guy, Tommy Wiezorek, and I told my best friend, Lori, all about him and how much I liked him. So one night at a party she told me she would get him alone and tell him a bunch of nice things about me and stuff, and I watched from the other side of the air-hockey table as Lori led him into the washroom where it was quieter and I waited through three stupid games of air hockey and then I couldn't take it any longer. I crept up to the door of the washroom to listen to what she was saying to him and I could hear them kissing in there. That was devastating."

"And now what?"

"What?"

"It ain't so bad, is it? It's just a blip. You aren't even that sure of the details, are you?"

"But Marc . . ."

"No, listen. In college didn't you have a whole semester to write some paper and didn't you put it off until the last moment and then didn't you cobble together some crap and you ended up getting a D and you were in big trouble and it ruined your GPA and all that stuff?"

What had happened was completely different than what he had described, but for the sake of furthering this philosophic dialogue I said, "Yeah, so?"

"Well, who cares now? Does that professor, what's his name? Do you?"

"No, but . . ."

"You graduated, right?"

"Yes."

"And remember not long ago you had brain cancer and were dying a' AIDS and the world was fallin' apart and all that shit? Well, up until today it wasn't so bad, was it? In six weeks, in six months, who gives a shit about this collarbone? You'll still be a great mountain biker. This collarbone is just a blip."

The cardboard Corona twelve-pack endtable was too far away, so I just let the phone drop into the blankets and stared out the open window into the late afternoon shadows of the So Cal winter afternoon, and listened to the yips of kids as they played soccer and skateboarded on the dead-end street, and thought about what Marc had said. I couldn't sleep so I thought about our trip in Europe when we were sitting in the baggage train drinking Jaegermeister dreaming about what a great thing it would be to sail around the world, and ride our bikes wherever we landed, and asking Marc what we would name the boat. He threw out a name, but it wasn't the usual sort of name that you see painted in big letters on the bows of boats. It wasn't *Indomitable* or *Intrepid* or *Independence*. It wasn't any of the words that you would think sailors would yell as they stormed ashore or would carve into ancient statues or weave into songs. He said, "*Indifference*."

And when I finished laughing I asked him what he thought it meant.

"It's a polite way of saying I don't give a fuck," he said.

"And you would be proud to have that on your dream boat?" I asked.

"Hey, millions of Buddhists have been striving for just that state of mind for thousands of years. Indifference is the state that Socrates had attained when he drank the poison hemlock. It's what Thoreau found at Walden Pond when he said the mass of men lead quiet lives of desperation. Indifference is the self-sustaining power that enabled Melville's Bartleby to become the center of the universe. It's what the stableboy, Wesley, conveyed to Princess Buttercup in that movie *The Princess Bride* every time she asked a demeaning chore of him.

"And I'm sure it's the best way to be when you have considered everything equally. It's just not an easy thing to maintain, that's all. You have to strive for indifference. Work for it."

I knew he was kidding, but not really.

The next day I asked Terence to hook up my StumpJumper bike to a wind trainer on the hardwood floor in the living room. He aimed it toward the big picture window and I rode it for hours each evening after work, my arm in a sling, trying to reach indifference. For the first few days the Vicadin pills helped, in a numbing way.

It would have been easy to quit. But I didn't. If anything, that broken collarbone made my determination much stronger. Each night sitting on the saddle, the sweat burning in my eyes just dripping off the tip off my nose, bereft of the benefit of a cooling breeze, pedaling circles that took me nowhere, my roommates gathered on the livingroom couch and during the commercial breaks of *Baywatch* pulled deep bong hits. And since I was right there an easy object for their shortened attentions, they heckled me, until on TV some girl in a high thigh-cut suit ran yet again into the surf. They weren't intentionally trying to be cruel, I was just more entertaining for them than channel surfing.

For the next few weeks I couldn't ride on trails, so at work, in between experiments, I exercised outside under the portico with the ocean right beneath me. Sit-ups for my stomach. On top of the picnic table, butterfly lifts for my back. Lunges for my thighs. Toe lifts on the cement stairs for my calves. Squats and leg stretches. I answered Dr. Fox's raised eyebrow that all this was "physical therapy." I had to do it. In truth it was probably as much mental therapy as well.

The local bike shop was kind enough to let me treat their magazine rack like a library. From the lab I borrowed a gram scale and weighed each component on my race bike, comparing my stuff to the trick parts that I couldn't afford in the magazines. But I was learning a lot. My old bike had metal cages and straps and you stuck your foot in and cinched down on the strap, and since your foot was so firmly attached you were able to transfer more power from each pedal stroke. They were called "toe clips" or sometimes just "clips." When Shimano came out with their new pedal system the straps and cages were eliminated and replaced with a spring attachment between the bottom of the shoe and the surface of the pedal. My race bike came with these new clipless pedals. You pushed your foot down and people said you were "clipped in" and to take your foot out you twisted your heel out and the spring released, and then people said your were "unclipped." I put my new bike on the stationary trainer and practiced clipping and unclipping my clipless clip pedals. That's how I had broken my collarbone in the first place: unable to unclip and then "endoing." The magazines even explained the differences between "mountain bike" and "mountainbike" and even threw in "all-terrain bike," just to add to the confusion.

I splurged on a cycle computer, which looked like a digital watch and mounted on my handlebar. It counted pedal strokes per minute, called *cadence,* miles ridden, and time ridden. It could derive average and top speed, and it recorded my heart rate. That helped pass the time on the stationary bike. I stared at the computer and listened to its beeps as *Melrose Place* droned on the television behind me. I wore a red bandana on my brow like Russ and Norm and pretended that they were chasing me.

Time passed.

My collarbone healed.

The Cactus Cup was the following weekend and I was given medical clearance to ride my bike on the trails. I never confided to the doctor that I planned on racing. Monday's commute on my circling string of trails to work by bike was shaky. I had no strength in my arms and had lost a "feel" for the ride. The street was safer than the trails so on the way home I was more careful, but still stressed. The doctor had told me my collarbone still wasn't fully knitted.

But Marc was reassuring and positive and that's what I wanted to hear.

Marc said he was planning to catch a ride from one of the racers he had come to know in Durango. We'd meet up sometime during the weekend and catch up on things. He promised that he'd cheer me on and pass me fresh water bottles in the feed zone, and said he wanted to be there at the finish when I won. I was looking forward to seeing him and finding out what he had been up to all winter. I wanted to show him how fast I had become. He was the only one I had told that I wanted to turn pro someday. I was too embarrassed to tell anybody else.

The race was on a Sunday in the Arizona desert. Friday after work, I drove Vidalia hard at night when it was cooler and arrived at dawn. Without sleeping I rode on the red clay carved trails and flatted within sight of Vidalia on the needles of Sonora cactus littering the course. I got back on course. I felt very cool. Most of the other racers were head to toe with logos and sponsor's names. Color coordinated. I was stealth. I was soul. My John Tomac-style plain black socks signifying to all my competition, despite the logos of my farm-team jersey, that I was a pure mountain biker. I hadn't sold out to ride. I memorized the sections where I hoped to attack and the turns where quick passes could be made. I was imagining that Julie Furtado was right behind me, possibly even gaining on me, when I almost crashed right into Marc.

He was off to the side of the trail, his very unracelike bike outfitted, as it was, with front and rear lights and loaded panniers leaning against a large red rock. Marc was lounging in a camp chair under a small umbrella reading *The New York Times* and drinking a beer. He had put on a few pounds since the day I dropped him off at the Greyhound station in Las Vegas almost a year earlier. His chin was trimmed tight so it was a dark shadow line beneath his longer-than-I-remembered, starting-to-curl-a-bit hair. Sort of cute.

I hugged him, but I didn't want to kiss him. Our embrace had been awkward; where were his elbows supposed to go and how should my head be cocked? That brief moment where a kiss would seem natural and right, frittered away. We agreed to meet up later under the giant Specialized tent. I didn't know what to think of him. It would be fun to see him again, but even just the few moments spent with him had been distracting. Next time, maybe, it wouldn't feel so funny. I hopped back on my bike to finish my practice duel with Julie Furtado and Marc sat back down to finish his newspaper.

Specialized, a big bike company, was the main sponsor of this race and had erected a circular white tent for registration and results, and orbiting it were the tents of other, smaller sponsors, and of race teams: Cannondale, Yeti, Ritchey, Mongoose, etc. Music boomed from speakers. Marc was standing off to the side trying to look cool in his tight bike shorts. His socks didn't match. What was I gonna do with this guy? All my new, cool, mountain-bike friends would see us together.

We rode into town to grab the requisite night-before-race chicken burritos, and before we made it back to Vidalia he had me laughing about how everyone in Durango assumed his accent was Australian. How he managed to bartend in a real cowboy honky-tonk during the height of the "Achey Breaky" dance craze by pretending that he was from "down under." "If they only knew I had voted for Dukakis and Clinton they would have gutted me right there on the pool table," he assured me.

The next morning Marc and I rode into Scottsdale for breakfast. From the sidewalk some of the leathered locals and wintering snowbirds from the northeast pointed and gawked at my tight shorts and pink and blue Lycra jersey. After dragging my bike inside the pancake house and leaning it up against the gumball and cigarette machines, I heard louder than the tapping of my SPD shoes onto the floor tiles such whispered comments as, "That's them mountain-style bikers. And one of 'em is a girl!" I was proud. Proud to be identified as a mountain biker.

My race was at one o'clock, six hours away. I ordered coffee black, toasted bagel no cream cheese. Marc got the Trailer Trash Triage with bacon.

"You know," he said to me, "you should eat some more. Get some eggs." He didn't know what he was talking about.

"You train so hard that you can eat almost whatever you want. You look great, but you're getting real thin." He had some eggy bits dangling from the corner of his moustache.

Over the top of his *USA Today* he observed, "I can see all your ribs and you have no muscles in your arms. The biggest part of your arm is your bony elbow."

Stashed in Vidalia were some oatmeal flavored energy bars and I planned on eating one a half hour before my start. I'd be fine. He wasn't a mountain biker anyway. What did he know?

"Are you going to finish up with apple pie and ice cream?" I said, twisting my face into Sarcastic Barbie.

"Nah. They only have Dairy Twirl in places like this and that stuff gives me the shits. But really, Marla, your legs look like they belong in the Olympics but from the waist up you look like one of those third world refugees you see on the cover of *Newsweek*. I'm just a little concerned. That's all."

I didn't want to hear this. He was supposed to suffuse me with confidence. But if I had seen myself as Marc saw me, I would have agreed with him. I did look like a Barbie doll and as unnatural.

I'm tall. Nearly six feet and I've always been hipless. A straight line practically from shoulders to my ankles. Skinny. I didn't even get boobs at all until my junior year of college when it was nearly too late to enjoy them. And besides when my boobs did arrive they were too big. They were no fun at all trying to skateboard, or free climbing the stone walls of the school's bell tower. But because of the past year's intense training and inadequate diet, my legs had cannibalized my upper body even more. The only part of me that retained healthy fat were my boobs. And they seemed way out of proportion, not freakish, but Barbieishly large since all else was rail thin.

Did I have an eating disorder? Was I one of those women on Oprah smiling for the cameras with teeth stained brown from vomiting up digestive juices and lettuce? No. I wasn't.

But I wasn't honest with myself when I looked in the mirror. "Watch what you eat!; Virginia Slims; Ten ways to lose ten pounds!" Magazine covers, billboards, and TV had screamed at me since I was a little girl, and though I wasn't aware, some of that propaganda must have sunk in. I had added all this extra training to my life but hadn't changed my "girl diet" of plain bagel no cream cheese, salad no dressing, pasta no sauce, and the once-a-week treat of chicken breast no skin. I hadn't changed the way I was supposed to view my own self-image. I wanted to be an athlete, but I still wanted to look like a girl was supposed to. But what was a girl supposed to look like?

Despite considering myself a well-educated woman with a high sense of self-esteem, I got snookered by Madison Avenue and the images of women in *Cosmo* and *Vogue*.

A person can only keep eating like a magazine cover girl and training like an athlete for so long before things start to break down. The pinky fingers of each hand had fractured. I'd tape 'em up and they'd be okay for a while and then I'd slide out in a turn and one of them would snap like peanut brittle. Once again, I was no longer menstruating. I had cut out most of the drinking but still binged occasionally, because that was "fun," wasn't it? I was trying to be healthy, but didn't know how—which was crazy because of all that money I had spent and still owed on a science education.

"How's the sailboat coming along?" I wanted to change the subject.

"Pretty good. Pretty good. In a couple of weeks the book says I should turn the lights down and then in a little while . . . bingo! Forty-foot sailboat."

"Really? Do you have it all figured it out?"

Marc went into a lengthy explanation of how he was growing cannabis in the basement of his apartment building. Marc
didn't smoke himself, and that worked to his advantage. He had
his dreams of a six-figure sale to help him get the boat. I wasn't
sure about any of this—my dreams of becoming a pro and
Marc's drug-funded sailboat.

Marc was wiping the runny eggs on his plate with a butter-
smeared slice of toast and I was thinking, Hey, sail around the
world. That's not too bad. That's an adventure! It'd be easy to
quit work to do that. And on a big enough boat I could take my
mountain bike with me. I'd need it. I know he says he wants to
ride the Great Wall of China, but the way he's digging into the
porcelain cracks of that plate prying out every last bit of choles-
terol, he won't be up for it. Besides I'd need that bike to get
away from him when he started ranting about politics and how
Clinton has pissed off so many people, like my innocent little
parents, that he'd probably get shot. I liked Marc a lot but I
didn't love him. I didn't know what it was. Maybe it was that
fleck of bacon on his plate that he wiped with his finger and
licked gone. Icchh.

I didn't win that day. Jeanette Denison won. I placed third.
Maybe I did have a brain tumor after all. Maybe I was a little crazy.

Even though I had only gotten third, and Jeannette had
beaten me once again, I still wanted more. I knew I could do better. I could get stronger, get faster.

Marc was cheering when I crossed the line as though I had
won. I thought I would have been crushed. Instead I was incredibly happy that I raced and raced well and that my collarbone
hadn't been any problem. My legs would ache lovingly for hours
afterward. The next day I would be joyfully stiff, each creaking
limb a testament to life lived on the edge of enlightenment. The
racing part was like a musical stage that I was performing a
piano piece on.

On the podium! Even if it was the lowest expert tier. My head was dizzy from the adulation of the adoring crowds. Maybe I was dizzy because of dehydration and the onset of heat stroke. And maybe the crowd's adulation wasn't for me. More likely for the swag: water bottles, bar grips, helmet covers, gloves, and chain-stay protectors that the race promoter was heaving into the crowd by the armful. No matter. It felt great to do well. It felt great that all these other people knew that the only way I'd gotten third was because of all the hard training I'd done and the sacrifices I'd made.

I didn't have to explain to these mountain bikers how hard it was to put in the miles or how scary some of the rock sections were. How much my collarbone worried me. They all knew. And now I knew dozens of others just like me. Mike Ferrentino was one of them. Marc had proudly told Mike to keep an eye on me. That I was going to do well. Mike yelled my name whenever he saw me on course and afterward we talked at length over sun-warmed draft beer about the new Rock Shox forks and chain wax, and whether the new Bell helmets might have better ventilation. Stimulating conversation and I was taking part! Mike and I, after having sweated out in the desert on the same race course together were, I imagine, like two draftees who had shared a foxhole during a nighttime artillery attack. If we ever met up again at another race or at a bike shop, or even a Taco Bell, I'd feel as though there had been no lapse of time. (I concede he might think differently.) I was living and breathing this sport. Mountain biking and how to go faster and how to get stronger—turning pro maybe!—was pushing most other thoughts out of my head.

The race was such an emotional high that saying good-bye to Marc was a little anticlimatic. Meeting dozens of new, like-minded mountain-bike racing freaks was overwhelming. There was a new language of gear ratios and training regimens to learn. I exchanged phone numbers with bunches of guys who promised to show me trails back in the So Cal area that I had never heard of. I felt like I had been initiated into a tribe. A tribe of pretty much all guys to be sure. And a tribe that Marc had no interest in joining.

"Why don't you want to sign up for a race in Colorado? If you do a couple maybe we can meet up in races and that way stay in touch?" I asked him. Vidalia was jammed with my grimy race stuff and Marc was standing beside his strange looking bike, loaded with camping gear, a soft-sided cooler and the fat Sunday *New York Times* wadded up under a bungee cord that held it all together.

He glanced toward his ride. They were still wrestling with partially disassembled bikes and sorting out seating priority.

We talked for a few minutes more about our differing views on bikes and racing. I was into the competitive part, Marc the more aesthetic and romantic. It was clear that another divide had widened.

I was standing beside Vidalia's open driver's door. I had washed up with a wet towel and changed into loose fitting shorts and a sweatshirt, but I was still grimy. My hair was a mop of sweat and desert dust. My mouth was dry and my nose stuffed with snot. Not a very romantic setting to say good-bye. And I was beat up from racing, and from all the socializing. I had to be in the lab tomorrow morning, smiling and fresh faced, and I dreaded that. Couldn't Marc make it easier for me to do this?

Couldn't he just tell me that he would ride more and do a couple of races?

"I want to ride mountain bikes forever."

"Me too."

"But you never ride."

"I do. Not as much as you. Not as fast as you. And I can't ride the way that you do. I pretty much just ride on the street, getting groceries, and going to work and stuff. Not all those switchbacks and drop offs like you do. But I'm trying to get us a sailboat so we can sail all over the world and ride single track that only goats and jungle critters have cut. To places where nobody has ever been before. Like we talked about on that train in Europe. We could ride for years."

That did sound pretty good. I didn't know what to say. I was thinking over the implications. Would I have to carry all the camping gear? Would Marc be able to keep up with me at all? Where would the money come from? Even if he could find a way to sell his garden to buy a boat, we'd still need money after that. Does he think we could manage a garden on a sailboat while we are traveling? Who would we sell the crop to?

Marc and I mumbled some more good-byes. We agreed it had been fun to see each and we promised to stay in touch.

He only got a kiss on the cheek.

I watched him walk his bike over to the only other car in the parking lot. I watched him wrestle breaking down his war pony of a bike. I suppose that in some ways I was suffering from "White Knight Syndrome," the belief that someday someone was going to come into my life and sweep me off my feet. Marc's bike was no white charger, and at that point I wasn't feeling too much like a princess. I was as mixed up as this tangled fairy tale explanation is. Besides, what was Marc thinking about when he said the way to be about life was "indifferent"? What a dolt! He needs to spend more time on his bike. What sailboat? Does he really think all that is possible? As he was fixing his forks to the car's roof racks I coaxed Vidalia into starting up, and tooted her horn.

We waved and then I clutched Vidalia out of the dirt lot and onto the asphalt, past the survey-staked lots just outside the park where we had raced, west toward the beach and the ocean beyond that.

As I drove Vidalia west through the desert I said to myself, "That's the last time I'll probably ever see him."

• • •

It was a few weeks later that I called Marc, once again from my room, lying on my bed on a sunny summer afternoon with another broken collarbone. The rest of the race season over for me. I had broken it this time trying to pass another girl on a little downhill section of a cross-country race. Her name was Mia Stockdale, a pro rider, and I knocked her down as well. She was able to ride away though. I don't think she heard me yell out that I was sorry. I had barely begun to tell Marc how sorry I truly was. I was holding back tears and a lump in my throat when he interrupted me.

"I'm coming out there," he said.

"It's okay. I can take take care of myself." A rush of stale trapped air was expelled from deep inside me. My open mouth curled into a slight smile. I didn't even know why I had picked up the phone to call him and now Marc was going to take care of me. He was rushing to my bedside! Before my eyes a vignette played. Marc would bring flowers and carry me to an ambulance that would howl off to a famous specialist who would have a radical new bone-knitting treatment that would miraculously heal the break in my collarbone.

"No. No. I'm coming out there 'cause my landlord just found out what I was doing in the basement. He's not gonna tell the cops 'cause I convinced him that they wouldn't believe he had no idea what I was doing in *his* basement and they'd seize his house."

What was he talking about? Was Marc coming out to help me or was I supposed to be helping him?

"Oh. So you still have time to do the thing with that 'trustafarian'? You know. Sell him all your buckets . . . of stuff?"

"Nope. I'm lucky I'm not getting raped in county jail right

now. I don't know what the landlord's wife is gonna convince him to do. So, the second he left I started ripping 'em all out and bagging 'em in trash bags and I rode down to the river and threw 'em all in that night. Every cent down the river."

"So, no deal. So why are you coming here?" I pulled the sheet tighter under my chin. Was he my hero or an orphan I hadn't known that I had somehow adopted and now had to take care of?

"Gotta get out of Dodge. I got another plan. I'll explain it all to you when I get out there. Gotta go, my housemates are coming through the door and they're real pissed at me 'cause they were 'jonesing' all winter and didn't know I had a grow room right beneath their feet."

"You must be pretty upset."

"I'm scared shitless. In this little town I could get screwed. But hey, it was only months of back breaking labor, and I only lost hundreds of thousands of dollars. Could be worse. And anyway, I got an even better plan. I'll be there by Labor Day. I already found another place to live on the other side of town. I'm just gonna lay low for a while. Gotta fix up this old motorcycle I bought for a dollar first."

I pulled the blanket over my head with my good arm. I was tired. That's the only reason I didn't try to talk Marc out of moving to San Diego. I was too exhausted.

I slumped into my pillow and tried to not disturb the sling and bag of dripping ice that puddled beneath my chin.

My mind raced with repercussions of Marc's impending next move. How did I feel about it? About him? About me and him? How would he mess up my mountain biking? He doesn't really ride much. I won't get any faster hanging out with him, that's for sure. And I'd feel bad telling him I couldn't play pool or go to the movies because I had to train. That's why I liked all my other boys. They really didn't mean much to me. That's one rarely acknowledged facet of girl power. I could drop any one of them if a good ride came up or if I felt that I should spend a night at home with my legs up resting on a pillow. What about my boy toys, Glenn from the lab, and the surfer guy Gene, and the skateboarder kid Rick? Marc would mess all that up.

Marc somehow imposed his presence on me. He demanded all my attention in very sneaky ways. Even though he is a thousand miles away my boy toys are sick of hearing Marc's name. I'm not sure I could handle having him here in town. I definitely couldn't live with him. That'd mess everything up. How he was always wallowing in the shallows of poverty. Him and his pretend sailboat. And no matter what Marc said about being liberal and open-minded, he'd be jealous and start problems with all my little boyfriends. They are just for play, but he's a dumb boy and he won't understand. He'll be put off and then won't want to make me laugh anymore. And I'd miss that.

He'll just have to get his own place that's all. I never told him he could stay with me. Not in any detail. Not really. He wouldn't be bringing flowers with him or any magical cures for my collarbone either. Looking back on it now I can see how confused and conflicted my feelings were for him. I could never settle into a comfortable position emotionally on the issue. Just like I'd hoped for a sudden inspiration, a moment of clarity that would help me decide about the direction my career life would take, I hoped for the same thing in my romantic life. Or maybe I just hoped I could go on forever with things in a kind of stasis.

I raced that season on the stationary trainer. I crunched sit-ups and leg lunges and read all the bike mags and watched old Tour de France videos, which I borrowed from Russell and still haven't returned. And I devoured the few cycling titles that the La Jolla public library stacked on its shelves. I religiously maintained the entries in my training journal. I was especially diligent about chronicling my calorie count. That was something over which I could have control, even if I couldn't keep my bones from breaking. I could still be proactive about limiting my protein intake! I totaled up every bran muffin, each strand of sauceless spaghetti, and denied myself any excesses.

In between experiments at Scripps I stalked the halls of adjoining buildings and staked out the waiting rooms of orthopedic surgeons looking for a doctor who might have a long-term solution for my collarbone. Almost every physician counseled that the best course of treatment was to stop riding. Give up racing. In their minds that was the least expensive method of treatment. San Diego is a very conservative part of the country. This Just-Say-No prescription wasn't working for the epidemic of crank in Mission Beach and Just Say No wasn't saving any lives from AIDS in Hillcrest either. And just saying no to mountain biking wouldn't work for me.

But what was the use of laboring at a research hospital risking opportune carcinogens or stray radioactive isotopes every day and risking AIDS from the slip of my own hand if I didn't avail myself of the generous health plan benefits?

A few doctors said that the long-term solution to my brittle collarbone was a change of diet. Much more protein, calcium from dairy, more calories in general. I was perniciously anemic. That was serious. Something for me to think about since it was a rare diagnosis in San Diego where the TV show *Bay Watch* was sometimes filmed, and where the beaches were slathered with the sunning shrunken bodies of coeds and strippers who thought bulimia was an Eastern European country. Most doctors figured that cause was hopeless. That girls around here just wanted to starve themselves to death. It seems that I did.

Many doctors, a whole nascent industry of health care, were scrambling to make the situation even worse. Breast augmentation, tummy tucks, and buttock lifts, among other procedures, were widely advertised in the newspaper, on billboards, over the radio, on the sides of city buses. Howard Stern, the self-proclaimed King of All Media, gave away boob jobs as prizes on his widely-listened-to radio show. Walking testimonials to the cosmetic surgeon's handiwork strutted on the beaches, along the flourescent aisles of the supermarkets, and dotted the beach boardwalk wall like funhouse curios. If you were a stripper, the medical costs were deductible as a business expense. If you were a mom of a certain age, the ego boost of uplifted breasts might just be worth all the hassle. And if you were a young woman, why learn to love your body when you can throw down some bucks for the "hop up" kit.

I was too skinny—maybe not for the same reasons as most women in San Diego's beach culture—but I was too skinny for wrong reasons all the same. I was struggling to reach the optimum strength-to-weight ratios for an elite cross-country mountain biker, which was not much smarter than starving myself to reach the perfect porportion of bust-to-waist size for a job at Hooter's.

I finally found one surgeon who was a surfer. He also rode a bike. He listened as I told him about my rash of broken bones, what I hoped to accomplish in mountain biking, and how I was too impatient to sit out a whole season for my bones to heal. How, to be competitive as a cross-country racer, I had to maintain a high power-to-weight ratio; and so the diet wasn't really a problem and more calories wouldn't really be a solution. I was this anemic, and amnoreic, for healthy reasons. He looked at my X rays and medical history. He saw that I was fully insured through my job at the Scripps lab. His proposed treatment was simple, immediate, and permanent.

"Take it out," he said.

Since I kept breaking the same section of collarbone repeatedly, and since I refused to modify my behavior in any reasonable fashion to diminish the odds of further injury, he offered this solution. And since I considered myself an athlete already committed to an ideal of self-sacrifice and inured to the Faustian bargain of temporal success, why not? Just remove a one-inch section of my collarbone where it has been breaking and be done with it. A large part of the danger of a broken collarbone is that a jagged edge of the bone could pierce through the skin. There are some some major arteries and veins and nerves that are better left intact in that area. Such a wound could easily become infected especially if suffered on a muddy trail. If a section was removed then the rest of the collarbone would "float" and easily avoid the impact of a fall. There would be no bone to break. If I fell, my collarbone would suffer no more consequence than a rag doll's. Conveniently collapsible.

Sounded good to me.

The surgery was scheduled for the following week. With some luck I'd be racing cyclocross, a cycling discipline I'd come across in the magazines, by autumn. It might not be mountain biking but at least it was a kind of racing on a bike.

The only painful part of this surgery for me would be telling my parents.

There is no lying to my mother. I mean you can. Lord knows that I did. But there is no use. She knows. Even long distance. And once she knows that I am lying, it is just a matter of time before she discovers what I am lying about.

So there was no point in lying to her about why I would be getting this operation. I knew that. I would have to tell her that I was modifying my body, inalterabley changing it, improving on God's handiwork . . . so that I could race a mountain bike. It wasn't a boob job so I could make more tips as an exotic dancer. It was so I could race faster without the chance of a sustaining a season-ending endo. Was there much difference between the two? Was this a committment to my sport, or an irrational, self-delusional ego boost? I could just see my father, fixed to the floor beside my mother, the kitchen telephone in her hand, as I told her and she told him, and he in turn stiffening against each whispered word. And how afterward, after she had placed the receiver back on the wall cradle, they would quietly sit side by side at the kitchen table.

It was easy for me to make that commitment, personally. But to make that same commitment publicly, like a recovering alcoholic at a meeting, standing up and saying loudly, "My name is Marla S. and I am an alcoholic," is very brave. I had let my parents believe that mountain biking was just a hobby for me. An innocent pastime like playing Frisbee. Now I would have to tell them that I was having an operation to add a sixth finger to each hand so I could catch a Frisbee better. Or having my tongue enlarged so I could better lick my stamps for a collection book more efficiently. That I really never had any intention of returning to school for a doctorate. That I was never interested in carving out a career as a research scientist. That rather than marrying a Nobel Prize–winning surgeon, I'd end up shacking up with some bike mechanic. They would think I was crazy and try their best to talk me out of it.

And I would have the operation anyway.

I put off making that phone call for as long as I could. That is a sound coping strategy. It works pretty well. As long as I could ride my stationary bike hard and fast, I wasn't troubled at all about making that phone call. As much as I could still do sit-ups at the foot of my bed until my manic movements had pushed the bed across the wood floor such that it was up against the wall, I wasn't bothered in the least about that phone call. While there were leg lifts and lunges and toe raises to make me so sore each day, I never even thought about making that call. If I did so many exercises again before going to bed that sheer exhaustion alone would ensure sound sleep by walling off the inevitability of that phone call, then everything was okay. Life was even more perfect if I draped my bedside Touch-Tone with a sweaty tie-dyed tee shirt. And unplugged it too.

And then the day arrived when I had to make that call. I had filled out all the insurance forms, scheduled for some time off work, packed up a gym bag with toiletries and pajamas, arranged for Glenn to give me a ride to the hospital, and hadn't eaten any solid food for twelve hours as outlined by the preoperative instructions, and all of a sudden the surgery was going to happen in the morning!

In the early evening, before it grew too late on the East Coast, I plugged my phone back into the wall jack and lifted the dusty tee shirt off my Bell Labs cordless, with intercom, redial, and answering machine capabilities, and punched in the numbers to . . . Marc's house.

"Of course, they'll be disappointed, Marla. And hurt, and scared for you. Short-term and long-term. They're your parents. That's their job. And it's your job as their child to do that to them. It's all very natural.

"But you gotta call 'em. Not even so much for their sake as for your own. You have to tell 'em how you feel about mountain biking. Like coming out of the closet. Out yourself. You'll feel a whole lot better about the way you've decided to live your life."

Marc was good at that. Justifying stuff. Explaining situations in a way that didn't sound too bad. Maybe it was from all those years of bartending. Listening to all those people drown in their sorrowful beer that he was able to put a well-practiced spin on things. I was twenty-seven years old and I knew of no way to explain to my parents that I wanted to chuck everything for a chance to ride a mountain bike professionally.

"Have you told your parents that you are a failed drug kingpin?" I asked.

"Well I told them half of it."

"What do you mean half? Which part?"

"I told them the part about me being a failure. The rest was just a detail."

When I had finished laughing Marc continued, "Marla, of course it's much easier for me to tell you what's the right thing to do, what's the smart thing to do, rather than for me to do it for myself. Distance lets you do that. You're too close right now to see it for yourself. That's why old people are so smart. The wisdom comes from distance that time provides. Don't worry, your parents are smart. They're old and therefore wise. They'll understand."

Distance huh.

I dialed the phone number to the house of my childhood, unchanged since I first put it to memory. That house on Glen Arm Road, the same as it ever was, a comfort so far away from where I now found myself. That number was an unbroken link to a time when everything was simpler. It was reassuring to hear the loud brrriiing, brrriiing of that kitchen phone a world away in Maryland, a world that would always be there for me, immutable.

I spoke first, as all kids do, imagining that there could be nothing at all of importance in their parents' lives. I gushed on about the collarbone and how it had broken twice now, and why I wanted and needed the surgery rather than just quit mountain biking. How I was sorry that I had deceived them about how much I loved this sport, how deeply committed I was to it, and how much I realized that I was throwing away my future, but how determined I was to have the surgery tomorrow morning. And how I was sure that I would be fine, and that I would call them as soon as I could right afterward.

I thought my mom was tired. She seemed exhausted as I made my confession. Her loud sighs and deep breaths had been her only response. Could that have drained her so much? My head felt light. Like when you stand up quickly after lying down for a while. I had said what I wanted to say and now I had to brace myself against her questions, suggestions, alternatives, and outright veto. I was still going to go through with the operation, I was just eager for this reprobation to be over.

The phone twitched a tiny bit in my hands. It seemed forever.

"Your father has been going to the hospital quite a bit too."

"Dad?"

My collarbone had knitted up enough so that that offending section could cleanly be removed and the ends knit tightly with scar tissue, but as I sat up in bed there was still a wince of pain.

"Dad? Is he okay?"

"Your father is fine. He will be fine. He is going to the hospital again later in the week. But this seems like as good a time as any to tell you that it looks like he has Parkinson's."

Save for the glow from the Touch-Tone pads of my phone and the weak moonlight through the window, my room was dark. The two sources of light cast competing shadow shapes on my wall.

My father is the most honest man I have ever known. He lives and works entirely for his family. He was about to retire in a few years from his job in Washington and I knew that he was really looking forward to spending the coming years with my mother, enjoying each other's company, and doing all those things that they had worked and sacrificed and saved for. They wanted to travel. Play with the grandkids at the beach. My father wanted to play some golf. Maybe even get back into sailing. Or start another project car.

When I was a kid Dad had bought and restored lots of VWs. Bugs mostly, but there was a camper bus that he had brought so much back to life, that he drove all of us kids and Mom down to Florida for a vacation. He respected the precision and the enduring qualities of the German engineering. One year, from the ground up, he rebuilt an old fire-engine red Porsche 356B. I remember a test drive with him. After months, in pieces meticulously laid out on the cement floor of the garage, he purred me down the length of Gun Powder Road. We sat side by side, both smiling ear to ear, in the wide open summer breeze, since the doors had yet to be hung.

Pretty daring for my father.

I always remember him being very stiff. Very controlled. Especially after my brother Mark died. But had he always been that way? I always thought that he kept everything bottled up inside and that was why he moved with such deliberation; after much consideration. I thought he was just trying to be safe. Safe for all of us. To think now that he didn't casually swivel his neck when the doorbell rang, but rather rotated his torso from his easy chair to face the door. That while standing in line at the supermarket his back was ramrod stiff, his arms straight at his sides, his whole body in tetanus except for a slight bend in his knees and an even slighter tremor in his hand as he fingered his credit card. That he no longer drank coffee. That the hesitancy with which he spoke wasn't just rumination, or a re-examination of his position, but all were symptoms of a disease.

"There is no cure right now. But Johns Hopkins has a wonderful research facility and they are a leader in this field. Your father is on some medications and we will see a specialist. It is fortunate that we have good insurance."

I was by no means "up" on the pathology of Parkinson's, but I knew that it takes a long time. The mind stays sharp and ever alert, yet the body fails. The fingers become less dextrous by degree, finally shaking uncontrollably. The whole body shaking, quivering, to the point that every muscle is constantly contracted so that there is no movement at all. Like a statue. Aware and helpless to stop it. This old lady disease, this palsied shaking of the hands, this infirmity of white-haired men sitting on park benches takes a long time, but it takes all. And my father would be aware of the whole distant process.

We talked around in this way that people do, my mother and I. No conclusions are ever reached in these circling conversations. They have no real beginning and no real end. I am still not sure who said good-bye to whom that night, but I slept not at all and instead stared at the play of lights on the wall until the sun rose and extinguished them.

My operation was a quick fix. In a few weeks I was able to ride on the road. A few weeks later, on the dirt once again.

Riding in the dirt with my new mountain-bike friends would be a way for me to put some distance between myself and my father's Parkinson's.

I am often guilty of that, I have learned. Blocking out unhappy thoughts. Not dealing with things. Not really thinking things through. In some ways that's a necessary evil for anyone who is driven to succeed. The tenacity and focus that's required to achieve can sometimes turn into a kind of tunnel vision, call it self-involvement if you will, but it works. But I also knew that I needed some help. My father was still doing well, and there was always hope, but I wanted something better than hope. So I reached out to Kathleeen. I called my old college roommate. She was always more talkative than I.

Kathleen Tubridy was my roommate for three of my four years at Mount Saint Mary's College in Maryland. Her nickname in school was "Tubs," from her last name, but I knew it made her self-conscious, depending on her current weight. She saved me from drowning during college. She taught me the things that my four brothers could not and my mother would not. Like how to wear lipstick and crop the tops and bottoms of my tee shirts. Kathleen tutored me on how to dress for Friday nights. She was also there for me when my brother Mark died.

We shared clothes and confidences, and rarely did we ever compete with each other for attention. I conceded to her pretty much. She had the power of making boys ask her to dance, and usually found one of their friends for me. Kathleen was outgoing, flirty, loud, funny, comfortable with herself, and able to make new friends easily. I was not. She let me tag along with her, a mixture of sympathy, and mission impossible.

After graduation we remained close. We vacationed together. Took long bikes trips together. Ran in the same social circle in Baltimore. She was the sister I never knew I wanted. Kathleen had gotten a degree in education and was teaching in the Baltimore public school system, and when she turned down a marriage proposal from the guy I always thought she would marry, she called me to commiserate. I immediately suggested to her that she come on out West.

I had told her that one of my housemates, Ari, would be moving into a new place in time for the fall semester freeing up a bedroom for her. So at summer's end Kathleen drove out with a U-Haul trailer and, quicker than it seemed possible, she was installed in my room and sharing my closet and her own half of my bed. This was a temporary solution imposed on both of us, I hoped, because Ari, whose room she was supposed to have taken over, had broken up with his girlfriend. He was now bunkered down in his drawn-curtained room comforted only by Jack Daniels and the grunge-music favorite reminders of their relationship thumping over and over on his boom box. I hadn't really planned for contingencies like sharing my room, for complications like Kathleen not understanding that I wanted to become a pro mountain biker, and certain other omissions. I had not prepared Kathleen for any of this.

A few weeks later Kathleen and I were playing pool in a surf bar on Garnet Street in our short shorts, wearing bare midriff tops and scrunchied ponytails, bathed in a warm evening breeze, surrounded by tanned beach boys. We looked like the Doublemint Twins. I mentioned to her for the first time that I expected Marc to arrive sometime soon.

Kathleen raised an eyebrow.

"Oh, I remember Marc. For a visit?"

"Yeah."

"Great. When?"

"Oh I don't know," I said. "He said something like Labor Day weekend."

"That's next weekend. Sounds like fun. We should have a party."

"But, he might probably stay."

"Really?"

"Yeah. I think."

"Where? I mean, is he going to find a place on his own?" she asked.

"Well, I sort of told him he could stay here, with me, you know with us. Until he finds something."

"Hmmph."

It was my turn to shoot and the recent surgery on my collarbone was still healing so I had to concentrate more than usual to keep from scratching. There still wasn't a complete range of motion as I lined up a bank shot. I was nervous. Too much top spin. Her turn.

Kathleen's face was a mask of equanimity. Her peach-colored lips held a smile and her ponytail bobbed with enthusiasm, but I knew her brain was in high gear running the dynamic tabulations of this new variable in our household's social algorithm. She possessed a feminine divination. She was aware of the meanings hidden to me in a casual dinner's seating arrangements, she could decode the pauses and coughs in a canceled date's voice mail, and decipher when a spilled drink was not an accident or when traffic was not the cause for being late or why some jokes weren't funny. She always filled me in later. I never had a clue. It's like she had eyes into a different world. She'd whisper in my ear which guy in the room was single. Which was in a relationship but fooling around, and which was definitely gay. Kathleen could sense the precise moment that a friend needed to cry and for those occasions she was prepared with a padded shoulder and a tissue. Kathleen refused to get into cars with the wrong kind of guy, and held my wrist firmly so I wouldn't either. But she never expected to be blindsided by me.

I felt bad, but I didn't know how I had gotten into this and could see no way out. Maybe they would be friends? Kathleen and Marc. I didn't want to hurt either of their feelings. I still beat Kathleen by three balls though. As we rode our bikes home that night we didn't talk much.

I hadn't considered how Kathleen would fit in with my new mountain biking friends. I hadn't figured out how Marc fit in at all either.

Marc had told me repeatedly in phone conversations to expect him by Labor Day weekend. There was no sign of him during Friday night's pool party, which Kathleen threw, or during Saturday's flag football and ultimate Frisbee tournament, which she had refereed. Not even a phone call by Sunday's beach volleyball fest, which she organized. Maybe Marc changed his mind, I thought. In the way a child is convinced school vacation will never end, I thought tomorrow is so far away I should revel in all that is good so far. That worked until Marc come through the open door late on Monday.

Kathleen really wanted to know why he was here. I wanted to know how I could have slept with this guy—more than once even. Marc's face was red and raw and the shadows around his eyes were dark and heavy. He brought with him a whiff of burning gasoline and the dank of high-school locker rooms and an undernote of McDonalds' French fries. He leaned a bicycle, touring bags front and rear, against the door jamb and then collapsed into an easy chair that Terence vacated for him. His arms had shrunk a little. Kathleen darted into the kitchen to get him a beer.

Marc: "My motorcycle started leaking oil, and no matter how often I stopped to top it off I couldn't keep up with it. That was three days ago."

Robbie: "Head gasket?"

Marc: "I wish."

Kathleen: "Where is the rest of your stuff?"

Marc: "I knew there was a small drip before I left, but I thought I could make it. Turns out it was the timing chain eating through the block."

Robbie: "No shit."

Terence: "So where did you get the mountain bike and those bags and stuff?"

"I brought 'em with me. On a rack I had some guy weld on the back of the motorcycle for me."

Again, Kathleen: "But where is the rest of your stuff?"

Ari: "You made a bike rack for a motorcycle? And you were carrying a bike on the back of a motorcycle all the way from Colorado? That's pretty stupid."

Ari was in premed. He was quite smart.

Marc: "Yeah, I thought so too, but I don't own a car, so . . ."

"So, now you are here," said Kathleen, handing him a cold bottle of beer, which Marc tried to drink in one long pull, but couldn't quite, and instead the beer foamed up and spilled down the front of his sweat-stained and otherwise filthy tee shirt that read in simple blocky letters, "Vote. It's Important."

I didn't know what to say. He didn't have any other stuff. Just what came through the door with him. I knew he would have a story. Which he did. It was amusing. Hardly believable.

He seemed to be trying to win Kathleen over more than me, and so far wasn't accomplishing much. But we all laughed, me the loudest; as he told how he had abandoned his motorcycle in a gas station's salvage yard in a dot of a town about twenty miles east of Yuma, Arizona. He imitated how the thin and gray gas station owner's words rang in his ears for hours, "You'll be bones when they find ya! Bones!" as he pedaled off on his mountain bike into the shimmering desert at noon during the middle of Labor Day weekend. How in Yuma it was so hot that truck tires were exploding and how he didn't have any spare tubes so he released as much air as he dared from his tires, knowing that each lost ounce of pressure in his knobbies would add many minutes to each thirsty, sweaty, ridiculous hour along Interstate 8's dirt shoulder. We visualized his wobbly ride through the desert, a gallon water jug hanging from the end of each handlebar, and howled as he described how he had to take equal sips from each jug to keep the weight balanced otherwise he'd ride off track into the traffic or out into the scrubby wasteland.

Did he really climb a billboard and sleep for a few early morning hours on its narrow platform because he was afraid of snakes? Does a pyramid squat out there in the desert not so far from the highway that you can see it if you squint? Is there really a place called Plaster City, the only outpost of civilization along that road—a giant, dusty, plaster factory with no water hose in its parking lot? Did he really ride about 180 miles? We didn't care. It was a good story.

A few beers later the laughs were dying down and the yawns were piling up. Kathleen made a big show of announcing that she was going to bed and marched off to my room. One by one my housemates peeled off and went to sleep leaving Marc and I alone for the first time.

"Are you going to be okay here in the chair? I'll give you a blanket."

"Yeah. I'll be fine. I'm so wiped out. Be asleep in a minute."

"You sure?" I asked. I didn't know how comfortable I was with the idea of leaving him in this chair. Him living in this chair. Eating and sleeping in this chair. Receiving mail—collection and past-due notices and warnings of unpaid parking fines—in this chair. In my living room.

"Yep. Be fine. Tomorrow I'll clean up and find a bartending job somewhere. And then we can start looking for a sailboat."

"A sailboat? That's a little premature, don't you think? I mean, don't you really have to have a job first? And get settled down somewhere? And don't we have to talk about it? The boat? I am supposed to go on a ride with Russ and Norm tomorrow after work. I don't have time to look at boats."

"Don't worry about me getting a job. And don't worry about your mountain biking either. Living on a sailboat will be better than living here. You'll be able to concentrate more, sleep better, train more seriously. You'll see."

"I don't know. I have a pretty good setup here, I think. This is a great house in La Jolla. Besides. A sailboat will cost money. And I have only a little bit saved. And I know you don't have any."

Marc reached into the pocket of his baggy shorts and pulled out a crumpled sweat-stained envelope. He waved it around. "This is a sailboat right here. At least a down payment." The envelope had been torn and its flap was creased as though he had opened it to check its contents many times. "A partial down payment anyway. Insurance settlement from my hand injury." He stuffed it back into his shorts. "Not a bad deal. I only lost the feeling in a couple of fingers."

Over the next few days it was obvious that Ari wasn't moving out. He rarely left his room during daylight hours. He'd go to work at night in the liquor store and bring back with him a pizza, and share it with Eddie Veder in his room. The grease-stained pizza boxes stacked up in the hallway. Marc was sleeping in Vidalia parked in the driveway outside my window. Only the window's thin screen was separating us. Kathleen slept beside me on my bed in her own sleeping bag. I was sandwiched in between the two of them. At night I tossed and turned fighting for more space. A space of my own. My housemates were tolerant but the house only had two bathrooms and one was in Robbie's bedroom so we all had to share the other in the hall. The dirty dishes in the sink didn't belong to anyone and weren't cleaning themselves. There were remote control battles for the TV. Phone messages were lost. There were battles over empty milk cartons, late video returns, and clogged shower drains. Marc and Kathleen struck an uneasy detente with each other. I tried to stay out of it. Ignoring uncomfortable situations around me was my stock in trade. I had no idea how they were going to work it out. I wanted to keep both as friends and I wanted both to move out, but I had invited each to stay with me. Maybe I would be the one to leave? What a mess.

It was a surprise a few days later as I skidded home from work into the driveway, and saw that Kathleen's stuff was packed up in her car. And Marc's bike on her roof. They had found a place together. Right off the beach down by the roller coaster. The neighborhood was a little seedy. The apartment tiny. But the rent was cheap. And each would have their own bedroom.

Marc did find work and he did start looking for a sailboat. I was passive. Sure, I told him. If you can find a boat and arrange everything and it won't mess up my training I'll go in with you. What was the harm? If he couldn't find a boat I still had my place. My job at the lab. And if he did, well, that wouldn't be so bad either. Getting a boat was the hard part. Maybe we really would sail around the world? I couldn't just tell him no. That I wasn't interested. That would be more crazy than relying on him to pull it off. The idea of traveling really appealed to me.

Sailing around the world. Seeing new stuff. Exploring. Adventure. Constant stimulation. If I kept moving I wouldn't have to worry about carving a respectable life. Perpetual motion would keep me one step ahead of the real world. It would provide plenty of distance from which to consider my father's illness. The distance could become a destination. After all, the lab was just a job; San Diego was turning out to be just another place. I had no sense of direction.

Eight hours a day I did what Dr. Fox told me. In grad school I had studied oysters because that was a condition of my grant. In college I learned what they wanted me to. I played piano the way the sheet music was written. Kathleen had picked out my clothes, and my mother picked over my boyfriends. Maybe it was because I was a girl, but I never felt encouraged to take charge. To go off in my own direction. My brother John, the oldest, left for California as soon as he could and now he had his own successful business in real estate. Dave, too, went his own way, a computer start-up, marrying outside the Catholic church and raising his kids to be bilingual. My brother Mark always set his own course regardless of the constraints of my parents' concerns. That's why despite his tragic accident and as much as I missed him, I knew that in some way his passing was a fulfillment of sorts. He died on a mission of his own choosing, for a cause he thought noble. He was doing what he wanted to do. Something I couldn't quite come to grips with. And even my little brother Chris, an ardent environmentalist, was pursuing his graduate degree in riparian ecology, despite my parents' desire that he become an engineer like my father. My parents respected the notion that boys will be boys, but I was a girl. I had been running away from their design my whole life.

I knew that sailing away was still running away. When I was riding my mountain bike I felt like I was headed in some direction. Even when I was hopelessly lost in the woods I knew that I was going somewhere. At least I was in charge. Myself. I determined left or right. I decided fast or slow. To keep going or to pause. And there was no shame if I got bruised or bloodied. No guilt if I was stronger than someone else. And those achievements affected everything else. Just like on a mountain-bike ride where I could yell, "No, this way!" and jump off onto a path separate from the pack. I now felt confident enough to tell my VW mechanic that I wanted him to just change the oil. No rebuilding the carburetor or valve jobs, thank you very much. Mountain biking helped me develop in the lab a sense of empowerment that let me speak up at staff meetings. That told me I had something to contribute to our published findings. Mountain biking was showing me the way to strike out on my own. Mountain biking was more than a phase. Like my rock-climbing phase. Or my surfing period. (That one lasted only a couple of weeks. The waves were too cold.) I relished the black and white of winning or losing a mountain-bike race. That clarity. There wasn't much of that in the lab. Sort of a moral gray area, killing monkeys to save people. The simplicity of making circles on a mountain bike to get from here to there was much more direct than the twisting turns, false starts, dead ends, and confusing roundabouts of the paths most people seemed to be on. Simple.

When I was riding my bike I wasn't remorseful about no longer playing music. I wasn't conflicted about going back to school for a doctorate. When I was riding in the woods or along the empty canyons, I chose whether or not I communed with my brother Mark. At times the bike was the only way to escape his loss. Other days it brought me closer to him. And recently, mountain biking kept at arm's length the degenerative disease that was every day inching further up my father's arm. A hard ride erased my concerns about whether I had agreed to go to the movies with both Kathleen and Marc or not, I couldn't please them both.

In the evenings after work, after I had finished hill repeats on Mount Soledad, the highest mound in La Jolla, I would put my legs up on the couch, savor a sip of iced water, and then the phone would start to ring. It would be Troy with an offer to play pool. Or Kathleen wanting me to go to dinner and meet some guys she just had bumped into. Or Marc wanting to come over and give my legs a massage and look through "for sale" sections in some sailing mags.

More and more I found myself choosing to spend time with Marc. It required less effort. He made it easy. And subsequently Kathleen and I began to see less of each other.

Something I wish had never happened.

Chapter 6

Stage 5—Morphing into a
Pro Mountain Biker

The trouble with most dreams is that they don't come with a set
of instructions for how to realize them. Rand McNally doesn't
have a map of Successville. Most of the time you have to make
your own way. If you're lucky, like I certainly am, you have a
few people along the way who are willing to lend you a hand,
maybe not point you in the right direction, but at least help you
get your bearings.

At night before Marc went to work at the bar, he would
swing by and massage my legs. While he was helping tune my
muscles, he'd try to tune up my head. He was smart enough to
wait until I was deeply under the spell of his magic thumbs before he'd begin. Marc was sure that I could turn pro, and when I
protested that no one was going to walk up and offer me a sponsorship, he jumped all over me.

"But did you know anybody at Scripps when you got your
job there? No. You didn't. You had to sneak in. Do a B and E.
No one is going to hand anything to you. You have to reach out
for it yourself. You know that."

"Do you think I could just make a pro racer resume? Who
would I give it to? Do I telephone first? Do I drive out to a bike

factory? What would be on it? You think it's easy. That it's so simple. Tell me how."

"I don't know. But you have to begin somewhere. You have to do something like that. I was hoping you would move to Durango when I was there. It would have been easier there. It is a small town full of pros already."

"Well, I'll just go to all the local bike shops and ask. That's all. I'll start by asking. I met this one guy, Eric something, at a race a few weeks ago. He works as a mechanic in a shop in PB. I'll ask him." While Marc continued to massage me, I plotted my strategy for the next Saturday. Eric was a tenuous connection, I figured, but if I picked up that thread it might lead somewhere.

Most bike shops are too busy to deal with vague and vacuous questions from people who have no intention of buying anything. They are, after all, trying to run a business. So I "scoped out" through the plateglass window my "friend," Eric, in the coffee shop around the corner from the store where he worked. I reasoned that it would be less onerous to pester someone on his "free time." I waited until he had nibbled the last of his morning bagel and dribbled most of his coffee before I "bumped" into him.

"Well. Small world. I am on my way right now to talk to the owner about sponsoring me." I blasted him my biggest and brightest smile.

We exchanged small talk for a while, established who I was and where we met before. Then I plunged in.

Eric sipped his coffee. And then took another sip. I imagined that I could actually detect the wispy hairs on his Gen-X chin growing thicker. Even though the cup was already half empty he blew into it as though it was still too hot. I was expecting a comment. Some acknowledgment. So far my casual encounter had gone exactly as scripted. This is where he was supposed to say,

"Wow, that's great! We've been looking to sponsor a rider for a while now. And you'd be perfect! Great timing! We just got a new shipment of race-ready, super cool bikes that are all just about your exact size. Why don't you come on over and pick out a couple!"

"Marla," he said softly. "It's not that simple. The owner, Bjarne, has four stores. He is a busy guy. He might not even drop by today."

"That's okay. I'll try today and if he is not around or too busy, I'll come back tomorrow."

"You have to understand that every day all sorts of Looney Tunes ride right through the front door and announce that they have turned pro, and that they have decided that our shop has been awarded the prize of sponsoring them. We just always say no."

"But, Eric, I'm not like that. I am not greedy. I know that I can win races and I just need some help."

This time Eric took even longer before answering. It was a contest between my bright smile and his chin hairs to see which would grow the largest.

"Okay. All right. Why don't you go on your ride and I'll talk to my manager. Jim is a good guy. Swing by after your ride and at least I'll have him a little bit buttered up for you."

"Thanks so much, Eric. You have . . ."

"But, I'm telling you he'll say no."

". . . no idea how how much this . . ."

"He always does. Racing doesn't really . . ."

". . . means to me."

". . . sell bikes."

"I know I can help you sell bikes," I promised. "I can."

I don't know if it was desperation or my unflagging intensity that won him over. I'd learned something though—don't be afraid to be bold—even if it's a sly kind of bold.

I hopped on my bike and beelined it for Tecolote Canyon where I did a lot of my "technical training." At the time I thought Tecolote was it. No better place for mountain biking available to man or woman in San Diego. In it I could chase after Julie Furtado on single track blazed by feral dogs and cats. Up its scarred walls I could outclimb Ned Overend and back down I could outwit Missy Giove.

A couple of hours later I wheeled my bike into the store still a little sweaty from my ride and caught Eric's eye. Eric was standing shoulder deep in the service area, surrounded by built-up bikes, broken bikes, repaired bikes, hopeless bikes, and trophy bikes. With a shrug of his shoulders, a weak smile, and a thrust chin, he signaled out to me Jim Norris, the store manager.

He was a roly-poly guy somewhere on either side of forty. He was outfitted in the beach community's retail uniform: sandals, knee-length shorts, and golf shirt.

"Hi. My name is Marla. Are you Jim?" A customer, a single mom wearing a bikini top and cut-off jeans, moved toward a BMX bike from whose handlebars dangled blue and white streamers. Jim's eyes tracked her.

"Marla. Yes, I'm Jim. Eric said you would be coming by but I'm quite busy."

Knowing that, I tried to talk about business instead of racing. I had absorbed the lesson just played out in front of me. Quickly I explained how I was going to provide them with more business. How I was going to increase sales and improve profits. Not how I was asking them to spend their money, part with their inventory, and cut a thin slice off their advertising budget. Jim's eyes scanned for the mother her and pudgy preteen son as they lingered by a toy mountain bike. I kept it brief. Stuck to some main points. I don't know where the words came from. Certainly none of my remarks were prepared. I made sure my voice was clear and strong. I stood tall, taller than Jim by nearly a foot, tall with confidence and capability. My shoulders were set back with conviction and, consequently, cast out my C-cup breasts with an uncompromising firmness at Jim's exact eye level. Sometimes a girl's gotta do what a girl's gotta do.

I concluded, "You can run one of those free ads in the back of the *Reader*. Something like 'LEARN TO RIDE WITH A PRO EVERY THURSDAY EVENING IN TECOLOTE CANYON. RIDES DEPART FROM BICYCLE NETWORK IN PACIFIC BEACH AT SIX O'CLOCK P.M.' And I'll make sure everyone buys spare tubes and pumps from the shop and after a couple of rides I'm sure some of the people will want to buy better bikes. I'll ride whatever kind of bike you want to sell the most and I'll make sure anybody who asks knows where they can buy one just like it."

I could see that Jim's eyes were lost in deep thought. His brow furrowed in concentration. His nostrils flared with decision.

Even though bike shops are businesses, they are not a real business. Not like General Electric, AT&T, or a Conglomerate Inc. That is, bike shops are about bikes, like small restaurants are about food. Sure there are some big bike-store chains, a few of which are actually pretty good, but for the most part bike shops are a mom-and-pop operation. And they do it because they were once kids themselves who were crazy about bikes. And that means that not every decision is necessarily a sound business decision. Like not every entree on a chef's menu is a moneymaker. And Jim Norris was a bike geek. There was no way supporting me as a racer made any kind of business sense.

"We couldn't do anything for you at the moment, aside from a tune up on your bike now and then. I'll run the ad and see how it works out. After a couple of weeks if everything is going okay I'll tell Bjarne, the owner, and see what he thinks. Maybe we can get you a deal on parts and stuff. Maybe."

"Great!"

"I'll ask Eric to keep an eye on you for the next couple of

races. Tell me how you're doing and stuff like that. You're racing in the pro class right?"

Not yet. But I said, "Oh yeah, I just moved up."

"And you haven't spoken with any other shop or company yet, have you?"

"No. Not for this season. I raced as an expert on a team last year for someone else, but I want to do better."

"Okay. Come by on Thursday and by then I should have scrounged up a jersey from somewhere with our logo on it," Jim said, before rushing over to the mom and son who were about to leave without having heard his sales pitch. Jim's nemesis, a skateboard shop, loomed large right across the street.

I was so excited that I could hardly lay still for Marc's massage that evening. I recounted it all. In exact detail, but with jumbled chronology and added hyperbole. As Marc finished up on my legs and began to work on my hands and arms, he grit his teeth together and sucked some air in, making a tiny whistling noise. He does that when he thinks he is going to say something important. Like giving an unconscious cue for an imagined stenographer to double check the paper and ink.

"Marla, you didn't sign anything did you?"

I was so mad at Marc that I was glad I didn't see him for the next couple of days. I was busy anyway, calling all my friends making sure that dozens would show up for my Thursday-night rides. Kathleen thought it was a great way to meet guys. And people did show up. They had read the ad and really did want to ride with a pro. Mountain biking was blowing up. Madonna and JFK, Jr., rode together in Central Park. Lifeguards on *Bay Watch* were rousting tourists on mountain bikes. They were under every Christmas tree and featured on dozens of TV commercials as valid reasons for selecting one Jeep over another pickup truck.

Lots of people wanted to ride with a pro to see for themselves what all the hoopla was about.

One thing though.

I had neglected to tell Jim Norris that I still had to apply for my pro NORBA license. I rushed the paperwork out and hoped I'd get my pro card before he asked to see it. But it seemed that my "sponsorship" was working out. Jim was cautiously pleased, and he told me that Bjarne would be by next Thursday to see for himself. A week later Jim let me use for the race season one of the shop's best bikes: a Univega Boralyn. It was made of some top-secret boron-aluminum compound and had all sorts of trick stuff on it. Grip-shift twisters, and an AMP-linkage front fork and bar ends, and all sorts of stuff that real pros were riding in the magazine photos.

Eric, the shop's mechanic, was doing so much work for me, truing my wobbly wheels, pacing me on long rides along the coast highway, balancing my out-of-whack barrel adjusters, and toeing in my brake pads, that I gave him as inadequate compensation my old and beat handpainted Rock Hopper. Bjarne, as it turned out, was an even bigger bike geek than Jim. Bjarne told me he would do his best to get me on the Univega race team for the next season.

A couple of weeks later my promise to Marc that I wouldn't sign anything with the bike shop without letting him read it first, was old news. We were back to the regular massage schedule. But it wasn't long before Marc was once again making that annoying whistling inhalation.

• • •

"Marla, you need a real coach. You have to stop letting every guy you meet on the trail or in the bike shop be your trainer for the day. One tells you you should work on intervals, another says you should do long slow rides, another you should only ride a road bike, and someone else tells you to stay on the dirt, 'keeping it real.' It's too much," Marc cautioned.

"But I have to learn. How else am I supposed to learn, if not by asking questions? And all these guys know more than you. They actually ride. On trails, not just to some bar room. And how would I find a coach? They're not really in the yellow pages. And I know it seems like I have a lot of money, but that's because I always work. Even still, how could I pay for a coach? How would I know that some coach's program would be the right one for me?"

"It doesn't make any difference which coach. Not really. Anyone is better than a whole bunch of different ones. You gotta choose one kinda program and stick with it."

Some of what he said was self-serving. There were a lot of guys that were eager to be helpful. I knew that. And I knew that he knew that. Those guys also wanted to invite me to dinner. Or to their apartment to view their Swiss spoke collection. Still, Marc made sense. I admit I was flailing around trying out whatever crazy stuff was recommended to me. My science background told me that I did need a baseline from which to start and measure my progress. I should turn myself into an experiment. Could I transform myself into a champion mountain biker? I should use the scientific method. Controls with variables. Quantify my results.

"But I think it should be a woman. You have to find a woman coach," he said. "You can't just trust all these guys. I mean you're beautiful and vulnerable to suggestions at this point and these guys know that. And you are already faster than most of them and they know that too. And nothing is free. Why would anybody want to spend time with you, dedicate some effort on your behalf without some sort of reward? And believe me you are better off giving a check to anybody than surrendering something more valuable."

"Just because you are suspicious by nature doesn't mean that you are right all the time," I argued. "There are nice people in the world too. Not just bad ones. Jaded ones, like you.

"Sure, there are. But you have to be realistic 'bout this if you really want to achieve what I know you can. You can be a champion, but there're no shortcuts. Any real coach expects to get paid. Ones that don't want to get paid aren't legit. Same as anything else. Free legal advice is worthless. Anybody offering you free magazine subscriptions is fulla shit. You know you can't even get a 'free estimate' from some carpet installer without expecting to have your stereo and TV ripped off a week later."

"That's just big-city talk. Tough talk. The world is not always like that. And even if it is, I don't want to operate in a world like that. That's why I am happy riding my bike. That's why I don't watch TV. I don't read three newspapers a day like you. The headlines are always about how bad the world is and how mean people are to one another. Disasters and accidents."

"Marla, if for no other reason, you should have a woman coach because only another woman can really draw up a training program for you. Guys don't or won't take into account that women are different."

"I'm just as fast, I work just as hard, I . . ."

"I know. I know you are. That's because I'm real sensitive. But, really, male coaches think girls are just playing. That chicks don't take sports seriously."

I knew that was true. Men often don't give women the consideration that they deserve in light of their anatomical differences. That was a dirty little secret of medical science. Many longitudinal studies of heart disease, diabetes, hypertension, and cancer even, had been conducted only on men, by men. Medical studies are flawed all the time because researchers don't factor in female physiology. Our hormones. Body mass. Bone density. Strength-to-weight ratios. And medical science makes incorrect diagnoses and prescribes ineffectual treatments and even harmful medications all the time because of that. Study results were often simply extrapolated for women—a practice the industry was just finding out produced disastrous results. "How do you know that?" I asked.

" 'Cause I'm a guy. Even though I'm pretty sensitive."

"So?"

"So you should get a woman coach. She'll know how to set up the bike for you. How to get you on a good diet. How to train you. Seriously. And you won't have to worry 'bout her trying to put any moves on you."

"You are just trying to scare me with that, because you are jealous of all my riding friends."

"True. I am jealous of all the time they spend with you. I know that I can't ride with you. You are too good. But I am not jealous of those guys as guys. They are all too skinny. I vood crush 'dem. And I also know it would be a disservice to you to pretend that I could help train you. I don't know enough. I'm trying to help you, that's all."

"But you said not to trust any guy that's helping me. So why should I trust you? You are a guy and you are trying to help me. And you are just a bartender after all."

"No. I said not to trust any guy who is helping you without knowing what he hopes to get from you."

"So, what do you want from me?"

"I want to sail around the world. With you. And that is just as stupid and silly and unrealistic as you becoming a world-champion mountain biker. But if you can do that, if I can help you do that in any way, then maybe you will help me. If you can succeed at something wild and dumb and impossible like that, maybe I can too. Sailing around the world is a pretty ridiculous goal for a guy who has never been on a sailboat in his life. Just a little help is all."

Marc shrugged. Marc can be good looking in certain, though very rare, lighting conditions. After a while he seems more handsome than he really is. His charm is never apparent in photos. When he talks in that awful Boston accent—I swear, it's thicker now that he has been away from Boston for years. "It doesn't make any difference that I love you."

I never knew what to say when he said stuff like that. I wasn't even comfortable thinking about an exclusive relationship with him.

Despite my good training rides that week, negative thoughts crept in while I was running gels at the lab. It is stupid to even think about being a pro mountain biker. I am twenty-seven years old, I thought. Way too late to play catch up. Pros begin racing as kids. You just can't jump into it. Even though I tried to wash away interior dialogue when I was in the shower, excuses and justifications stained my morning ablutions. According to the mountain-bike magazines most of the great mountain bikers come from California or Colorado. There are no pros from Maryland. They come from places where there is some history of mountain biking. Or downhill skiing. Where there are mountains. In the kitchen on Colima Street standing in front of the stovetop, staring into the swirling steam of my pasta, I rationalized that you need to learn bike-handling tricks and techniques as a kid when your brain is a sponge. It is incredibly hard to learn the piano as an adult. I knew. I tried teaching a few. An adult will never develop a good ear. And the inner ear, which is close to a good ear, is responsible for balance, one of the most crucial elements of mountain biking.

So why was I attempting it? Trying to become a pro? Why was I stalling? Was I just putting off making the commitment I knew it would require? Ever since my brother Mark died, I have avoided commitments. I didn't want to be hurt again, the way I was when I lost him. It hurt too much to love someone, and then just continue on afterwards, alone. That's why I had no serious boyfriends. Even Marc. No commitments. That's why I wasn't in a doctoral program. Why I liked paying cash. Why I persisted in acting like an adolescent. But my mind kept reaching the same conclusion over and over again. If I give my love to a sport, to mountain-bike racing, it will stay true to me. It won't ever lie to me, can't cheat on me, and will never die on me.

After thinking things through for a while, I told Marc that I was willing to hire a coach. But would he find one and talk to her to see if it would work out? And she had to be local. And not too expensive. I was just swamped with work, and training, and maintaining my friendship with Kathleen, and too exhausted from fighting off Marc's amorous advances to deal with it. If he was serious about finding me a coach he would see to it. It would be a little test. Like with the sailboat that he was supposedly searching for all day.

A few days later Marc was laying on his back in the driveway. The top half of his body was buried under Vidalia's engine skirts. A mishmash of tools was scattered at his feet. Marc was excitedly telling me all about Doreen Smith Williams, while I was supposed to be training a flashlight on a round thing with a belt on it.

"She lives in San Diego. Used to race herself. On the Canadian national team. She retired only a few years ago. She's a roadie but mountain biking is so new no one has been able yet to race, and then retire and become a coach. All the mountain-bike coaches around right now are coaching 'cause they couldn't make it as a top pro mountain biker. She is certified by USA Cycling, and there was a blurb in VeloNews recommending her. When I'm finished I'll dig out the article. I brought it with me. It's in a back issue."

"Good. I'd like to read that. Find out some more about her. What did you tell her about me?"

"I explained that you are twenty-seven . . ."

I frowned, but Marc's voice in the engine compartment, amplified in the process, went on regardless. "Marla you have to be honest with your coach. That's the whole point. I know you told the bike shop that you are only twenty-four. That you are afraid that everybody thinks you will be too old and won't give you a chance. But you can't hide your real age from your coach."

"Well, what else did you tell her?"

"I said that you were highly motivated, driven. That you had a master's degree that proves that once you set a goal for yourself you are willing to do the work necessary to attain it. That you have an incredible tolerance for pain and that you have already won top expert races your first season of racing."

"How much does she cost?"

"I don't know. I didn't get into that."

"What do you mean? What is the point of even discussing this if I can't afford her?"

"Marla, if you want to do this you have to do it right. You have to spend the money. I know that you deny yourself all sorts of simple pleasures. Most women, with the job you have, have a closetful of clothes, and a nice new car, and jewelry and stuff. They spend lots of money on perms and makeup."

"But you know none of that stuff interests me."

"I know. You think it a waste. An extravagance. Look at this old bus. The only stuff you wear are tee shirts that you get when you enter a race. Or from old boyfriends. You have only a couplea nice skirts and a few blouses. But a coach is not like splurging money on a mud bath. Or a pair of shoes from Saks."

"Ralph Nader," I countered, "says that the greatest environmental problem the world faces is fashion."

"A tee shirt, is a tee shirt, is a tee shirt. I agree. I get all my stuff from the Goodwill, but if you want to be a pro, you no longer will be able to live like that."

"I can save a lot of money by not spending it. You wouldn't know anything about that. The not spending part."

"Marla, I don't want to discuss how we each value money.

I'm trying to convince you that whatever the cost, you can afford this coach. You should afford this coach. That you can't afford to keep getting sick from overtraining. That you can't afford different guys adjusting and readjusting your saddle height. You can't afford constantly wondering if what you are doing is the right thing, the wrong thing, the smart or dumb thing. You have done real well on your own getting this far. But you need a little help."

Why was I being so resistant? Was I reluctant to admit that I couldn't do it on my own? Was asking for help, a coach, a sign of weakness? That I couldn't do it all by myself? Isn't mountain biking all about doing it by yourself? Isn't that why we race by the "no outside help" rule? Just the rider, alone, against the mountain? Or was it something else? Was I afraid of the commitment? The commitment I would have to make to this coach to do what she thought was best. The commitment to a program. The commitment to honesty that my effort would require. Honesty to her. And to myself. Ever since I was a kid I'd been a little fibber. I thought the little white lies were shortcuts, evasive easements, conveniently there for the taking. But there are no shortcuts to winning a mountain-bike race.

But were all these concerns really impediments? Like my age. I wasn't crazy about revealing my age to this coach. None of my little boyfriends knew I was twenty-seven and I liked it that way. I didn't want the Bicycle Network to know. At times I regretted not telling them that I had just turned twenty-one, but I didn't know how to explain having a master's and my job at Scripps before I could legally drink wine. So, twenty-four sounded okay.

Marc has no idea how age affects women. How the world looks at and treats us differently relative to our age. What is the difference between a sexpot and a spinster if not age? Both could be just as horny. What are the implications of being considered a girl or ma'am or lady by a waiter? By a stud muffin? By an employer? Men can wear the same blue suit only differing in size from first communion to funeral, and from looking at pictures I know some of them do. But women are always aware, or made aware, that they are too old for this dress, or too young for that bathing suit. If I told this coach how old I was, would she treat me differently? Less seriously? Would she tell me to not even bother trying, that I'd be wasting both our time? Would she go easier on me? And what would be next? What else would I have to tell her?

Who I was? Would she have to know that I was riding a bike away from things as much as toward something? Would I have to deal with that rationalization myself? Mountain biking, my perfect escape path, my effort to avoid commitments by riding away from them, would be twisted and turned in on itself like I was riding on a giant Möbius strip where there was no escape from ending up where it all began. What else would I have to confront and then confide to her?

I knew I should be eating more and better. But I wanted to be skinny too. Not sick skinny, but healthy skinny. Fit. It was better for my cycling. Or was I just kidding myself? Was I deceiving myself that the mountain biking gave me an excuse to be skinny. A reason that I could hold out in defense of starving myself. I never threw up or anything. Never took any of those diet pills, but I was always mindful of what I weighed each morning and what I ate each day and how much I worked out. Am I normal?

Did I really want to do this mountain biking thing? Or was I just playing with it? Amusing myself with it? Would being honest with myself that I had tried my hardest be worth acknowledging possible failure? Suppose I gave it my all and got nowhere? And everybody knew? Would they laugh? Would Kathleen understand that I had to have tried?

If I hired a coach—if I was really going to pay for a coach—I'd have given my parents another indication of how seriously I was taking all this cycling stuff. Was I up for that phone call too?

This coach would tell me next that in order to train I would have to quit my job, and then how would I be able to afford her, and my apartment and all my bike stuff? I had about a year of savings and could always camp out in Vidalia, but would it be worth it? To put everything I had on the line? How foolish would I feel if I sucked? Easy for Marc to tell me I should just write a check. How could I count on him for anything?

"So, what's next?" I groaned.

"I told her that you would ride over to her place next week. She lives just north of here. Talk things over, together." Marc grunted and his legs squirmed.

"Marla, please don't shine that flashlight right in my eyes. Try to keep the light on this thingy," Marc tapped the tip of his screwdriver against the greasy metal assortment of rods, nuts, and bolts that comprised the assembly of the dreaded "ball joint." I focused the weak beam of light where he had asked me, making an effort as he had helping me.

"I told her," Marc's voice, emanating unseen from deep inside Vidalia's entrails and therefore seeming omniscient like an ancient click-clacking oracle, "that I was interviewing a couple of coaches for you, but that you'd make the final selection yourself. Just ride over and talk to her. That's all."

"Did you talk to some other coaches?"

"A few. Some seemed like those personal trainers. You know the ones that wear black Reeboks and march up and down a little plastic step all day. There were a couple of spiritual types . . . inner strengths and incense and twelve-step programs that I knew you wouldn't be interested in. And I did call one or two guys, but I got the feeling that they wouldn't take you, you know . . . just some girl . . . seriously."

"So, this Doreen Smith Williams, is really the only one," I said.

"She's the only real one."

"Okay, I'll call her."

"Great! And then we can start checking out some boats."

• • •

In a few months Doreen Smith Williams had already become one of the most important figures in my life. Doreen, a proudly fit woman in her late thirties, commanded a very strong presence in a room. When she spoke, I listened. I didn't anticipate how quickly I would come to depend on her. How much I would value her expert opinions on training techniques and racing tactics, on the benefits of nutrition, recovery, and sleep. Just a short while ago I was trying it all on my own, and just going in circles. And now I consulted with Doreen about everything. I had told her that my goal is to turn pro for next season and win NORBA cross-country races, and she drew a road map for me to get there.

Doreen was an inspiration. She had chosen a field, world-class cycling, a sport dominated by the machoistic ethos of the classic tours, six-day races and the velodrome in which to compete. She had done it. And she believed I could do it too. If I made an honest effort.

I had about nine months before the Cactus Cup Classic would kick off the '93 race season. My rides were planned. My races scheduled. Doreen put me on a weight-training and exercise program. We talked a lot about nutrition. I trained with her other pro athletes, like Kiomi Waller, a BMX racer who was getting into mountain biking.

Doreen led our group rides. There were a lot of miles in her legs, she said, even if she didn't look like she was in great shape. Doreen Smith Williams was an imposing figure of a woman. Standing on slim ankles her calves were long and lean, slimming at the knees which swelled to powerfully defined thighs front and back. The strong features of her face were softened by a large smile that flashed whenever she felt like she was about to be too harsh, or too severe in her coaching duties. She wore her short hair carelessly, this way once, over that way the next, seeming whichever way the wind blew it. Strands of auburn and blonde twined comfortably with a smattering of gray. Small wrinkles winked from the corners of her large eyes, but I couldn't guess her age with any certainty. I couldn't say that she was pretty like a TV actress, but my eyes lingered on the strength of her chin, the fullness of her slightly chapped lips, and the wide planes of her smoothly tanned brow, and that made her beautiful.

Once, we were riding side by side on the narrow asphalt around the cool blue of Lake Hodges, among the tropically landscaped five-acre lots of Rancho Sante Fe, stealing conversation in snatches between the roar of BMWs and Audis that swerved past. I told Doreen that I was playing with the idea of buying an old sailboat and living on it. In case I wasn't able to make it as a pro. If I wasn't fast enough, strong enough.

"Don't be negative," she said. "If you want a sailboat, get one. Just be sure that you do want one. Just like you are sure that you want to race. You do want to race, don't you?"

"It's all I dream about. Racing. The sailboat is something else. I'm not sure, but I feel like I want one. I know I'll be able to focus on training more. More than I have been able to sharing a house with a bunch of people," I said.

Doreen and I discussed the pros and cons of my living arrangements. Turns out that she'd owned a sailboat once when she lived in New Zealand. Finally we got to the heart of the matter.

"The deal is, I plan to go in with a guy. Split the down payment fifty-fifty and he says he can do all the fixing up and stuff."

"This is Marc, your boyfriend? The guy who called me at first?"

"Well, he is not really my boyfriend, but yeah he's the one."

"What do you mean? Is he your boyfriend or not?"

It was tough to hold my line. I was squirming all over the road. Must have been a gust of wind. "I don't think of him as a boyfriend."

"Does he think he is your boyfriend?"

"He swears he doesn't, but I think he secretly does."

"Marla, I'm only your coach," Doreen's heading was straight and steady. She was breathing easy and deep, and on top of her pedal stroke. "And I've only been that for a couple of months, so I'm not going to go too much into this. But if you are going to get a sailboat it could help you focus on training. And you've shown potential. And all that could be lost if you get yourself messed up with boy problems." She was making it difficult for me to stay with her. "I'm not saying you can't have one. A boyfriend. I'm saying you have to know if you already have one." I find it very frustrating when someone rides a half wheel ahead of me, always out of reach, so that I feel I am always playing catch up. "He thinks he's your boyfriend, and you are buying a boat together, and you are going to live together on it and you don't think that you are his girlfriend. All sounds to me like you are setting yourself up for boy problems."

• • •

That evening while massaging me Marc said, "I don't want to hurt you." His hands were always soft. Soft from washing glasses at the bar. Soft from all the massage oil. He joked about never having worked a hard day in his life.

"You won't," I said. "Can't you feel that? It feels like a golf ball, right there in my calf."

"Okay. Okay," Marc cautioned. "A guy would be screaming right now if I was doing this to him."

Marc's thumb was buried in my gastronemus, his elbow bent at ninety degrees and his mouth hung open breathing in whistling sheets.

"If we look at this boat and we decide to buy it," I began, "what would that mean? You know I am not looking to get married. It'd be like sharing a house, right?"

"Come on, Marla. A boat is small. There is only one bed. You know that since I came out here I've been patient. But you know that whenever I talk about a boat, I'm really talking about us. Me and you."

"But Marc. I never promised you anything. And now I am starting to feel like the boat is a trap. That you are trying to trick me with the boat and sailing around the world and riding everywhere."

"I am not trying to trick you. I am trying to help you. And I am willing to stick it out until you figure that out. Till you figure that, yes, I love you and just because I have no money, no real job, no great looks, and not much prospect for the future, I can't stop loving you. Of course, it is all a trick."

"That doesn't make any sense."

"I know."

"You love me even though I tell you that I am not sure that I love you the same way. You say you want to help me even though you don't know how you'll be able to do that."

"Exactly."

"Marc, why can't we just be good friends?"

"Marla, I am sorry. But I am in love with you. I always have been. Even before we went to Europe. I thought it would go away, but it hasn't. I thought maybe when I was in Durango I'd meet up with some girl and then another and then maybe you would go away but you didn't. I wouldn't think about you anymore. And then I thought I'll go to San Diego and you wouldn't be the same. I'd see you and it would be different. You'd be someone else. Just a girl I used to know. But that didn't happen either."

"I don't know what to say."

"Don't say anything."

The knot in my calf was dissolving as his thumb rubbed circles along the grain of my muscle fibers. I was able to let out a full breath. Stale air had been trapped in the bottom of my lungs since the ride with Doreen earlier.

"Let's just do this and if doesn't work out, I'll buy out your half of the boat and sail to Mexico myself."

"You'd go to Mexico without me?"

"Yeah. I mean that's the point about it not working out, right?"

Marc was now working on my foot. Twisting and pulling at the ankle joint beyond the point it was pleasurable to where it was rapturous. Popping and snapping sounds emanated from my ankle joint as he moved it through its full range of motion. It sounded like there was beach sand trapped in there and he was grinding down the coarse grains between the mortar and pestle of my bones. I lay on my back staring at the stucco swirls on the ceiling. Searching for a pattern.

"What about if we get a boat and I turn pro and do okay?"

"And me and you are doing okay?"

"Yeah. And I am doing okay racing, you wouldn't rush me would you?"

"Marla, if we get a boat, and things are working out between us, of course I wouldn't rush you."

"You wouldn't?"

"No."

"No promises about us? We'd just try it out and if it works and I'm racing well . . . no problems with that either?"

"No. If you and I are working out okay, instead of sailing away as soon as we can, we'll wait until you're done racing. In two more years you'll be thirty. You don't really plan on racing past that do you?"

"I don't know. I've never even thought of when I might stop.

I'm just trying to figure out how to get started." I propped my self up on my elbows.

He had bent my foot back, stretching the achilles. Pointed back at me, my toes waved at me under the steady strain.

"Okay," I said. "We'll take Vidalia to Los Angeles and look at this boat. But you will have to handle everything. I am going to be swamped. If we get this boat, I'll have to call my parents. They'll be worried. I'll have to talk to Kathleen." My toes were waving good-bye. I raised a hand to wave back and winced a bit as the gap in my still-healing collarbone widened under the strain. "Kathleen is not going to understand."

• • •

We did go look at that sailboat. The sellers, a nice couple, the Levys, even took us for a sail. Marc was funny. Once under sail poor Mr. Levy asked Marc if he wanted to take the tiller. Marc had no idea what Mr. Levy was talking about. He pointed to the long smoothly sanded hardwood, which was resting in a salty notch in the crook of Mr. Levy's arm and asked, "You mean that wooden thingy?"

Marc lost a lot of his negotiating power in that exchange with Mr. Levy. I grabbed the tiller and pointed in to the wind until we were heeled over, the decks awash, and the rig was humming. I had been doing a lot of negotiating myself. A rep from one of the bike companies, Iron Horse, had been coming by the Bicycle Network quite a bit in the last few weeks. The shop carried Schwinns of course. I had one when I was a kid. It was my brother Mark's, an Orange Krate, and pretty beat up by the time it was mine to ride. The shop carried GTs, the mountain bikes that Julie Furtado, the national champ, raced on. And Uni-vegas. That was the bike they tried to sell the most. I guess they had a good deal on them. I replayed the highlights of my conver-sations with Jeff as Marc white knuckled the cockpit coaming and the Levys puzzled out whom to address the boat's selling points to.

This bike rep, Jeff, was trying to get the owner of the shop to sell Iron Horse bikes. He was a persistent guy. He'd even gone on a couple of my Thursday night rides. He was trying to convince me to do a cyclocross race next week. My collarbone was okay for road rides and easy mountain-bike trails, but I wasn't sure about cyclocross. Doreen was bringing me along slowly. She wanted me to spend a lot of time in the gym, lifting weights and building muscle in my upper body she said. She wanted me to be able to race a complete season without injury. I hadn't told her yet about this cyclocross race. It was nearby. At UCSD on trails under the eucalyptus trees on which I had been commuting to work at Scripps for months now.

Jeff was persuasive. He told me that Toby Henderson would be there. I had no idea who Toby Henderson was, and Jeff explained that Toby was a downhiller. I raced cross country and thought downhill was sort of dumb. The thing that didn't seem sort of dumb was the fact that Toby was looking to sign a rookie female for his team. That caught my attention. Opportunity seemed to be knocking.

I brought the boat around, the large headsail snapping across the bow and the mainsail booming over the cockpit to catch the afternoon on-shore breeze. Marc's eyes watered, perhaps from the cold wind, as Los Angeles sunk into the wake behind us. I saw myself racing cyclocross next weekend. Lapping the women's field. Dicing my way through the men's pack. "A mysterious unknown dueling with the pros," the announcer would baritone. "This Racer X has just taken the lead, passing Toby Henderson! Get ready for this fans," the announcer would crow to the shoulder-tight crowd that hemmed the course, "Racer X is a woman!" On the bell lap I'd be pulling away, putting the hammer down on the chase group, only one final obstacle to clear before the finish line. I dismounted, and raised my bike in one fluid motion to shoulder height, resting the top tube on my rotator cuff in the classic cyclocross manner, the toe of my left bike shoe planted at the base of the twelve-inch high plywood obstacle. I saw my right leg arc in a flashing parabola over the obstacle's crest and gracefully land beside my bike's wheels onto the soft soil on the other side. Cameras snapped and the crowds cooed at the momentum I carried and at the great form I showed, and all were shocked at the sight of tangled tubes and limbs, none having seen my right toe catch the top of the obstacle and none realizing more than I, that once again my collarbone was broken.

"I'll do it, Jeff," I had said. That diplomatic tactic is known as the "cave in."

The mainsail was starving the headsail so I yanked the tiller flipping the boom over and let the traveler out all the way so that both sails puffed out on each side of the boat like a bird's wings. I had told Jeff I'd enter a race that I hadn't yet told my coach about. A type of race, cyclocross, I'd never done before and only seen photos of in VeloNews. Months earlier I had signed a contract with Bicycle Network that I promised Marc I wouldn't. And I was hoping that this complete stranger, Toby Henderson, would make me an offer I couldn't refuse. How much trouble would I be in with Jim and Bjarne? I had no idea what I was going to say about this to my parents or to Kathleen. I knew that somehow Marc was going to be able to talk the price of this boat down. And I was going to do that race no matter who said what.

Los Angeles' infamous pollution paints the twilight sky Disney oranges and van Gogh yellows. Maybe it would just be easier to slip over that slim horizon with the wind, I thought. Maybe that's why we'll buy this boat. In case things don't work out.

• • •

The yellow ribbons strung out among the eucalyptus trees on the UCSD campus were less than a quarter mile south from the Scripps lab. I had ridden on some of these trails only the day before on my way to my lab cubicle. Many times during lunch I'd snuck off to these trufula trees shading the windswept trails pretending that I was a pro, and now here I was with a chance to "try out" for a real pro team. Jeff had made no promises beyond an introduction to Toby. I wanted it so badly that any possibility other than a contract was inconceivable!

As I warmed up on the course, it seemed that on each quadrant of my circling laps there was a force that exerted a pull on me. It was as though I was riding atop a giant divining rod that tweaked this way and that of its own volition. Some mineral element in the Boralyn tubing of my bike, like a compass needle swinging to mysterious magnetic forces, pointed me toward scattered directions.

I pedaled along under these strange influences searching for Toby as slyly as I could. Right in front of me was the solid outline of the Scripps Reasearch Institute, and the secure future it guaranteed. I could stick to that path and who could fault me. That was the direction that people were supposed to take. A good job. A good future. Health benefits. The pull was weak, but palpable. Risk free and blameless.

One hundred and eighty degrees from Scripps stood Kathleen and my housemates grouped in a sunny cheering chorus. The whistles and clapping of my friends were echoes of a past that I no longer felt close to. I'd convinced myself for a while now that, although they were supportive, they didn't really want me to succeed. Not out of malice or jealousy but still they hoped that I'd give up trying to be a pro. If I gave up it would just be easier for them. As though one day I just decided out of the blue to be a strict vegetarian, and my personal decision made them feel bad about their own personal decisions. My soy burger took the pleasure out of their baby-back ribs or kung pao chicken. And in little, seeming unintentional ways, they all crumbled bacon bits into my salad or tossed pepperoni into my linguini. The failure of an aquaintance is very comforting in a way. We Germans call the concept *schadenfreude*.

I imagine that Kathleen felt a little threatened by the prospect that I might really become a pro mountain biker and leave her and our friendship behind. Although Kathleen recognized that she was a great schoolteacher, she considered herself to be a surfer, and a snow boarder, and a rock climber too. I looked up to her as though she was my big sister. And now I think she felt we were playing a sibling rivalry zero-sum game, where a gain for one was perceived as a loss for the other. Every boy who asked her to dance was one who didn't ask me. Every bike race I won was a snow-board competition that she didn't. Teaching grade school was a real job and could be as boring as my lab work, but if I could escape from my drudgery then she too would have to try and escape hers. Or admit that the risk was too daunting. Kathleen's pool parties in the backyard, or stick-ball games in the driveway, seemed to me to be challenges of a sort. Maybe I was crazy but I imagined that she planned these fun-filled events to present me with the choice of playing or training. I had to make the unpopular choice. Sometimes I felt like I was a little kid trying to do math sums on a sunny afternoon in my bedroom while being tortured by the sounds of hopscotch through the open window, and I resented that a little too.

The truth is often painful, and I'd come to believe that on every day that Terence punched insurance data into a hospital mainframe, he knew that his hovercrafts wouldn't fly, and the computer programs he wrote for games would likely crash. Forty hours a week Robbie changed oil in one of those quick-lube operations, and he knew that his El Camino would never be put back together again. Ari was wrestling with his premed studies, cramming for his MCAT exam, and a little fearful of how difficult medical school and an internship would be. I had come to believe that my housemates' invitations to drink schooners of beer at Coasters, play Hacky Sack in the living room, or tailgate at a Chargers' game, although genuine, were also disingenuous attempts to derail my training. If I slept late in bed with a hangover and missed my morning training ride, Terence didn't feel so bad about stalling work on his gaming programs. If my bike was in the work stand and I was having a hard time dialing in my shifting, Robbie wasn't as troubled about not getting around to reboring his El Camino's engine block. Somehow my bike tools often ended up on Robbie's workbench or under Terence's hovercraft. As bruised and bloodied and beat as I was, as long as I climbed on my bike each morning, Ari had no reason to not crack open his medical texts.

I circled round and round the cyclocross course concentrating on what gear I should be in, memorizing where the wooden obstacles were, holding my breath through the fog of ganja that marked where my housemates were cheering me on. What was fun for them, this little cyclocross race, was serious to me. To just get a chance to become a pro mountain biker I had to race this cyclocross race first. Not exactly a straight-line progression.

My brother John and his wife, Elaina, had come out to watch my race too, and their presence pulled at me, invisible familial strings that stretched east unbroken all the way back to Baltimore to my mom and dad, the master martinets. My family thought mountain biking was a hobby, like "extreme" golf. There was no harm in it, as long as it didn't interfere with the grand plan's trinity of career, marriage, and kids. This mountain biking would pass. Fade from memory, an embarrassment like disco, and in a few years around the holidays they would pull

out old Polaroids and we'd all laugh at the white suits and platform shoes.

On the ocean side, the pull was the strongest. On the western
horizon was the sea, and against the blue-on-blue backdrop
were the silhouettes of Marc and Doreen Smith Williams. They
both wanted me to do well, but each exerted earnest influences
in ways that tangled and twisted the direction I wanted to pur-
sue. Doreen wanted me to be aggressive in this race. Doreen told
me to ride with Toby as much as possible. Marc was afraid I was
flirting. Doreen told me to expect no easy way out, and Marc
was actively preparing an escape vehicle, a sailboat. Doreen told
me to not worry about the course. Just ride it and take what it
gives me, work with it during the race, and seek an advantage
where there might not appear to be one at all.

And circling the course with me, adding to the swirling con-
fluences of irresistible forces and immovable objects, was Toby
Henderson. At that moment he might as well have been a god.
Toby was a big guy, big for a mountain biker, I thought. The
guys I was used to racing with were sleek and wiry. Toby was
well muscled; a powerful man. His nickname during his BMX
racing days was "Captain Elbows," so aggressive was his racing
style, and I could see evidence of it as he dropped off the lips of
steep embankments only to charge up the vertical wall on the
other side. Toby was riding a mountain bike, green and white
and blue, the colors of his uniform, the colors of his team: Team
Iron Horse. A few other mountain bikes roamed the course. I
was on my Boralyn Univega. The cyclocross bikes, lighter and
skinnier, whizzed around and I struggled with lifting my mountain bike over the wooden barricades. I was amazed by the way
that Toby flashed past me during practice, bunny hopping as he
did through sections that everybody else ran.

The race was a small affair organized by a frantic, enthusias-
tic promoter, and a couple of his friends, laid back and lack-

adaisical. The volunteers grouped us racers together near the starting line only a few minutes behind schedule. There were about fifty entrants, maybe a dozen women. Prodded by Jeff's encouraging head nods, I wheeled my bike alongside Toby's while the race promoter talked about how many laps we would race, where to pin our numbers, where to expect the final lap bell, etc.

"Hi, my name is Marla Streb."

"Hi," said Toby. He held out his hand. I had forgotten to extend mine when I introduced myself. Now that I had his hand in mine I didn't want to let go. Toby's fingers were large and thick like carrot sticks. My tongue swelled to the size of a bath towel and my voice cracked. Jeff rescued me.

"Marla is the one I was telling you about," Jeff said. "A real cross-country honch."

"So, you're Marla," Toby said. His voice lingered with confidence and he smiled with the healthy ease of a lifelong milk drinker. Toby was that California blend of suntan and blonde hair and blue eyes that jumped off the mountain-bike magazine covers. Other racers were already giving him a new nickname, "Hollywood Henderson." "Are you going to take it easy on me this morning?" he teased with an easy familiarity I found alarming.

In an instant I was once again the too-tall, bucktoothed, skinny girl in eighth grade. Reflexively I rounded my shoulders and lowered my chin so that I appeared shorter than Toby. How could this be happening? Wasn't I a twenty-seven-year-old woman? Hadn't I delivered an oral defense of my master's thesis? Didn't I believe that I was faster than he? Our elbows were no longer pumping in the acceptably polite handshake fashion. Our handshake was beyond the awkwardly long stage by now. I still couldn't speak. My education was failing me. What good were all the hours I'd invested on my mountain bike if I couldn't cash in on this moment? All my bruises and scrapes and scars were IOUs I had issued myself, and now refused to redeem. I should have enjoyed the pig-roast barbecue last Thanksgiving rather than wasting my time on a road ride up to Oceanside. Maybe Kathleen was right. Maybe I'm just a mountain-bike rider, and nothing more. Not a mountain biker. Certainly not a pro.

"Thirty seconds!" a voice called out. The race promoter jumped down from his milk crate. "Senior men in front! Master's men. Then women, then juniors. Come on, line up!"

"I have to go," I blurted out. "Nice to have met you."

"Good luck, Marla," Toby said. "I'll be watching you."

I didn't crash. I risked crashing on every turn, cased every jump and sometimes washed out on smooth flat straightaways, but I stayed on my bike. Marc yelled for me to be more careful. Doreen watched with discerning detachment. I knew that Toby was watching me too. The women started thirty seconds after the men. I caught up to the slower guys after the first lap, and then began picking off the faster ones one by one whenever a straightaway gave me an opportunity, a turn, a chance, or luck presented itself. I reached a point during the race when I was dueling with a pack of guys, a half dozen, and Toby was one of them. I'd surge on a small climb and pass two of them and I'd mis-shift through a sandy patch and three would pass me. I wanted to show Doreen that I possessed self-control and I wanted Toby to see that I was fearless. Toby and I diced in that way for the remaining laps and I finished just ahead of him. I wanted to show them both that I didn't ride "like a girl."

That was about the worst thing anybody could say about you. That you ride like a girl. That insult, or variations of it, antedated mountain biking for sure. You throw like a girl. Or you hit like one. Or run like one or even pee like one. Words like those made both little boys and girls cry and grown men angry or embarrassed. And words like those had separated some women from sport, segregated many from having an equal chance.

I wanted in. I wanted Toby Henderson to think that I rode like a guy. Even if it meant that I spent more time with my ass in the dirt than in the saddle.

After the race Doreen, shaking her head, said my bike handling skills needed a lot of work. That I was scary to watch and a danger to myself and to others on the course. Jeff, too, said my bike handling skills needed a lot of work and echoed that I was a danger to myself and others, but he was smiling.

This was my big chance. Like being noticed in a high-school play by a big movie producer. Or a sandlot pitcher discovered by a major-league scout.

In the bathroom at home in preparation for meeting Toby Henderson, like a student actor ripping De Niro in *Taxi Driver,* I had rehearsed my line, "I *want* to be a pro mountain biker." And then, with my head cocked, "I want *to be* a pro mountain biker." My roommates stood in the hallway banging on the door waiting for their showers while I convinced myself in the mirror. "*I* want to be *a pro* mountain biker." I had blown my introduction with Toby before the race, and had punished myself for it during the race. I made myself hurt with exertion. I rode like the rocking horse winner, wild eyed and feverish. Like I could wipe away my shame with sweat. A mantra under strained breath, on each lap I repeated the line that I had practiced the night before and choked on during our introduction.

After the race I wobbled up to Toby and said, "Iwanttobeapromountainbiker." The words came out. Flat and lifeless. Soft and surely unrecognizable. Toby nodded his head politely with incomprehension the way a traveler does when on vacation in some country where there is no MTV or McDonald's. He smiled patiently, like the uninitiated, in response to the baby talk of a new grandchild.

"It's obvious you don't mind taking risks," Toby ventured. He was still smiling. "I almost took you out on that second chicane back there; but you went for the pass anyway."

This was the occasion for reliving the race; when the racers talk in jargon about root sections and rock gardens and washboards or a shared history of misery and elation, that cements the bonds between competitors. There is a semiestablished flow of conversation about the race results. The winner speaks first about the defining moment. The instance where the race was won, the approach to a particular turn that has now earned a name in that race's mythology like the whirlpool, Charybdis, in Homeric poems. The winner is allowed to proclaim this triumphant turn for the whole car ride home. The slowest then gets to tragedize the first excuse. The chorus of competitors shake heads in commiseration then wail in baritone, "I almost dropped my chain on that climb too!" Then each verse recounts every small dramatic moment of the race culminating in the refrain about the triumphant turn.

Toby was giving me the stage to sing about my pass on the second chicane section according to custom, but all I could peep was, "Iwanttobeapromountainbiker."

"Everybody wants to be a pro mountain biker, Marla," Toby conceded. "But tell you what. Why don't you come up to LA next week and I'll introduce you to our west-coast distributor."

"Great!" I beamed.

"And bring some photos. A head shot and some action photos. Race pictures. And we'll see what happens."

The interview at the Iron Horse office made me nervous, but at least I stood straight. Afterward in the lobby Toby told me to it would be a couple of weeks before any decisions were made.

Marc and I bought the boat from the Levy's. We sailed her

Me standing in front of my favorite companion and bike part storage locker, Vidalia. (*Author*)

down to San Diego and tied her up at the cheapest available berth in Seaforth Marina across the street from SeaWorld. In the marina parking lot Vidalia established residence and assumed a new occupation as my bike shop/storage locker. Her polka-dot curtains and Kryptonited sliding door guarded my mountain and road bikes. Cardboard boxes of parts and tools and milk crates of spirited chamois and rain gear were stacked on top of a set of Kreitler Rollers that Marc had "borrowed" from a friend and even to this day still hasn't returned. We stowed aboard our dream boat the rest of our wordly possessions inside the nooks and crannies of her nine-foot beamy width, under the cabin sole into her six-foot keel, from stem to stern of her thirty-seven-foot length. We didn't have much: some books and a shoe box of music cassettes, duffel bags of tee shirts and shorts and baseball caps—enough for about four unique outfits—my answering machine, and a beat-up Radio Shack telephone. Marc right away began restoring and repairing our "fixer upper" sloop, and I trained and worked out before and after my day at Scripps lab, and waited for Toby's phone call, which finally came a few weeks later. A contract followed in the mail.

As a girl, my signature had been a soft scribble of rounded consonants and looping vowels, neat and meticulous. Had it required the letter "i" it would have been topped with a heart-shaped dot. My signature was now a screech of jagged loops and vertical slashes and stared at me from the bottom of this professional mountain-bike contract. The deal was for one year at zero salary but provided two new Iron Horse bikes, race fees, travel and accommodations, and allowed me to keep all my prize winnings. There was an option to renew for another year with the same terms, and the right of first refusal! My signature transformed me into a pro mountain biker.

Just a few squiggles with a blue and white toothworn Bic pen? A wave of a magic wand? Was it magic, or would it be hard work?

That night Marc barbecued boneless, skinless, nonfat chicken breasts on the back of our little sailboat and we twisted open the plastic cap on a bottle of "sparkling wine," and after the sun sank below the green flash of the horizon, and as the fireworks from SeaWorld lit the sky, I asked Marc to shave my head, mohawk style. I needed some part of my shoulder-length hair on my scalp otherwise my bike helmet would no longer fit. Clenching the half-dozen pages of my pro contract I marvelled under the exploding colors of bottle rockets and pin wheels at the signature that made it real and at the clumps of my hair falling all over, which sealed the deal.

"Ow!"

"Sorry. The boat moved."

"That's okay. I want you to cut my hair off, but I don't need my ears lopped off. My sunglasses won't sit right without ears."

"Sorry."

"That's okay." A thatch of hair was floating in my coffee mug of champagne but I drank it down anyway. "Ith there anymore?" I asked, pulling some bubbly strands of hair from my mouth.

"Yeah, there's another bottle. It was two for five bucks. Want me to get it?"

"No. I don't want anymore. I was just asking. I wanted to know if this bottle was empty. If this was my last glass of champagne."

"Let me get the other bottle. There's not enough ice in the ice box to keep it cold for tomorrow. We should celebrate."

"No, I don't want anymore. Whooh." I blew the hair off the contract and smoothed the edges where it was beginning to curl, "I'm not going to drink anymore."

"You mean forever?"

"I don't know. But not for a while. At least a year. That's why I want you to cut my hair. I have to do things differently now that I am a pro. There's no turning back now. No more candy, no more sweets. No more playing pool and no more late nights. No more beer or margaritas. No more of any of that stuff. And I have to stop seeing any friends who will tempt me."

"Really?"

"Of course. Why do you think I wanted to buy a boat? I have to leave a lot of stuff behind if I want to make good on the commitment this contract here in my hand means."

"Marla, if you want to win races, I know you can. But let me help. I can help."

"How?"

"Quit your job. I'll pay the bills."

"You can't do that. I mean, I don't want to hurt your feelings, but you are not the most responsible guy around."

"I know. I know. But I will be. I can pay the slip fee and the phone bill and do the shopping and stuff. I can do it for at least one year."

"But this boat needs a lot of work. Look around." The fiber-glass deck and cabin top were a robin's-egg blue, faded and chalky with age. Even in the sixties when our boat was built that color couldn't have been too popular. The wood grain on the coaming that surrounded the cockpit and the tiller itself was raised and almost black with the particulates from Los Angeles' smog. The deck was missing railings and cleats and winches and lots of other stuff that was required to make her safe and sea-worthy and livable. And down below in the small galley kitchen and in the V-shaped bedroom in the bow was where the real work needed to be done.

"Marla, you could be great. Or you could stink. I really have no idea. But I'll help you anyway. Who knows? Look at Larry Bird. He was a garbage man before he went back to college and made the Final Four. And Joe Montana was practically the last football player drafted out of college. And Greg LeMond was shot in the chest and still has a bullet lodged in his heart and he came back to win the Tour de France, again."

I had heard of Larry Bird. He played basketball. He looked out of place on TV with those short shorts, flabby pale skin, and wispy blonde mustache. He did look like he could have been a garbage man with that funny haircut, parted down the middle with bangs and shaved over his ears, practically a mullet. I didn't know who Joe Montana was. But of course I knew who Greg LeMond was. The greatest American cyclist ever. A hero. That's right. His brother-in-law did shoot him by accident on a hunting trip after he had won the Tour twice and he did come back after a year off, when no one thought he could, and win it for the third time.

"You'll probably be so good," Marc was saying, "that we'll be able to fix up this boat better than new and we'll be able to sail around the world and ride our bikes anywhere we want."

"Quit trying to swell my head." But it did feel good. Just when I was beginning to have doubts. Marc had been great. So far, the only other guy coming close to believing in me was another local racer, Gene Hamilton. Gene was a snowboarder trying to turn pro as a mountain biker. He had told me to quit fooling around and buy myself a heartrate monitor so that I could train to the utmost limits of my beating heart. He knew how hard mountain-bike racing was and what the sport demanded and how slim the odds were that I would even have a zero-salary contract in my hands. But Marc really didn't know anything. He only rode his bike to the bar where he tended. Why should I believe him? Why should I believe him when he says I can win races? There's even less reason to believe him when he says he can help out financially. But I wanted to believe him anyway. I wanted to believe in myself too.

"I'm not trying to swell your head. But I am trying to maneuver you into bed." Marc had set aside the disposable razor and safety scissors and was rubbing moisturizing lotion all over my bright white scalp and now his fingers were on my shoulders, squeezing and pulling the ache of the day's road ride right out of them.

I knew what that kind of shoulder massage meant.

"I am giving that up too," I said. "Remember. I have to concentrate. Stay focused. For at least a year."

Of course I was only teasing but he didn't need to know that right away. Marc's fingers kept their constant pressure on my shoulders. My head flopped from side to side in a steady rhythm to the beat laid down by his fingers.

"I am not riding to Scripps tomorrow."

"No?"

"Nope. Tomorrow I am going to start my new job. Just riding my mountain bike."

One of the best perks in academia is the sabbatical, or leave of absence. When you work for a university or research institute you might not make a lot of money, the opportunity for tenure might be remote, the publish-or-perish mentality may be pervasive, but you can take long vacations that are euphemized as sabbaticals. Sabbatical is from Latin and it means, "this vacation is a pretty good deal and it makes up for a lot of aggravation, but let's keep it sort of quiet, if you know what I mean."

So, to hedge my mountain-bike gamble, Dr. Fox agreed to reduce my status to part time, and when the racing season really began, granted me a leave of absence for the summer. I would be able to remain in the Scripps health plan while competing. If I was a complete bomb as a mountain biker I could slink my way back to the lab if I wanted to.

Doreen thought I should continue working right up until the races began. She believed that work provided a structure around which I would be forced to train. Too many athletes quit their jobs or schooling to devote themselves to training and then discover a wonderful facility for procrastination, she said. Doreen said if I knew I only had a few hours a day to train, I would make the most of my opportunities. I think now, Doreen's unstated reason for encouraging me to work for as long as possible was to prevent the more debilitating rookie syndrome of overtraining.

Doreen was a great coach and a woman to look up to.

• • •

That rookie pro season in 1993, I won every cross-country race I entered and crushed all my competition. In my dust I left behind Julie Furtado, Alison Sydor, and other names now enshrined in the Mountain Bike Hall of Fame. I dominated the field so that the race itself was a prelude, a ritualized exercise like the bestowing of flower bouquets and opening of champagne, before I climbed to the top of the podium to receive my uncontested gold medal. Demoralized women were refusing to line up alongside me at the start, and those who weren't were clamoring for me to race with the men. I had hired a public relations firm to respond to the loads of fan mail, the breakfast at the White House, and the rumors of my secret marriage to Brad Pitt—all distractions that I handled with aplomb as I raced toward the first undefeated season the sport of mountain biking had known.

Not really.

In reality, my first pro season was a qualified disaster. I didn't win a single cross-country race. Didn't even make the podium. But I did learn that compromising a little is sometimes better than conceding the whole. That, better than retreating, moving laterally, opening up a new direction, can still lead to achievement. That sometimes the shortest distance between two points can be a circle.

The 1993 Cactus Cup was my pro debut. It was called the "practice cup" because, as it was the first race of the season, new bike designs were on the line, new equipment was tested, new uniforms were sported, and all these elements were thrown together in the desert and expected to perform flawlessly despite the strain of competition and the scrutiny of team sponsors and the small mountain of biking press. The Cactus Cup was a stage race, comprised of a one-lap time trial the first day, the big cross-country event the next, and that night as a finale, the crowd-pleasing fat-boy slick criterium.

My new Team Iron Horse cross-country bike was sandwiched in the back of Vidalia's living room as I chugged along the asphalt ribbon of Route 8 to Scottsdale, Arizona. I drank from my Team Iron Horse water bottle at each mile marker along the way and grooved at fifty miles an hour to the hissing cassette of the Stone Temple Pilots. Marc was my copilot and his nonstop monologue about how great I would be made it easy to imagine an undefeated season. By the time I had parked Vidalia at Pinnacle Peak, Marc had filled my head with more hot air than the surrounding desert waves of shimmering red rocks, towering saguaro cactus, and white sandy single track. Marc checked Vidalia's oil and popped open her roof and set up camp while I changed into my Team Iron Horse uniform. Dozens of other pickup trucks and station wagons had already set up camp as bike shop and field kitchen, product display and keg party. Ford Explorers and Jeep Cherokees weren't known then as SUVs. I rode past them on my shiny bike in my crisp uniform and pretended that all eyes were on me, noticing what gear I was in, approving of my tire pressure, in awe of my pro deal.

The Team Iron Horse truck showed up at the venue just after I had finished a practice lap. I washed the dirt off my face and smacked the dust off my brand new uniform and pedaled over to my pro-team truck, blue and green and white, logoed and stickered up with the official race team sponsors. There was on the bottom, the last of all, under the heading Factory Riders: *Marla Streb*.

Toby made the introductions and as a team we all shook hands, nodded heads and smiled. Tom Buzzelli, tanned and ripply with muscle, was another cross-country rookie. Johnny Bottema, the team mechanic, fluttered around our bikes, stoop shouldered and bent at the knee, an Allen wrench in his hand, tightening stem bolts and tweaking bar ends. Kenny Adams, a veteran cross-country rider, floated up and down the dusty road on his bike, in and out of our group, as Toby talked. Kenny was a bundle of energy, and his long dark hair flitted out from under the scooped air vents of his helmet with every manic pedal stroke. When Toby mentioned Kenny's name, Kenny shot into our circle and skidded to a track stand, which he held as he shook hands all around. And then Toby gestured to a tall girl with short blonde hair, page-boy

My first factory ride. Seeing my name on the truck was surreal. (*Author*)

style, who smiled shyly as he listed all her accomplishments: NORBA downhill champion. Dual slalom champion. World cup downhill winner. World cup slalom winner. Kim Sonier. Toby's wife, Shauna, patted her clipboard, coughed without raising her hand to cover her mouth, and tapped her foot into the dirt. She was the team manager. And these were the subtle signs, that even Toby picked up on, that the team had a schedule to keep. So Toby blurted my name to everyone and said that I'd be racing cross country, and then he bounded into the driver's seat of the rented minivan and blasted the air conditioning. I waved awkwardly to my new teammates as Shauna read off the time slots that each of us would be allowed on course in the morning for practice, handed out our race numbers, and informed us that we had fifteen minutes to tell Johnny about anything special we wanted done to our bikes before we piled into the minivan for dinner and the night's sleep at the luxurious Ramada Inn conveniently located only forty-five miles away. I pedaled over to Marc and told him I'd see him in the morning, gave him a quick kiss, and as I scooted back to the team truck with my duffel bag full of shower things, race gear uniforms, and stuff, I hoped he wouldn't get too drunk with Russell and Norm. At least those guys were racing.

Dinner in a strip-mall stucco-walled Italianeria was pasta with a smidgen of sauce and salad with oil and vinegar. I thought the meal was fantastic. I wasn't paying for it! The team picked up the bill. Toby alone topped his angel hair pasta with a sprinkled mound of grated parmesan cheese. The rest of us made do with black pepper. The talk was small and polite and muted except when Toby was speaking.

Tom Buzzelli and I, as rookies, naturally sat next to each other and remained quiet. I wasn't even chewing loud.

Kim Sonier was by nature a quiet woman and when she did speak it was in a high reedy voice that barely carried across the dinner table. The high pitch of her voice was incongruent with her broad shoulders, narrow hips, and straight-backed posture. Anyone could tell with one glance that she was an athlete. That she possessed a confidence and sense of purpose. I thought she looked like Joan of Arc, as depicted in my Catholic school history books. Except that Kim's voice was too Minnie Mouseish to ever command armies. I had always imagined that downhillers were loud and outgoing, flashy and edgy, like the type of racing that they chased after. Missy Giove, I thought, personified the downhill discipline with her blue mohawk, numerous tatoos, nose piercings and a mummified piranha dangling around her neck. I wanted to race cross country like John Tomac so I wore black socks. I had just assumed that, since Kim Sonier raced as fast as Missy, she would have green hair and tongue piercings, wear a necklace of shark teeth or something.

Kenny Adams flirted with the waitress who was probably wondering why he was wearing sunglasses indoors at nine o'clock at night. He looked like Bono's healthier, more tanned, not-quite-as-cool little brother.

Toby lectured us on who the sponsors were and what they expected of us. What he expected of us as racers and as teammates. That this team, since Kim was a champion and Toby himself a downhiller, would have more of a gravity focus than most factory trade teams. Kim met and held Toby's gaze as he said that he expected her to win a lot of races again this season. Toby then looked toward Kenny, who from behind his sunglasses was gaining ground on the waitress as she made her way around the table replenishing our water glasses. In the deeply competitive pro cross-country class Kenny would get some cross top-ten finishes and have a good chance to podium at some races. Then Toby shifted and leveled his bues eyes on Tom Buzzelli. Tom looked down for something of great interest in his crumpled dinner napkin as Toby stated that Tom would shoot for top-twenty, maybe top-ten finishes. Toby pushed his empty dinner plate toward the center of the table. With the side of his hand he brushed some parmesan crumbs off the table. Because the women's cross-country field wasn't as deep as the men's, I might sneak in for some top-ten finishes, he said. My face flushed red. Then Toby brushed off the crumbs that had fallen from the table onto his shirt. Since I was such a rookie, he said, I might as well race downhill too. He signaled for the check. Kim stood up from the table and headed off to the bathroom. "Then," Toby said, "we'll see what happens." Wow! Another bike, I thought. One of those fancy ones that had shocks in the back too! As the waitress was processing his credit card Toby drummed into our heads a checklist for organizing our gear that we were supposed go through before we went to bed. We were to lay out on top of our dresser or beside our bed, wherever the cramped rooms left space: our helmet, glasses, gloves, socks, shoes, shorts, jersey, tube, pump, patch, and number. As Toby figured out the tip, I repeated over and over silently to myself the checklist he had given us. Filing out of the air-conditioned restaurant, Toby first and then Kim and then the rest of us with me in last place, into the nighttime blast furnace of Scottsdale, I mouthed that checklist speeding up the rhythm of the words nonsensically, searing their order into my brain.

The night before races even now I still go through Toby's list, the items spilling from my lips with the unconscious speed of a Social Security number.

At the motel Kim and I were sharing a room as we would all season. I felt like a freshman in college dorming with a senior. She opened the door and under the flickering fluorescent light surveyed the twin beds, the mini fridge in between, the curtained window off to one side and the bathroom opposite. I still found it hard to believe that my team was paying to put me up in a motel. This was going to be so much better than camping out in Vidalia. I stood on the soggy red carpet of the hallway behind her and to the side, the thin straps of my overstuffed duffel digging into the soft of my shoulder, and watched the profile of her high angular cheekbones twitch ever so slightly and her clear

blue eyes squint momentarily into the shadows of the room as
she assigned and then tabulated numerical values to the anticipated angle of the morning sun, inevitable middle-of-the-night
parking-lot noise, the location of the wall switch, the proximity
of the nightstand, and the orientation of the beds to the bathroom. I just looked around a little. What was she seeing? I
waited till she threw her duffel bag onto the bed closest to the
air conditioner near the window and so I "chose" the other one
by the bathroom. I was mindful to let her use the bathroom first.
She did not turn on the television, so I made no move to either.
We laid out our gear in silence in the order that Toby had told
us, Kim quickly and methodically, as though she need not have
been lectured; like anyone who wins world cup races. Me, a lot
slower and conscious about not copying her every movement too
closely. She turned down the cover of her bed all the way to the
foot and then crawled under the thin blanket in between the
sheets. I didn't want to do everything she did. That would be too
much. I was my own person, so defiantly I pulled the blanket
cover spread right up to my chin. Weeks later I discovered that
Kim kicked off the cover spread because, although motel cleaning crews changed and washed sheets every day, and blankets
now and then, they never, ever, laundered cover spreads. Somebody had to die in that motel bed before they would launder the
bed cover. Every germ that was ever sneezed onto its inscrutable
paisley pattern by a traveling salesman was probably still there,
mutating. Every snot wiped onto its embroidery by mischievous
boys still lurked in its folds, crusty and virulent.

I lay in bed squirming with questions. There was so much I
wanted to ask of her. You know girl to girl, now pro to pro, during the few moments after the light blinks out but before the
room grows dark with sleep. During those moments of wrestling
with the pillow and stretching legs against the tightness of the
sheets, when breaths are still arythmic and conscious, as thought

fades away and dreams tiptoe in. I wanted to ask her how long she had been a pro. When did she first start racing? How did she get into it? I knew she had a motorcycle, a dirt bike. Was that how? Did motoing lead to downhilling? Would this be her only cross-country race of the season? How did she feel about racing a cross-country expert when she was such a big-time pro down-hiller? What were other teams she had been on like? What was it like to win races and be a national champion? I wanted to ask her about her training even though she was only a downhiller. I'd read in magazines that Kim had a master's degree in mathematics and I was curious about how she felt about leaving that world behind. Did people think she was as crazy as me? Whom do I give my receipts for gas money to, Toby or Shauna? Was there good riding in Flagstaff where she lived? Did she ever ride so hard that colors turned into sounds, and was it really okay to eat red meat, and what should I do about birth control?

Kim leaned over to the nightstand. She took one last sip from her water bottle. I had forgotten mine in my duffel and now was too timid to crawl out and get it. I'd wait till she was asleep and then sneak into the bathroom and fill it. She set the alarm for five a.m. and then she shut off the light.

A perfect moment for girl talk. "It feels like our first night at summer camp. This is going to be such fun," I gushed. "I can't wait."

Kim took one deep breath and exhaled into the darkness in a voice louder than I had heard her use all evening, "Welcome to the world of pro mountain-bike racing," and it seemed she was asleep as the last syllable left her lips.

She wasn't trying to be mean, I knew, as I lay sleepless in bed all that night. She didn't hurt my feelings, not really. This was her job. She was trying to win races. I was the newbie, the rookie, the first-day trainee. I would be in her way this weekend. All season. I would ask questions. I wouldn't know how to do the simplest things. I would slow the team down checking in at airports. I was one more person whose baggage would get lost. One more body to squeeze into a rented minivan. I would forget equipment. I wasn't to be trusted with the grocery shopping or directions to the motel or with picking up the race registration forms. I was to be endured, tolerated, and ignored. For the whole season Kim would have to share a room with me. The bathroom and the alarm clock. For the next four months we would practically be living together. And athletes, I have come to understand, by their very nature are selfish.

Only one person gets to win. There is no sharing in that respect. No point in playing nice. The winner seeks out every advantage. It sounds mean I know, but that is the nature of sport. And sport has been recognized, even before both *Rollerball* movies explained it in simplistic fashion, as a substitute for war. One team wins; the other loses. One team "beats" the other. It's easy to see in ball sports, like baseball, football, and hockey. We "out hit" them. Or they "prevailed" against us. Our guys got "murdered." It was a "slaughter." We "creamed" 'em. Even in track and field and swimming one team is "stronger" than the other. One team uses its "big guns" against the other. Any sport in which there is a score, or points, like golf, bass fishing, or figure skating, there is a winner and that means there is a loser. Especially in solo sports like boxing or marathoning or an extreme sport like mountain biking. Mountain bikers are not allowed help from mechanics during a race, like the roadies are allowed. There are no pit stops like in car races. No in between rounds to rest on a stool and have your boo-boos attended to. In mountain-bike racing once the gun goes off it's every man for himself. The mountain-bike rule book even forbids helping another competitor during the race. Loaning a tire pump or giving away a patch kit is automatic disqualification for both parties. In mountain-bike racing the winner has to consider his own needs in every way. And that means the winner has to be self-aware, that the winner must want to win more than the other guy. Winners never want to share the top spot on the podium. The winningest athlete in a room is almost always the most selfish. It is a quality that a winning athlete has to cultivate. If you want to win on race day you must be selfishly confident, egotistically aware of your body, completely in tune with your id. And to achieve that heightened level of self-actualization on race day the athlete must practice, practice, practice every day. Selfishly.

Selfishness is drummed out of normal people, rightly so, when we are children. Ask any little kid what they learned in kindergarten that day and most of the time you'll get the same stuff-nosed, snaggle-toothed, shy response, "Shaaarinngg." But athletes aren't normal people. Especially mountain bikers. I can laugh now at the memory of watching Lisa Sher, a recent NORBA champ and teammate when I was on Team Marin, haggle, cajole, complain, and beg for an airline to honor her reserved aisle seat in the bulkhead row. Bulkhead seats are the first in the row. There are no seats in front of them. That means in front there is no seat that leans back on your lap. No seat in front under which you have to cram your foot-room-stealing carry-on luggage. Bulkhead rows are a few extra inches wide, and in them you can push deep into the seat of your chair and prop your feet up against the bulkhead wall. The elevation is good for the blood's circulation, diminishes the swelling of the feet and ankles, and means that, upon arrival, a bike racer will need fewer miles to warm up the next day. And an aisle seat makes it easy to get up and walk around frequently. An aisle seat means a little more breathing room, which all bike racers prize. I can remember the blood rising on Lisa's face as she tried to explain how much she wanted the airline to honor her reserved seat, and how she didn't care that a honeymooning couple had checked in just prior and had been "upgraded" to those seats for "privacy." I can laugh now because I understand, but then I was intimidated by her vehemence that she get that aisle seat in the bulkhead row. She taught me a valuable lesson, and in years since, I have tapped nursing mothers on the shoulder and asked them to get out of my aisle seat in the bulkhead row.

Being an athlete, the cultivation of selfishness can be difficult for the people who you share your life with. Every potential meal is weighed as a component of a winning-race strategy. If a racer is crazy enough to dine with spectator friends the night before a race, then the racer is not really being whiny or demanding about insisting on institutional-grade pasta from a chain rather than adventurous sushi of dubious quality from a not-too-clean and not-enough-cars-in-the-parking-lot roadhouse. The racer is not being a prima donna about vetoing Bubba's House of Brisket. The racer is simply being selfish. Trying to win.

If no water glass is provided when given a menu by a server, I have to ask for it. When the server brings the salad and forgets the water, I have to insist on it. When the spaghetti arrives and still no water, I must rise from the table, schlepp to the car, retrieve a water bottle, fill it in the bathroom sink, and then set it down next to the dinner plate. You have to do that if you want the best chance of winning the next day. I learned that first pro season to carry a water bottle with me everywhere I go. Marc calls it my "baw baw."

After I signed as a pro with Team Iron Horse I made life very difficult for Marc. I am not sure he knew what he was agreeing to when he said he would help me. Countless times he was the one who trudged out to the car to get my baw baw during the middle of a movie. He made light of it by squirting a splash on his wrist, like one does with a baby's milk bottle, but it was a chore. That first year living on the sailboat with Marc I spent a lot of energy developing my awesome powers of selfishness. I don't know what it is, but others agree with me, when you live on a boat you always feel the need to to go the bathroom. It's like you can't stand a single drop in your bladder. Maybe it is the wave motion of the boat sloshing us around so much. . . . I was constantly going to the bathroom, and that made me even more thirsty. I wanted to replace each droplet. I wanted to stay fully hydrated. Perhaps the salt air drove my thirst. Some weird kind of osmosis. But I would wake up in the middle of the night, my vacuum-collapsed water bottle clutched in my hand, wimpering for more water. And faithfully Marc would rise in the dark, throw on a pair of shorts, walk the dock barefoot to the marina office, and fill my bottle with springwater from the upturned five-gallon-bottle dispenser. I refused to drink from our boat's water tanks. I thought the water tasted "funny." Like from a plastic thermos.

Selfishness can be especially difficult for women to embrace. We carry the eggs, we have the breasts; we are the nurturers. We are expected to be polite, respectful of others' feelings, sensitive. Guys who want to win, and act accordingly, are just headstrong. Or aggressive, determined, intense. Kim and I were polite to each other in our cozily cramped motel room. We had to be—we are girls. This veneer of congeniality is an added strain. So even if Kim would prefer the fresh air of the desert night through the open window rather than the recirculating, legionairing, droning air-conditioning, she would have asked me. A guy racer would have just thrown open the window with the challenge, "You got a problem with that?" Neither of us girls would ever consider for a second leaning over after the lights were out to sneer, "Tomorrow, I am going to kick your ass," the way guys are expected to act. Women who act the same way as winning men are often awarded just the one syllable: bitch. And we cringe from that label. But if women want to compete as athletes, then we sometimes have to live with that. Kim dealt with it by remaining quiet. Reticent. I think that recently, in some way, the word *bitch,* which was originally bestowed on us for being competitive, outspoken, or a threat, is being transformed by the "girl power" movement. The tiny cotton tee shirt shirts that can be seen on preteen girls that proclaim, "Girls Love Dirt!" or "Girl Power," or on the slightly larger shirts of more adult women, "Dirty Girl" or even "Luna Chick," show that we have embraced some of the concepts of that word *bitch,* and we can happily live with that.

During that first team dinner Toby had surprised everyone with the idea that I'd be racing downhill too, that Kim and I would be competing against each other. Not that Kim had anything to worry about. I'm sure she knew that.

Maybe it flitted through her mind before she turned off the light. I had no clue then as I lay in bed wide awake, that I was now a competitor of hers. Not so much on the downhill course as for the team's resources. Race teams have budgets. I was one more downhill bike that Johnny, the time-strapped and sleep-deprived mechanic, would have to service and tune and adjust on race day. I was one more groupo of Shimano race components, which meant that Kim had one less set of spares. The same with forks and tires and wheels. I know a lot of people think that pros get everything for free, as much as they want, when they want. But the way it works, even if you are the fastest in the world, is that your team is allotted by the companies that sponsor them a certain number of tires, spokes, and helmets, etc. Sure, during the great mountain-bike boom of the early nineties budgets were flush and there was a lot of swag handed out, but even so, resources were finite.

Kim was just being realistic. After all, she was a math major. She was probably adding up what my addition to the team, even as a part-time downhiller who wasn't drawing a salary, would cost her.

I waited at least an hour, until I was sure that Kim was asleep, before I filled my water bottle from the bathroom sink. I stubbed my toe in the darkness. I snuck back into bed where Doreen's coaching tips floated in my head and got all jumbled up with Marc's predictions that I'd win easily. College friends from Mount Saint Mary's chased me through the desert. My mother appeared on a white thundercloud and told me to be careful about sharing water bottles with strangers: cooties.

I did okay in Saturday's time trial. Dinner was at the same Italian place. The table talk was about bike parts and cactus needles. Toby spoke about how important it was to keep our race uniforms clean and neat. Our bikes shiny and unscratched. Back at the motel Kim and I washed our uniforms in the sink. I watched how she laid hers out flat on a dry bath towel and then rolled the towel up, and then how she stood on one end and twisted the towel tight, hand over hand, ringing almost every drop from her uniform. I knew the demonstration was for me, but she didn't say anything.

On Sunday morning before the desert heated up, the pro women's class kicked up a cloud of dust.

That was the only race where I cried.

I didn't cry when I totaled my Acura.

Didn't cry when I found out that Chuck cheated on me.

Not after I watched the neighborhood bully feed my pet gerbil to his snake.

Just a teeny bit when I thought I had a brain tumor or AIDS.

The time I cried a little when I said good-bye to Marc in Las Vegas doesn't really count.

And to my parents' shame and my own confusion, I didn't cry enough when my brother Mark was killed.

I kept it together until I crossed the finish line, but I cried after this race.

I cried sobbing streams of muddy tears. Nose stuffed with dusty snot. Elbows and knees weak with emotion as I pedaled, dead last, across the finish line right past Marc who was standing in the middle of the dirt road waiting for me with water and a clean towel, my two flat tires nearly squishing and squashing off the rims every inch of the way.

He trotted alongside me as I slunk off away from the crowds, away from my team. I didn't want him to stop me. I didn't want him to hug me. I didn't want him to touch me. I didn't want him to say anything. I didn't even want him to be there. I wanted to be alone. I wanted to be somewhere else.

He kept saying my name over and over again and then he grabbed my handlebars and stopped me in my tracks.

"You said I was going to win," I sobbed. "You told me I was going to win. That I was good enough to be a pro. You told me."

Marc just kept saying my name over and over again, held my arms and squeezed my hands, as I poured out.

"You told me I was good enough to quit my job and that I could do it. And Toby's watching, and so many people think I can't do it, maybe he won't either . . ."

I rambled and then mumbled and after a while was too dehydrated to continue crying. I drank some of the water Marc thrust under my helmet. The water brought me around. Marc asked what happened.

"I was doing good. Didn't have a great start, but I was passing people and moving up after the first lap . . ."

Marc interrupted me, his voice was positive and upbeat, "I know, I was watching! You looked great!"

". . . I felt strong. But then on the second lap I got a flat. In the front. I swapped tubes, but lost all that I had gained. And then I got another flat. In the rear. I had to patch that one. And practically everybody passed me. And on the last lap that patch started to lose air and I was wobbling on the trail and slammed right into a rock and pinch-flatted the front again. I didn't have any more tubes or patches and everybody else was long gone."

Marc waited until he was sure I had said it all. Then he tried to console me. "Marla you flatted. That's all."

I shook my head in protest.

"Everybody flats."

"I'm last."

"Marla, you finished." He made me look right at him. "With two flats. And now you want to quit?"

"No. I don't want to quit, but now it's not gonna work out. This deal with Iron Horse is for one year, and I have to win races so I can get them to sign me up a again."

"Baby."

"But you told me." I shook my hands free from his grip. "You said I was going to be good. And I believed you, and now look. I'm last. All that hard work."

"Baby, baby. Come on. This is only the first race of the year. Who cares? It's the practice cup for chrissakes. This is just a blip."

"A blip?"

"Yeah. A blip. Won't be worth a damn by the end of the year when you are winning races."

"But you told me. I believed you."

"So believe me. This is just a blip. Remember how much it sucks and how upset you are, but realize it doesn't change things. This doesn't change who you are and what you can do. Remember how much it's making you cry and then don't let it happen again. Use it when you are training. When you don't want to get on the bike one more time. But don't end it. You can do this. You really can. I know you will."

While he was talking my breathing became regular. The edges of the world crept into my vision. There were people, little kids, staring. I coughed. I realized I was just being selfish, but not in a winning way. Every athlete assumes all eyes are on them. That there is great interest for others in their every training ride, in each race result. Marc handed me the towel. It was damp and cold and felt clean on my face.

"You have the fat-boy crit tonight. Go over to your mechanic and let him swap out your tires. I'm gonna go over to the timer's tent and see if I can get your lap splits. I know you were doing good on that first lap. Top fifteen, maybe top ten."

With my tears dried and drool wiped off, I walked my bike back to the Iron Horse pit. To my factory ride. Everyone who counted in my immediate world was waiting there it seemed for my reason, my excuse for doing so poorly. Toby and Shauna, my manager, Doreen, my coach, even Bruce Galloway the stringer of sponsorship fate from Shimano happened to be standing under the shade of our pit area's team tent. They could plainly see my puffy eyes and red nose.

Shrugging I blurted out, "I guess my breasts weren't properly aligned."

Bruce Galloway broke the awkward silence with a chuckle, and I guess that was good enough for Toby.

A few months later, while Kim and Toby were racing on the World Cup circuit in Europe, Doreen scheduled a VO2 Max test for me at the Olympic training center in Alpine in western San Diego county. I was earning some good results in the NORBA races, mostly top twenties. By the season's end I would be ranked thirteenth in the whole country. At the NORBA race in Atlanta, on what would become the Olympic course in 1996, I placed eighth. I was even surprising Toby, and myself, in the downhill events. Crashing of course, but still going pretty fast. But Doreen knew that the training regimen she was drawing up for me was limited.

The training efforts that compose a single workout, and the training schedule for a whole season, range from the easiest to the hardest and are arbitrarily divided into five zones. Zone one is riding your bike delivering newspapers and picking your nose at the stop signs. Zone five is trying so hard that you are at the edge of passing out, sweating blood and vomiting tears. One way to gauge these zones is by heart rate. It was simple for Doreen to place her finger on my wrist before we began a warm-up ride, count the pulses of my heart for ten seconds, and then multipy that by six. That product number indicated how many times my heart was beating a minute while at rest and could be used to set the upper limit of exertion for zone one. If I wore a heartrate monitor Doreen could estimate with some accuracy when zone one became zone two. She could could discern with a little less accuracy when zone two became three and even less when three became four. But Doreen had no way to recognize when I reached the ceiling of my hardest efforts. A heart rate of nearly two hundred beats per minute really didn't tell her much except that my heart was about to explode. Without knowing for sure what my top end of exertion was, Doreen was limited in devising a training regimen that progressed through these zones in such a way that I was able to stress my body and let it recover so that I could prolong the duration that I could race in zone four, reaching up to five when I needed to attack a hill climb, bridge to the lead group, or flick a chaser from my wheel.

A two-hour cross-country mountain-bike race is not a contest of brute muscle strength, nor a measure of bike handling over technical terrain, but rather it is an experiment to see which racer can most efficiently fuel the muscles with oxygenated blood. That's really all a cross-country bike race is: a contest of who has the biggest lungs, the best circulation, and the strongest heart. The human body cannot sustain maximum exertion longer than twenty or thirty seconds or so. Even Olympic medalers in the hundred-yard dash have to breathe while they run, otherwise their bodies slow down and eventually shut down with muscle cramps. The heartrate monitor told Doreen the beats per minute that my heart pumped the hemoglobin-rich, oxygen-laden dark bluish-green blood through my arteries into my muscles. In the cells of my muscles, the mitochondria—the cellular work engines—burned up the oxygen, creating carbon dioxide as a waste by-product. During the capillary exchange the blood's hemoglobin can only refuel my muscle cells with oxygen as fast at it carries away the carbon dioxide. So the blood's hemoglobin, now red and rich with carbon dioxide, pulses back through the venous system to my lungs where another exchange is made. Each sputtering, hot, wet exhalation throws off carbon dioxide and each gasping, cool, dry inhalation draws oxygen back into the lungs refueling my hungry muscles. What Doreen wanted to know is how much could my lungs take in to re-energize my muscles with each breath?

A VO2 Max test, a test to measure the maximum volume amount of oxygen that a single breath can draw, is not the type of test that you can study for. You can't improve your VO2 Max test by training or dieting, or by praying to the appropriate saint of heavy breathing. Though the Italians are so crazy about cycling that I am sure that in some small village along the race route of the Giro d'Italia there is a patron saint of lung capacity. The VO2 Max test is like a pregnancy test. You either are or you aren't: You either have a high VO2 Max or you don't.

It turns out that I didn't.

I could cheat though. The sports pages of even the smallest towns in America repeat in smaller type the gigantic headline scandals of the European road scene. Aside from steroids that the cyclist can use to recover from the nagging micromuscle tears, and the amphetamines that can boost a racer's heartbeat, the sneakiest way to cheat is by using EPO. A drug first developed to help combat anemia and now conscripted by bicycle racers to thicken the blood and elevate the amount of oxygen their blood can carry. Sure, I could do that. I am a research scientist. It would be easy to source some EPO and develop a doping protocol that would avoid detection. Or I could more simply draw off my blood in small amounts during the off season. Spin the blood in a centrifuge separating the blood cells from the plasma and freeze it. Then during the race season I could defrost it and inject it back into my blood like a car racer adds high-octane fuel treatments to his gasoline. But I knew that I wouldn't. I didn't want to give up the moral superiority that honesty provided. Doping my way to the podium would be as unsatisfying as taking an illegal shortcut through a dark section of the woods. It was too much fun anyway snickering at all the other mountain-bike racers I saw, even at the smaller local events, grasping for their "asthma inhalers" just before the start gun goes off. Mountain biking, aside from asthma-inhaler abuse, is free from drug-enhanced performances, as far as I can tell. Most downhillers are free from even taking caffeine. Although I admit I now drink half a Red Bull one half hour before all my downhills. But that's not cheating.

While I stared at the graph paper's columns of indifferent numbers, Doreen gently explained to me what this VO2 Max score meant. I understood the science. I used to trace the anatomy and physiology of the cardiopulmonary system on a wall chart for dozing college kids. But she sketched out what the test meant for me as a pro cross-country mountain biker. The upshot was, as hard as I trained, and as much as I would try, even if I was able to race for two hours in zone five at two hundred heartbeats a minute without passing out, I still would be stuffing less oxygenated fuel into my muscles than my competitors who might be gliding along happily in zone three. A bike race is not like baseball where a struggling pitcher can be crafty with a knuckler, or an aging batter pluckily punching the ball to the opposite field. Unlike in basketball there are no head fakes that an older, slower Larry Bird can throw, juking out a younger, faster, stronger defender. A cross-country mountain-bike race, all other things being equal, is an individual effort about one thing: pain. Whoever is willing to endure the most pain racing at a level just below where the lungs want to burst and the heart explode, wins. This test result just showed me, however, all other things *weren't* equal. I had been racing with a governor on my carburetor. There were weights in my track shoes. Lead in my bat. If I wanted to race road bikes, like in Europe in the classic stage races, Doreen consoled, I could have probably been a good *domestique*. If I had started racing many years earlier and spoke better French. A *domestique* is usually a younger rider who has shown promise, but needs some seasoning. Or an older one with many miles under the wheels who doesn't want to let go of the sport just yet. A *domestique* carries the water bottle for the team leader, pulls the leader up hills, chases down threats. A *domestique* finishes the races, if at all, in the back with the pack. A *domestique* is an anonymous workhorse, often without even an individual time for the race effort since the whole pack is assigned the same time. *Domestiques* have to be truly crazy for bike racing. And in road racing, women weren't even allowed to race the Tour de France! In road racing there are fewer women's races, smaller fields, tinier salaries. As a mountain biker I was already racing for zero salary. I couldn't afford any kind of pay cut to switch to the road.

"But," Doreen continued, "your road cycling handling skills are so scary that I'm not sure anybody would hire you if you switched over right now."

I was crushed. Clutched in my shaking hands were the graph papers, the squiggly lines and discordant bell curves that I wanted to rip up. The compelling reason why I wanted to race mountain bikes in the first place was because it was such a solo effort. It wasn't a team sport like field hockey or soccer. I had gotten into the sport believing it was just me against anybody else at the starting line, and that we all had pretty much an equal chance of winning. It just came down to who wanted it more and who could suffer more.

If I couldn't ever win a race, then mountain biking would just be a hobby that I was good at. And I was already pretty good at a lot of meaningless hobbies. Why had I been putting my parents through all this anguish?

This first pro season had slowly forced me to accept that the more I raced the better my competition would become until the point where not only the quality of my bike's manufacture made a difference, but also its design, the tires, the shoes, and the suspension; not only did I have to be on a team, but a team with a great mechanic and a smart manager; that in order to be on this team I had to sell the bikes and the equipment of the team's sponsors; and now this wad of paper in my hand was telling me that I was wasting my time. So much for solo effort. I had made all those compromises and for what?

Had I just been deluding myself all along? Had I been tilting at windmills thinking that attaining a level of excellence in sport was possible? That somehow being number one in the world would be transformational, that because I could be great at mountain biking made up for only being an average pianist. That winning a bike race would make bearable working as a lab drone when I was an old crone. That I would achieve my goal in memory of my brother Mark whose chance to make a difference had been taken away from him. That I would have no need to say I was Mrs. Somebody or Mother of Anybody, because I had made myself into a champion. Did I simply choose the wrong sport? A VO2 Max test doesn't mean anything in archery. What about pro bowling? I already had plenty of plaid pants. Was it a mistake to even focus on a sport at all? Okay, so maybe I didn't have a great burning desire for science like Madame Curie or

Jane Goodall, not enough zeal for research to win a Nobel Prize, but why couldn't I have become a real estate agent and been satisfied with a framed certificate of achievement of high sales for the year in my office, or won a pink Cadillac selling Mary Kay cosmetics?

My hands stopped shaking. Except for the hair on the back of my neck, which began to tingle, my body froze between the interval of two heartbeats. There was a silence all around. The focus of my unblinking eyes on the damning graph paper blurred and I began to perceive a premonition on the periphery. What was it? I could almost puzzle it out. Its reification was like the tenuous hesitation before a sneeze. Time stretched like it was waiting for me to realize this moment. I needed a flash of light. Just as I was on the intellectual verge of making an existential breakthrough into realizing my own sense of self in relation to the universe, like the epiphany of Proust's Madeline cookie-triggering a *Remembrance of Things Past* or the thunderclap of an unfolding idea like Crick and Watson's double-stranded helix of DNA, "Oh well," Doreen chimed, crashing my train of thought, "You could always be a downhiller!"

The rest, as they say, is history. Or maybe they say the past is prologue. Something like that. In any case, the irony of my cycling life taking off by me going downhill isn't lost on me. Nor is the fact that gravity is the force that assists me as I pedal ferociously down the course. My dreams of riding a bike full time were realized, I was continuing to undergo the transformative stages of my own evolution, was about to migrate to a place where I'd be surrounded by like-minded individuals, was returning to the womb where legend has it that the sport was born. What had once seemed lofty and out of reach was now all within my grasp. I was about to climb the mountaintop, and that's supposedly where we go to seek enlightenment. I still had a lot to learn.

I'd started off by being bitten by a mountain-biking bug, been smitten, head over heels in love with it, but now riding a bike became my livelihood, and there were certain realities that I had to deal with. Making your passionate avocation your vocation, your pay-the-bills, make-or-break financial future, is like the transition from the larval stage to the adult stage. I had to stretch my wings and explore a bit, and learn a lot more about myself, the sport I was in, and the larger industry it was a part of.

Like any scientist, I've learned to observe. As Jerry and the fellas once sang, "What a long strange trip it's been."

PART II

Goddess Under a Microscope

Chapter 7

The Powers of a Gravity Goddess

The Powerful Ability to Learn Childhood Lessons Late in Life

I could never have become a gravity goddess without trying to race downhill. That's elemental, but regardless, a point I didn't recognize until quite recently. I did not become a gravity goddess when I won the Red Bull Mountain Bike Festival at Lake Tahoe in 1999. I became a goddess simply because years earlier I decided to make a commitment to mountain biking. And the greatest power granted to me from that commitment was the ability to learn, as an adult, lessons that I should have learned as a child.

One of several realizations that mountain biking allowed me to appreciate was that compromise can be a great step forward.

Downhilling at first did not excite me like cross-country riding. It just didn't seem as universal or life affirming. Downhilling didn't present opportunities for self-reflection or communion with nature. I couldn't ride downhill for five hours like I could on my cross-country bike through a winding valley or over the top of a snow-capped mountain or across a painted desert.

Downhilling's need for protective pads and clanking cadence lacked the calming appeal of simplicity. In order to downhill I had to ride a chairlift or shuttle in a pickup truck to start from the top. What fun was that? Where was the soul and freedom and sense of escape if riding was restricted to summer at ski resorts? I doubted there was the opportunity for rhythm and modulation of effort and endurance that was necessary for me to get lost in a sense of accomplishment, which was another special reward of riding a bike.

But downhilling would pay, I began to realize. It would pay me enough to ride my bike more than messengering ever could have. The first time I won as a pro, a Downhill Mania, I received a winner's check of a few thousand dollars from the title sponsor: Paul Mitchell Pro Salon Hair Care Products. I admit I won in large part because I was lucky. I was too dumb to know how easily I could have crashed, and I relied on my cross-country fitness throughout the multiple rounds so that, by the final race, I was still pretty fresh compared to the rest of the downhillers. Holding that oversized check in my hands as I stood on top of the podium, even though I was in love with cross country, it was easy to see that if I wanted a future in this sport, if I didn't want to return to the lab or go back to school, if I wanted to get my picture in the magazines and to win races, if I wanted to get paid to ride my bike in the woods, then I would have to race downhill.

Just another compromise. Nothing will ever be perfect. At every level of existence we can only approach perfection, closer and closer, but never quite attain it. I pursued a career in science because I thought it offered clear-cut answers, definite rights and wrongs, numbers that added up, and conclusions that were logical. But I had learned there are no absolutes, not even in science. Even at the subatomic level the Heisenberg principle explains how compromise is the rule of order. That the best scientists and the highest-callibrated equipment can never know where anything actually is at the same instant that they can determine how fast anything is traveling. Trying to realize both at the same time is a compromise. That my work as a researcher required sacrificing monkeys was a compromise that I was eventually unable to make. Mountain biking, I slowly was realizing, was also a compromise, but I could happily accept its terms.

Doreen was right. I would never win cross-country races. Not against the top pros like Julie Furtado, Alison Sydor, and Ruthie Matthis. But if I raced downhill I would still be a pro mountain biker. I'd still be able to sneak in "training rides" in between downhill practices along Mr. Toad's Wild Ride in Lake Tahoe, or through the Jurassic-park jungles of Hawaii. I'd get to ride my bike in Europe, and this time somebody else would pay for my airfare, and I would be able to take a shower every day in a hotel room! I wouldn't have to buy tires or patch kits or new brake pads. And maybe if I trained hard enough I could still one day be fastest in the world, if only for a few minutes of one afternoon.

But there was a possibility that I could qualify in downhill for the world championships in Vail, Colorado, that year. And though the odds were more likely that Sting wanted to take me to dinner, there was still a chance I could win. I could count on anything happening on race day. I could also count on the help and guidance of other people.

One of the things I enjoy about Marc, aside from his cooking, is that he is extremely well-read. I guess like most bartenders he can bullshit a little about almost anything. Maybe he didn't have too many good ideas. But without someone to hash all this out with I would have gone crazy. I was aware of the aphorism that behind every great man, there was a woman, and despite the gender reversal in our case, I had to admit its validity.

That without Marc's encouragement and counsel, his massages and errand running and his toleration of my selfishness, I wouldn't have been able to make it through my first pro season.

But was relying on him also a compromise? Hadn't I started in on this racing stuff to find out what my own potential was? Or, had I just learned something?

For the second half of my first pro season in 1993 I resolved to become a better downhiller. That is, I tried to crash less often. That was pretty much all I could do. Even if Kim Sonier, or Toby, had the time there weren't many coaching tips that either could give me.

There was nothing that I had learned as a research scientist that I could apply to this new discipline of downhilling. Setting up a gel set for an experiment wasn't helpful for setting up how to take an off-camber turn. Knowing how to operate an auto-clave machine had not prepared me for manualing some stutter bumps. But I had proved to myself that I could learn to play the piano. I had learned about science. Just last year I had learned to race a cross-country bike. Now I would have to learn to ride a downhill bike. That's all.

As well-meaning and as helpful as perhaps the other down-hillers wanted to be, most of the top riders gave advice consisting of hand gestures, head nods, and grunting noises. "You know that section where it goes all ack ack ack? Well if you whip into it and let the bike get all, you know, then you are all set up for next whoop section, and you won't argh argh in too big a gear." Consider that some of the top riders might also be European, speaking English as a second language, and learning downhill lingo as they went along, you can imagine the mountain of Babel we were racing down.

I listened to their every word, but really didn't learn much. The only way to ride like these winners did was to learn as they had. The hard way. On the trails.

This inability that we all faced to clearly articulate what the bike was doing compared to what we really wanted the bike to do made life difficult for the team mechanic and even the bike's designer. After a practice ride, a racer would complain to a mechanic that the bike is all "Wheek! Wheek! Wheek!" when riding through some stutter bumps. Some helpful pantomine would elaborate. The poor wrench would tighten the handlebar. Adjust the suspension a little. Lube the chain a bit. What could he do? He had never raced a bike like this on a course like that in these weather conditions. Some of the top mechanics had tooled in the Tour de France, big road races with history and tradition where there was an accepted, a right, way to do everything. In a downhill race there was no manual or historical record he could reference. No old guy sporting a jaunty velo cap on his wizened head who was the embodiment of the sport's history to give him a hint as to what the rider wanted. And most riders could give even less feedback to the designer.

Imagine the situation. A bike company hands to some bike-racing fool the most expensive, cool prototype, slick paint, one-of-a-kind downhill bike in the world, tells him to ride for a week. Trash it. Ride it into the ground. Then the company asks the racer to evaluate its performance. Most racers in that situation wouldn't provide any worthwhile criticism or feedback because the ear to ear stupid grins plastered on their dirty faces prevented any thoughts from being vocalized.

There were many downhill-bike ideas, but no consensus on what worked. Kim had a lot of experience racing motorcycles and so she switched the positions of her downhill bike's brake levers to the way they were set up on her motorcycle. My experience on motorcycles was limited to holding onto the waist of a boyfriend, and tootling around the Bahamas' shoreline on a rented moped during a vacation. So Kim couldn't have helped me much there.

Toby had eliminated his front derailleur and instead ran a single gigantic front-chain ring, but I was such a strong pedaler I was reluctant to give up my three chain rings.

It seemed like each race weekend the stems got shorter and the saddles moved further back. Bar ends and water bottles disappeared, the inner tubes and tires grew fatter, and crank arms grew stiffer and shorter.

I just tried to hang on. My race strategy was to pedal as fast as I could, and make up for time lost in the inevitable crashes by taking ridiculous risks. I was attending a graduate school in hard knocks. My tactic was to try every conceivable bike setup my mechanic, Johnny Boy, would tolerate.

I bombed at Worlds, but I was learning. Iron Horse was so pleased with me that they told me they were planning to exercise their option on me for another year. I'd race for them next year too! For the same zero salary! Another lesson that mountain biking clued me into late in life is that you can't expect others to value you if you don't value yourself. Just don't make the mistake of confusing value and money.

With the race season now over and as mountain biking's most influential journalist, Zapata Espinoza, calls the "silly season" of contract negotiations, sponsor signings, team switching, rookies and retirements, underway, I made the long drive north to Marin County, arguably the birthplace of mountain biking. One of the guys I trained with, Sean Heimdahl, had mentioned that Marin Mountain Bikes was looking to sign another woman downhiller.

Twenty-four hours later I was driving south again, an offer from Marin Mountain Bike's owner, Bob Buckley, burning a hole in the naugahyde seat beside me.

At about the same time an English bike company, Saracen, called me out of the blue and made me an offer. And then Mongoose called too, and even though I told them I was still trying to get a release from Iron Horse and was probably going to sign with Marin, they told me they'd double anybody's offer.

Understand that my race results hadn't been that great. I was lucky that mountain bike sales had just reached their all-time peak. There were not enough women available to race downhill for all the teams that wanted to hire one. That these teams wanted to give us girls the same opportunity as the boys to join a pro team is a testament to their sense of fairness.

I was dizzy. Even while laying down on one of the boat's cushioned seats my head was spinning. Stuff was happening too fast. The offer from Marin was a good one. But if Mongoose wanted to double the salary that Marin was offering, then the next season I could make more money racing a bike than I had earned the year before as a research scientist. True, the money from Scripps hadn't been great, but these bike companies were talking about legitimate career opportunities.

These offers came with nondisclosure agreements, no-complete clauses, right of first refusals, time-is-of-the-essence language. "Marla, you decide what you want and I'll help you sign," Marc promised.

I dug out a sheet of notebook paper and scribbled two headings across the top. One for Marin and one for Mongoose. And beneath I listed the positives and negatives for each. Mongoose was promising more money. They were close by, right in Los Angeles. It was a big company. Marin, on the other hand, was much smaller. It had sort of a hippie reputation more than a racing history. The money wasn't nearly as good, and it was much farther away, so if I wanted access to the team's mechanic or spare parts or little things like that I'd either have to make a long drive north or consider moving to Marin County.

Drawing up a cost-benefit analysis like that made it much

easier to make an informed decision. An important consideration was Oakley. Oakely eyewear was not only the best protection from dust and mud, it was the coolest. A pair of Oakleys meant you were an elite athlete. And Pat Mac, the new Oakley rep, had told me that there was a chance that Oakley might sponsor me for next season. But, he said, Iron Horse already had a team deal in place for eyewear with a competitor. So if I rode for Marin I might be able to wear Oakleys! A good education often pays for itself.

After I had figured out where I wanted to go I told Marc. "I want to sign with Marin." Marc then helped me submit Marin's offer to Iron Horse. After Iron Horse decided not to match, Marc asked them for their official release in return.

My motivation to race mountain bikes wasn't the money, even though Marc and I were barely getting by, so Mongoose's generous offer really didn't sway me. That Mongoose was close by in Los Angeles wasn't a positive either. That would have meant that I would have had to fight all that traffic up to smoggy, sprawling, soot-splashed Los Angeles a whole lot. I had met Bob Buckley, the owner of Marin Mountain Bikes, and had shaken his hand. His company offices were at the foot of fog-shrouded Mount Tamalpais where mountain bikes had been invented and first raced down its tree-covered fire roads. And I wanted to move to Marin. During my short visit there I had fallen in love with the bay and the crooked streets and the microclimates of sun and shade, rain and mud, dust and fog, all in one afternoon's ride of single track on Mount Tam.

Joining Team Marin meant that I was no longer a faux pro, but now a real pro.

And again, another lesson, that as you grow, you move apart. Kathleen and I were drifting farther apart. Kathleen was a sister to me and in some ways a mother figure too. She had practically adopted me at Mount Saint Mary's after my brother Mark's death. She took me under her wing and protected me from my-self. But I was now taking off on my own, and this was causing as much pain for Kathleen as it was for my own mom. Kathleen and I saw each other less and less. I told her that after my first race season on Team Marin, in the fall, if the team resigned me, I'd be leaving San Diego. It's possible that this planned separa-tion, this nest leaving, hurt Kathleen even more than my mom, because Kathleen was largely unaware herself of the maternal role she had been playing for me. She is naturally a nurturer, a teacher, but I know I still hurt her feelings when it was time for me to fly up north to Marin.

It turned out that Kathleen would leave San Diego before I did, having learned way before me that you can never reach back and relive those simpler days of youth. She would move back to Maryland, marry, and a short while later have a baby on the way. I was looking forward in another direction.

I now proudly listed my occupation as "professional moun-tain biker" on my tax return. An envelope was now arriving each month that contained my paycheck for riding a mountain bike. My parents weren't quite thrilled by all this, but at least they were consoled with the idea that I was being compensated for the risk of breaking my bones.

"Isn't it about time that you thought about settling down and having a baby," my mom began to ask over the phone, "like Kathleen?"

Doreen too, had moved on soon after I signed with Marin. Her husband had accepted a great job offer in Atlanta (my mom also didn't need to know that Doreen was now happily wall-papering a baby's room). I knew that I would miss her support and expertise, but she admitted that she really didn't know that much about downhilling and wasn't sure how much more she could help me.

To use a technical term, I didn't know "squat" about downhilling

Always supportive but not always thrilled by my choices, my mom and dad have always been there. (*Author*)

either. I was deep at the bottom of the learning curve, but eager to use all my power to ramp up to speed.

The Power of Momentum

One of the greatest powers in a gravity goddess' quiver is momentum. That applies to winning a race and shaping a career.

My career benefitted from the mountain-biking boom of the nineties and the explosion of coverage on cable television. I was smart enough to take advantage of what came my way.

For example, even before I won a single big race I was featured on a nationwide television and magazine campaign for an energy bar, called VO2 MAX. The whole story is painful to tell. Especially describing how those things tasted. But it is more painful to remember making the commercial. I had run into a tree once as a goof for one of the bike magazines and an ad guy in New York thumbing through "extreme" magazines gave me a call out of the blue. Over and over again they filmed me running into a tree for two whole days screaming and smiling three words only. I knew it was cheesy but even more important than the pay was that my name would appear on screen and be mentioned by the narrator.

That summer during the Tour de France broadcast, the VO2 MAX commercial ran at every break. My name and face were on screen almost as much as the gods of the peloton who were winning the race. My riding friends groaned whenever they saw me on screen. Even though I was teased quite a bit, after that commercial whenever I called a potential sponsor to beg some product they at least knew who I was: that strange biker chick who ran into trees and yelled, *"Are you serious?!"*

A few months after that commercial aired, I won my first big race during the Crested Butte Winter X Games in 1999. At the time I had no idea how important that event would prove to be. How much my sponsors and mainstream America cared about what I considered a made-for-TV race. I thought myself to be a serious athlete. All the competitors take the sport of downhilling seriously. But to ESPN we were "content." We were not much more to ESPN than than contestants on *The Gong Show,* or a police car chase during the six o'clock news. That is, we were supposed to generate ratings and viewers. That's how we ended up racing in the snow. It's just business.

I felt a little bit silly standing on the frozen X-Games podium after winning the Dual-Speed Run. It wasn't as goofy as running into a redwood tree, but racing on snow, metal spikes on my wheels, wrapped as warmly as possible in Lycra and long johns, at speeds up to fifty miles an hour was not what I trained for. None of us did. But when Red Bull said they would give me a thousand dollars just to hold a can of Red Bull in the air while I was being awarded my medal, I quickly caught on. "Hey, this is pretty big!"

A few weeks before those X Games I had just signed with a new team, Team Yeti. Probably because of the VO2 MAX commercial, ESPN had called while I was still under contract with Marin. They wanted to use me in one of their athlete profiles, which would be broadcast in between the events. They wanted some slice-of-life footage of an extreme athlete.

I suggested that the ESPN film crew go on the Critical Mass ride with me. Yeti stepped in to take advantage of the exposure and shipped out a hard-tail bike and some uniforms. A crew of technicians were duct-taping stalks for the lipstick-sized cameras all over my bike while a two-wheeled crowd of thousands milled about until a critical mass thought the ride should begin. For the next hour all through San Francisco's hills and valleys, alleys and promenades, I weaved in and out of a rushing stream of cyclists with a tiny camera in my face. I even detoured into a high-ceilinged glass-walled bookstore to check out the best-sellers.

Having that footage in heavy rotation on ESPN was worth more to my sponsors than anything I thought I could do in the race itself. That coverage guaranteed more value, more media impressions for my sponsors than any individual win, I thought. So when I won a gold medal in the X Games Dual Speed event my accomplishment didn't really sink in until much later. To this day when I am haggling at the United Airlines ticket counter, trying to get my bike bag checked without having to pay an oversize penalty, watching all the while as surf boards, golf clubs, musical instruments of a marching band check in with impunity, it's magical when I wave my gold medal from the X Games and say that I am on my way to try out for the *Survivor* show.

A few months later at the season's first NORBA Big Bear race I finished second. On the podium with one of my heros Missy Giove! So when my team manager congratulated me by telling me I did "okay," I didn't understand. Not at first. To the team, placing second in a real race was not as good as winning a fake race like the X Games. In the real world, the world where millions of Americans live, the X Games are the new Olympics. In our much smaller world of professional mountain biking the X Games are a little bit hokey. But I understood that our small world of professional mountain biking exists only as long as we can provide a commercial service to our sponsors. Later that summer when I won my first NORBA downhill race in Pennsylvania I felt vindicated. Standing on top of that podium in front of a crowd of other mountain bikers, opening that champagne, and sharing it with my competitors was so rewarding because that much smaller world knew how hard it was to win one of those races. I'd had a sip of that champagne and even though I was now thirty-three years old I wanted more. If that meant I had to occasionally run into trees and race on snow so what.

During the three years I was on Team Yeti I was lucky enough, and had worked hard enough, to win a couple of races a year. At least one NORBA downhill and then any other "classic" that I could get away with. Winning at least that much made my sponsors happy and winning only that much kept me hungry.

Some of these classics were Red Bull events. I first encountered the Red Bull beverage when I was racing in Europe for Team Marin. From a base in Austria I had seen how Red Bull had expanded all over Europe. It was a mysterious company with a mystique marketing campaign. It wasn't long before Red Bull was sponsoring mountain bike events in America. During my first summer racing for Yeti, Red Bull sponsored the Lake Tahoe Fat Tire Festival. The Fat Tire Festival was usually a small local event, fun, but not really a race that too many pros attended. That year it was strategically placed in between a couple of NORBA races and Red Bull had done a great job of promoting it. The winners were to be crowned gravity god and goddess.

Myles Rockwell and I ended up winning the event, a series of races: a downhill, a "miss and out" roostmaster-type thing, a slalom, and a downhill mania-style event. Squeezing past my ex-teammate, Kim Sonier, for the top spot on the podium helped my confidence. But the real prize was catching the eye of the Red Bull athlete representative, Jim Gunning. I knew that the big prize of that weekend's race would be his business card.

Red Bull has sponsored me ever since. Aside from shipping me cases of Red Bull anywhere in the world that I ask, they have helped my racing in so many other ways. Some of their races that I have entered have been higher profile than the X Games. The cool factor of the Red Bull Ice Tube Race was off the charts. I went the fastest I have ever gone on a mountain bike—seventy-three miles per hour for first place—racing down the ice-covered concrete curves of an Olympic bobsled track in Cortina, Italy.

Red Bull also staged a race one mile underground in a salt mine in what used to be East Germany. We raced two at a time in the subterranean blackness, our headlights bobbing with each pedal stroke, breathing stale air so dry from the salt that our lungs burned. In the finals I lined up against Anne Caroline Chausson, whose snap at the start was so quick that I knew I would be playing catch up the whole way. So a few seconds into the race I shut off my light, becoming invisible, and as quietly as possible I sat on her tail waiting for her to think that I had crashed or given up. She looked back a couple of times and didn't see me in the blackness. She eased up bit, took a breath. I clicked into a bigger gear and pedaled as hard as I could but her snap is so automatic that the second she heard me she jumped out of her saddle and dropped me again. After the race all the competitors and a thousand fans who had won entrance in a special lottery danced to a Euro groove and drank Red Bull and vodka in a giant dome carved out of the salt rock deep underground. All the top athletes now look forward to being invited to these special Red Bull events held all over the world.

I won the downhill at the Sea Otter, the spring season opener at the Laguna Seca Raceway, a couple of times. That is a smart race to win since all the sponsors and media are in attendance and a podium there can be leveraged for the rest of the race season.

After a win, a powerful momentum can carry you quite a ways. Your competitors, who are your friends, pat you on the back. You feel like a superhero rolling through the pits on your race-winning bike. Back at the team truck anything you say is now important. If you laugh, others laugh with you. If you want to sit, some one gives you a chair. If you feel like a beer, somebody thrusts a cold microbrew in your hand. On race day I find it difficult to eat well at all. Too many butterflies. I have been so lucky to be sponsored by Team Luna and Clif Bar, because those bars have been all that I have been eating. But after a win my stomach is grumbling for a different kind of food. The glycogen window during which food can help refill your empty tank is only open for a limited time. Forbidden food treats like ice cream, yogurt, chocolate-chip cookies, a turkey sandwich smothered in mustard, whatever your pleasure, tastes especially fattening and rewarding when served during this window after a win.

There is another window, sometimes open for as long as few weeks or as short as a few hours, depending on when the next race is set to go off. It's called the "schwag" window. After a win is the very best time to coast by your tire sponsor for a visit. Smile. It helps if the race announcer is still talking about your win, or the video is replaying on the Jumbotron screen. Let your fingers tickle the tacky knobs and ridges of a set of High Rollers in the display booth. Be sure to thank your tire sponsor for making your win possible. There's a good chance your tire sponsor will hook you up with another pair. Don't be shy.

Next race you could flat and not even finish. It might be a long while before you get your hands on any more schwag.

I have never won a national championship. I still hope to. So far I haven't been able to put together a whole season of consistently good finishes to win the title. Missy Giove has recently won three years in a row, and Lisa Sher was able to break that streak by racing well for a whole season. I am still learning I guess. But I did win one world championship race once.

The first Single Speed World Championship was held a few years ago at a secret location somewhere in the Inland Empire of Southern California. This race was underground and unsanctioned. Secret invitation into a self-selected tribe, first prize was a tattoo. The tattoo wasn't optional. The race organizer warned everybody that if "you don't want the ink, don't win."

Downhillers typically do not race single-speed bikes. Single speeds are antithetical to the heavy, fully suspended, multi-geared, gravity-guided downhill rigs that I normally race. A single-speed bike is usually cobbled together from cast-off parts onto a hard-tail frame (one that has no rear suspension). Single speeds are simple and light and quiet. Choose too big a gear for climbing and you'll suffer on the way to the top. Choose a gear too small for the descent and you'll spin out long before others grind past you. Touch your brakes at any time and the only way to make up time is with your thighs. No mechanical advantage to get you back up to speed. So once you are up to speed you have to maintain that momentum at all costs. Racing a single speed is a special kind of pain fest.

One of the guys I trained with in Marin, my friend Cameron, clued me in to this race and convinced me to go. He even built up my Yeti hard tail that had been languishing in my shed since the ESPN Critical Mass ride, into a lean, mean, single-speed machine. Before the race I had zero minutes of riding time on that bike. Maybe that explains why my legs were so fresh. I felt good wheeling around the parking lot of the abandoned restaurant that was serving as a staging area. The weight difference was incredible. That Yeti could not have weighed more than seventeen pounds, almost two-thirds less than my downhill bike. Some racers were serious. Some weren't. Some were already drunk.

Travis Brown, who had raced in the Olympics; Daryl Price; and some other big guns were there. A lot of very competitive Californian girls, but no big names in cross country, had shown up. I, of course, was the only downhiller of either gender. Some bikes were titanium thoroughbreds. Others were clunking junkers. Chris D'Stefano, the Shimano office hero, rode laps around the parking lot smartly thumb-shifting the race field's only rear derailleur across a stack of cogs: nine gears all the same size. Cameron had chosen the perfect climbing gear for me. I ride my bike through the woods a lot, so I floated to the top feeling so strong that I even had time to chat with Mike Ferrentino, a good friend whose face was as red as a fire engine, yet another rider grinding too large a gear. On the way down, I screamed my bike into a frantic cadence, leaning it down into the turns, my tires only hooking up on the smooth sidewalls, my V-brakes never once uttering so much as a peep.

In the parking lot, the sun now high across the sky and hot despite the LA-basin haze, I hunched over my bike, still sweaty and dusty, a bottle of tequila in my hand, my chamois shorts pulled down beyond where I normally apply sunscreen protection and my butt high in the air to receive my first prize for winning a world championship. The tattoo artist was a talented guy. I am told this tattoo is an excellent example of single-needle work, exceedingly rare, and requiring an extremely high level of skill. For years after winning this race I have coasted on that ink. Innumerable double mocha nonfat creme lattes have been bought for me after Saturday morning road rides in various coffee shops in Marin just by exhibiting the fine quality of this ink work to any rider who asked.

I always look to see if there are any kids around first.

The Power of Confidence

Mountain biking has given me so much confidence in other parts of my life that I am no longer the meek little science nerd I was at age twenty-eight. Throwing myself wholeheartedly into this sport has empowered me in so many ways and opened up so many doors on which I would never have had the temerity to knock. Tattooing my butt is a good example. A little bit of tequila helped, but not a drop was actually necessary.

Years earlier while on that bike trip through Europe with Marc I wanted a tattoo. I had always wanted one. At least since high school when I had snuck into a B-52s concert and was wowed by all the colorful art displayed on biceps, ankles, and midriffs. But I knew my parents would never approve of one. After college while I was working in the lab I knew that the only employees who sported tattoos without recrimination were custodians. So in Marseilles with Marc, far from my career and parents, I got the teeniest tiniest tattoo conceivable on my earlobe and thought myself brave. But really I was just drunk. For months afterward, back in Baltimore when visiting my parents, I dabbed behind my earlobe with makeup, and toiled at my lab bench with my hair down.

No. I am no longer the meek little science nerd. I am now a true-blue, full-fledged, third-degree bike geek. A great personal development and quite a social advancement. The thin lines of that tattoo on my butt cheek, in ways that the cursive script on my master's degree never could, really have provided for me a sense of self.

It was relatively easy to get hired for a position in a science lab. Personality doesn't count at all. What mattered was your education, your experience, and how well your skill set matched the job criteria. I had even been hired at Scripps, not because of who I was, but because of who they thought I was. Getting the small sponsorship from the Bicycle Network had been completely different. They couldn't have sponsored me based on my experience or how well I suited their needs. They took me on because of how strongly I projected myself. I was so forceful simply because I was confident that I was a better rider than anybody else who walked into that shop.

A few years later I would need to dig deep into a well of confidence that I am sure was dug deeper every time I endoed into the dirt.

In 1997 I was having a pretty good season on Team Marin. I had just won the gravity goddess title at the Lake Tahoe Red Bull Mountain Bike Festival. I felt very confident going into the next NORBA race at Mammouth Mountain. Mammouth Mountain ran its downhill course, from the barren lunarlike volcanic top, fast and wide open, screaming through the tree line, skidding along a rutted, dirt, fire road at speeds approaching sixty miles an hour, loose shale kicking into the air with every turn of the wheel. The course was appropriately called the Kamikazi. This type of course was perfectly suited to my limited downhill technical skills, and it required pushing a huge gear, which I like because I worked so hard at staying fit.

I usually did not enter the NORBA dual slalom event. It is not really suited to my riding style. It is a very quick BMX-style course with lots of sharp turns and peaky jumps. But I was fired up from doing well at the dual slalom and "roostmaster" at Lake Tahoe, so I intended on winning the slalom at Mammouth too.

I can still remember walking up that slalom course in Mammouth, Marc pushing my bike beside me, for my second practice run. Marc huffing, "Marla, you can win the downhill tomorrow. The Kamikaze! Why are you messing around with this slalom stuff?"

I had just bought a house with money from the VO2 MAX commercial. My parents were beginning to think that riding a bike may not be such a bad way for me to earn a living. My brothers were proud of me. I had just won my last race, beating a world champ. A Red Bull rep had stuffed some business cards into my pocket and told me to call about sponsorship. Everything was perfect.

And I can remember sitting in the starting gate waiting for my turn on the course. I was riding a full-suspension cross-country bike called the Quake. I was sporting two water bottles, 175mm-length cranks, bar ends, clipless pedals, triple-chain rings, long stem with a ten-degree rise, and a seat post way up high. Not the standard slalom setup. Simply, the completely wrong setup. I had made it down once, safely, on the other course. Now my turn on this course was coming up when Toby Henderson sauntered over shaking his head. He fiddled with my bar ends and tapped my water bottles. He asked me what I was doing in the small-chain ring. So I shifted up to the big ring like everybody else. Then he shook his head and told me to watch out for the back side of the second set of doubles. Be careful there. And a few seconds later "there" was where I broke my wrist. Marc told me later that it happened in slow-motion ugly.

My season was over. There was no way I would even be able to qualify for the world championships. Marc brought my handlebar into the emergency room anyway and the doctor formed the cast around my hand as I clutched onto the bar. I learned right there in the emergency room to appreciate the specific skills required for slalom. In slalom you just couldn't tough out a good result like in cross country. You couldn't just swallow your fear and let go of the brakes like I had been getting away with in downhill. In slalom you had to really know what you were doing, and it obviously required lots of practice. Sitting in the emergency room is where I first laid out in my mind the slalom jump course that I would start to build that winter in my backyard. As it turned out I was able to make the world's team that year, but not for downhill. Because I was thirty years old I was able to race in the cross-country veteran class, and I ended up getting second.

Driving home from Mammouth, the cast on my wrist across my lap, Marc and I were quiet. There wasn't much to say. When we stopped for gas in Manteca I said, "Well, at least I signed a two-year deal so we won't have to worry about where I'll be racing next season."

Marc remained quiet for a long time. "You just heal up. I'm gonna spend some time at Kinko's anyway. Make up a couple of resumes to hand out at Interbike."

Interbike is the largest bike convention in America. It is not open to the public. Every drooling bike geek in America looks forward to Interbike. That year it was held over four days at the Anaheim Convention Center. All the deals are put together there. Bike shops order bikes. Bike builders commit to components. Manufacturers demo their products. Headhunters look to

fill open sales and management positions. Marketing departments strut their stuff. Pagers beep, people whisper, meetings
take place in closed rooms. It is a bazaar of bikes. The Italian
pavilion is a showcase for traditional road bikes and skinny-tire
stuff. The big American mountain bike companies tout all their
innovations. The BMX stuff, in a small slump at the moment,
ran ragged around the edges. And the Taiwanese pavillion offered to manufacture knockoffs of anything for bottom-dollar
prices. Crazy guys stood in their booths preaching and handing
out flyers to convert the world to the recumbent bike religion.
Interbike was an opportunity to thank in person the owners of
smaller companies like Brave Soldier, which made a line of road
rash and first-aid products, and B.O.B. Trailers for any support
they might have given me over the year. And bike racers get
signed by the big teams. Teams like to have their riders there to
hand out posters, and also to keep an eye on them to make sure
they aren't talking to any other teams.

The owner of Marin Mountain Bikes told me he wanted me
at Interbike to sign some posters and hand out catalogs to potential dealers. I was in the middle of a two-year deal so I wasn't
worried about scrambling around for a ride. That's why I was so
floored the morning of the first day when Rachel, a training
buddy, told me that Bob Buckley, the owner of Marin Mountain
Bikes, had told her she was wasting her time asking him for a
deal. Bob was going to fold the team he told her. All the rider
contracts would expire soon and he was going to "release" me
from my contract.

Even though I tried to compose myself during my meeting
with Bob later in the day I really don't remember all he said. I
know you are not supposed to take things like that personally,
but I couldn't help it. I was doing a great job. Bob had helped
me secure the mortgage for my house by telling the bank that I
was one of the top athletes in the world, that I had a guaranteed

contract and should be able to anticipate a higher income in years to come. Why was I one of the last to know that he was dumping me? If he had clued me in earlier in the season, I would have been more prepared to talk to other teams. Getting a pro ride is like playing musical chairs. There are always more people looking for positions than there are opportunities. During the season all the racers jockey for places on the podium, and also for rides for the next season. After Interbike, when the music stops, racers that you pal around with, that you know and respect, often have no place to go. I didn't know that I should have been shopping around all season.

Back at the motel that night I broke down a little. "So, what am I supposed to do now? I've just been fired," I asked Marc.

"Tomorrow you'll get a ride with another team. That's all. Hand out some resumes, shake some hands. Try to get some sleep. I know you are not a quitter. Try to get some sleep, Marla."

Sleep was out of the question. I had used up all my savings to buy that house. The bank had wanted twenty percent down since extreme athletes are in a special credit-risk category. There was no pile of cash under my pillow. I wrestled with all my blankets. I kicked my legs this way and that. Marc can sleep through anything. I hated him for that. The mortgage payments weren't too large, but there were property taxes, and the house needed repairs. We had a slip payment for the boat, and although Marc was taking care of that, we were stretched pretty thin.

Should I consider this a good time to move on? It had been a fun experience, but now should I go into San Francisco and get a real job with a biotech company? After all, how much more could I hope to accomplish on a bike? Should I tell Marc that I am ready to sail away and continue that bike trip that we first had started in Europe? In that meeting Bob admitted that my contract was guaranteed, and if I wanted to I could sail down to

Mexico for that year and he would still be obligated to send me a check each month. Was I ready to go on a long sailing trip now? I could rent the house out, probably for enough to pay for itself and sail away, or we could move back onto the boat and scramble around for next year while I continued to race. Or I could sell the house, take all that money, and never come back. Or I could set all these doubts aside and sleep like a champion, confident that tomorrow would be new day. Confident that I would find a new deal.

At ten a.m. when the doors first opened for the second day of Interbike I was more prepared. There were a half-dozen teams where I had a chance of carving out a spot for myself. Under my arm I carried a proposal package tailored for each team. Marc had anticipated this and done a bang-up job. He had even supplied me with stacks of cool businesscards. At the top of my list was Yeti.

Yeti was one of the pioneers of the sport and a team of many past champions. My hero, John Tomac, and other great racers such as Julie Furtado, Missy Giove, Myles Rockwell, and Jimmy Deaton rode for Yeti. It was a cult company founded in Durango by the legendary John Parker. Yeti recently had fallen on tough times, and had been bought by Schwinn, a much larger corporation. Along with the storied name, Schwinn had bought the Yeti factory and the services of motorcycle hero Mert Lawwill. Mert designed the downhill bikes.

There were other companies that might have been willing to offer me a larger contract, but none could offer me what Yeti could in Mert. I was determined to ride the best bike available. The staid Marin designs hadn't really improved in the three years I had been riding them. I was probably the only factory downhill rider on V-brakes, instead of the more powerful disc brakes. The Marin design limited the FOX Shock to only four inches of rear travel. The Lawwill-designed Yeti Straight 8 had twice the rear travel, though that meant switching to a Rock Shox pull shock. The pull shock was a concept that Mert really believed in, but FOX had no interest in making a pull shock. Leaving FOX would be the only negative to riding for Yeti, that, and a big pay cut. Still, a big reason why I wanted to ride for Yeti was because Mert lived in Marin. If a brainstorm came to him in the night for a new set out of drop outs, he would machine them in his garage by noon and I wanted to be able to ride them that afternoon.

But getting on Yeti would be twice as tricky since I would have to convince the Yeti guys and then convince the Schwinn guys, since they were writing the checks. And there were plenty of other riders lined up ahead of me.

My talk with Mert went over pretty well. He was interested, but said the ultimate decision would be up to the Schwinn guy, Dave MacLaughlin. For two days I circled around the Schwinn booth like a shark looking for the opportunity to pounce on Dave Mac. Dave was a busy guy that weekend trying to seal a deal with Sean Palmer, the extreme athlete wonder guy.

I didn't want to seem like a pest, or really desperate for a ride either. Both of those things can work against you. So I strolled farther away from their location, confident that Marc would whistle if Dave Mac showed his face. Across the aisle in the Oakley booth I spotted Lance Armstrong talking with a few product reps. Everybody in a few years would admire his story, but for now, all we knew was that this world champion road rider had gotten cancer, and then had been dumped by his team, Cofidis. He had lost a lot of weight. His swimmer's shoulders had disappeared. Of all the sponsors he had had at Interbikes in the past, only Oakley was sticking by him now. And here he was with his chin up, lining up to look for work like the rest of us. Seeing Lance like that put things in perspective for me. If he could do it, so could I. I wasn't even sick! I had only broken my wrist, that's all.

I always regretted not approaching Lance that afternoon. Just to give him a bit of encouragement. And get some in return. We were both Oakley athletes so had I wanted to, I could have marched right up to him, introduced myself, and asked him how things were going. But I lacked the confidence. Lance Armstrong was just too much of a world champion, even then.

And when Dave Mac finally did give me two minutes of time I confidently laid it on pretty thick about how well I was planning on racing. Yeti would be getting a big bang for their buck since I planned on racing cross country, downhill, and cyclocross.

It took a lot of discussions that weekend and many phone calls followed, but a few months later I did sign a deal with Yeti. And even though it was only a one-year deal for exactly half the salary that I had earned the year before, I was ecstatic. I was confident that even though I was racing for less money it would still pay off. I was sure that I wasn't making a mistake signing with Yeti. I was positive that Marin was making a big mistake by breaking my contract. I'd show them.

That winter, a few weeks after Marin stopped payment on my contract, I won my first big race: a gold medal at the X Games. I was thirty-two years old.

It wasn't that much later that I would be on the cover of *Outside* magazine riding not a Marin, but a Yeti. And on the inside, I confidently posed on my Yeti Straight 8, wearing only my Single Speed World Championship tattoo and a pair of sunglasses.

The Power of Just One Glass of Wine

The power of confidence that mountain biking has given me also probably saved me from getting in trouble with alcohol. Shaving my head, moving onto that small sailboat with Marc, and signing that contract with Iron Horse was a new lease on life.

Maybe riding a mountain bike and progressing through the pro ranks is like climbing up the rungs of some twelve-step program.

I did quit drinking for my whole rookie season. It wasn't hard to do. I just substituted mountain biking for alcohol as an organizing principle of my life.

Looking back I can see how in Baltimore when I was younger I fell into a pattern of drinking, and then drinking too much. If you learn one thing from four years of college it should be how to drink socially, responsibly. I hadn't. Instead I had learned how to drink in binges, frequently. Two more years of graduate school hadn't taught me that important life lesson either. Even more years in a doctoral program might have resulted in me being as pickled as the anatomical specimens I was studying.

Marc, maybe as a bartender or more likely because he can recognize patterns, saw in me the potential for getting in trouble with tequila. That's one of the reasons why he encouraged me so much to embrace mountain biking. When we first went out to Fells Point or to the beach the drinking was fun, but he noticed that, even though we didn't drink on every date, when we did drink, we drank a lot. Relatively a whole lot more for me than for him. I wasn't drinking every night. Usually I didn't even have a drop during the whole work week. I was a quiet, reserved, science nerd. I had good grades, a great job. But I was still greiving in my own way about the loss of my brother Mark. As long as I had a tray of oyster cultures in front of me to concentrate on I could block out those black feelings of remorse. If, in the middle of the night I couldn't sleep because of Mark, the only way to wait out the dawn was on my skateboard grinding the cobblestones and "ollieing" the granite curbs of Federal Hill. After work on Friday night if I had a few beers, and then twice as many more, and a couple shots and so on, so that I blacked out completely during the weekend, then it was even easier not to think about Mark.

When we were living in Durham and I had even more stuff to not think about, Marc didn't press it. He often let me get drunk while he sipped his beer and kept an eye on me. Training for the Boston Marathon was his way to subtly cut down on my binging. No one likes to wake up at dawn, especially me, and run some miles after a night of pub crawling. I realized a few years ago, actually, watching a romp of downhill pros tear apart a quaint beer garden in Kaprun, that, during our drive across the country in Vidalia, Marc was trying to show me how I could enjoy one beer after a long mountain-bike ride. One beer, and no more.

That's the kind of thing you have to learn on your own. It's not like learning musical scales or organic chemistry tables by having a Catholic nun pound them repeatedly into your skull. You can only learn something like that when you are ready. When you really want to.

When I signed with Iron Horse I simply stopped drinking for a year. I stopped so I could train better, keep my weight down, and because I knew that none of the other top pros would be lining up with a hangover on race day. I didn't want to handicap myself any more than my age and lack of skill already did. But not drinking is not really the same as controlling your drinking. For the first year of racing pro, while I was lining up behind Julie Furtado, Susan Demattie, Tammy Jacques, and other cross-country goddesses, it was easy not to drink at all. And when I signed with Marin I was so proud about earning my paycheck that I didn't want to drink on a whole lot of occasions. Many times when we were sailing on San Francisco Bay on a beautiful autumn afternoon I'd scold Marc for cracking open a cold one, because I knew I had an epic single-track ride planned the next day on Tam. Just the smell of hops would disgust me, because I knew it was no more than "go-slow juice."

The more I got into downhilling, however, and away from cross country, the more opportunities there were for having a few too many beers. Or all of the beer for that matter. This may be hard to believe but hanging around with a bunch of pro downhillers was like being back in college. There was way too much drinking, no introspection, and not enough adult supervision.

Downhillers do train. They work just as hard, maybe harder, because of all the cross training that is required on motorcycles, BMX bikes, road bikes, and in the weight room. Compared to the solitary monklike daily ritual of cross-country training— waking early and drinking coffee, a long hard morning ride, and then legs elevated for the rest of the afternoon and early to bed— downhilling might seem like spring break. Depending on the training schedule downhillers sometimes do spend more time sitting on a chairlift than on their saddles. Cross-country racers often train alone since their discipline requires developing a mental resolve to deal with the drawn-out self-inflicted pain. Downhillers usually train in small groups. It's a lot easier to see the line selection off a drop off if you can watch someone else do it first. The collegial atmosphere of mutual support, and its ugly twin sister, peer pressure, are instrumental for screwing up the nerve to ride down rocky spines at breakneck speeds. The nervous tension of downhilling is frequently relieved by laughter and giggles when someone clears a rough section safely. Laughing would be a sacrilege for cross-country riders mired in the middle of a muscle cramp. Cross-country riders typically down "Grande Ventes" on a grand scale, since they will be riding for hours on a dawn-patrol isolation exercise, and need to get fired up for the effort. Downhillers eschew caffeine because the jumps, gravity drops, and tree smacks already ensure that their nervous system will be stimulated enough. Maybe such an afternoon of close calls, lucky breaks, and body plunges of adrenaline does call for a cold beer to relax with and wind down. It might be just the competitive nature of group dynamics that leads to seeing who can drink the next one faster. Call it the Shaun Palmer Effect.

Although I believe that Shaun Palmer, the X-Games king, extreme athlete of all Gen-X sports, really never drank as much as he let on once he got a taste of mountain biking. He might have partied hard while snowboarding his way into the hall of fame because he was so much better than his competition. But once he got on his downhill bike, and especially after he came within a hair of upsetting Nicholas Voillois, the godlike downhill world champion, I think "the Palm" might have been playing mind games with the other racers. All that stuff about how he really didn't work out and instead drank Jack Daniels all night was a bit of a ploy to lull his competitors into adopting his "winning ways." He was probably training like crazy, eating right, napping in the afternoons. Extreme. Yes. Extremely smart.

I was the only downhiller on my team the first year with Team Luna. I spent the summer on the road with the world champion, Alison Dunlap, and other girls who wanted to be world champ. The first day in a condo at altitude I like to buy a six pack of Guinness. I put it on top of the fridge and have one a night. I have convinced myself that the dark, malty, iron-rich Irish beer is good for improving my hemoglobin uptake in the thin air. Once, I was able to talk the other girls into trying some. One drank half a glass, another had one sip, and another would only hold the bottle beneath her nose and sniff!

Straddling these two very different worlds of mountain biking, and striking my own balance, has given me special appreciations for each.

Really, it was only a few years ago that I learned how to enjoy a glass of pinot grigio while Marc whipped up a pot of fresh paella in the kitchen. During dinner the saffron and garlic infused the air so deeply, and would overpower any wine so easily, that a glass of water was best.

Moderation. Striking a balance. Find a happy medium. Choose your euphemism. Each is as empty as the next if you've never exerted yourself and learned the difference. For me going fast on a downhill bike was easy. Winning wasn't. Learning the difference was developing an appreciation for moderation. And balance.

In order to win on a downhill course I had to learn that I could not race absolutely as hard as possible over every inch of the course. That would require a perfect run. And you should never plan on a perfect run as part of a winning race strategy. I had to squirrel away a reserve of strength for the inevitible loose rock or broken branch that would pop up. I had to learn to attack the course where I was the weakest and reserve a bit on those sections where I was the strongest. I'm not saying to go slow. You never go slow. If you plan on going slow why bother racing. You just have to moderate a bit if you want to win.

Once I had understood that lesson of moderation on the mountain it was abundantly clear how to behave with merlot. Mountain biking has done so much for me it was my obligation to try to be a better role model and not tempt my Luna Chick teammates into intemperance.

Even though mountain biking was initially just one more way of not dealing with Mark's loss, it now allows me to put my brother's death into some sort of personal perspective by striving every day for some small improvement. Because of that I sleep better at night and wake eager to begin each day. Even with all that mountain biking has done for me, in and of itself, it couldn't protect me from perhaps harming myself. I never had the morning shakes, never secretly drank vanilla extract in the kitchen or traded sexual favors in a dark alley for a paper bag of scotch, but more than a few glasses of wine on any one occasion can be unhealthy.

After many years of learning the same lesson, I finally did straighten it all out on my own.

Chapter 8

The Achilles' Heel of a Gravity Goddess

Hubris: Being a Small-Time God in a Big-Time World

By the end of that first season in 1995 with Team Marin I figured that since I was now a big-time pro I could do a better job for Marin Mountain Bikes, boost their sales, improve their product, develop better distribution modalities if I was close by. How that company had managed the last year without my close presence was a miracle, I believed.

San Diego was a very small pond for a big-time mountain-bike frog like me, I thought. Besides, San Diego is kind of flat and Marin has the steep slopes of Mount Tamalpais. The bigger bike world of Marin would suit me better, I thought.

Marc agreed it would be smart to leave San Diego and move to Marin. So before I had boarded the plane for World's, we had packed up Vidalia with all my bike equipment, uniforms, tools, and whatever stuff couldn't be crammed into our boat. We donated books and tee shirts and stacks of old VeloNews and *Mountain Bike* magazines to the Goodwill and jettisoned the rest. Our plan was that he would sail our boat north while I raced in Kaprun, and when I got back I would drive up Vidalia and we would rendezvous in Sausalito. There we'd live on the boat for a while until we could scrounge up a cheap cottage to rent.

Marc was working his way north less than a hundred miles a day in our sailboat, along the coast to our new home sweet home, which would be somewhere in Marin. I was a little bit worried about him. We hadn't even spoken over the phone during the two weeks while I was at World's. He had no idea that I had placed seventh! Likewise I had no idea if he had beached our boat up on some rocks or if he'd been hit by storms or rogue waves.

Marc had fixed up our little boat, *Indifference,* all by himself. I had painted the inside cabin, but the list of stuff that Marc had rebuilt, replaced, bought secondhand and installed as new, fiberglassed, sanded, painted, fabricated, and fastened was long enough to make me sleepy as he told me at night in bed. Our boat didn't have an autopilot, so he would have to keep a hand on the tiller the whole time during his trip to Marin. We didn't have a GPS so he would have to maintain a good position on his paper charts. Our boat lacked radar, so he would have to keep a sharp eye out for the giant tankers that could sneak up on you near Los Angeles. The puny gasoline engine, not much more powerful than a VW's, was limited to getting in and out of a slip. Not great for powering against northern swells. We had sailed a dozen or so times, but there isn't much wind in San Diego and I was afraid there hadn't been much that I had been able to teach him. He was pretty much on his own. Sailing north from San Diego to San Francisco against the wind and current the whole way would be slow going and exhausting.

After World's as I drove north myself, and where the highway paralleled the surf near Newport Beach I kept sneaking glances toward the western horizon, looking for the silhouette of our little boat's sails against the sky.

That I was that worried surprised me a bit. I didn't think I was capable of that much concern. I'm not the mushy type. Marc would be fine. I should enjoy the drive.

Alone I pushed Vidalia, huffing and puffing, overladen with all my bikes and equipment and tools and spare parts, away from the coast along a stretch of highway strewn with industrial parks, discount auto-part stores, and uniform tracts of housing with bars on the windows. I was bobbing my head to the recently departed Jerry and the Dead. I had raced in a world championship just a few days earlier, not too far from where Marc and I had toured on bikes years earlier grimy and poor. The size of my head was expanding so rapidly that there was danger of attracting the attention of sci-fi moviemakers. Quite pleased with myself I was considering riding my bike every day on Mount Tamalpais, and maybe an evening sail on San Francisco Bay, and did not notice the smell of burning oil or the billowing gray smoke clinging to Vidalia's skirts until all the cars around me began to honk and flash their high beams.

I swerved off the highway at the first exit, which led me down an off ramp to one of Los Angeles' infamous "hoods." Vidalia coasted to a shuddering stop along a stretch of road illuminated in the distance by the flickering neon of a liquor store and not much else. Nikes dangled like strange fruit from the broken street lamps. Vidalia's windows shuddered at the booming deep base of low-riding Chevy Novas as they rolled slowly past. Young kids with gold teeth and old eyes smiled at me and flipped Vidalia's locked door handles as I bent over her open engine compartment groping for her dipstick in the slanting light.

This is where people die, I thought. The dipstick in my hand was as dry as my mouth.

Down the street the public telephone, which was bolted to a pole in the liquor store parking lot, dangled a broken chain instead of a phone book. No way would AAA send a tow truck to this neighborhood, they said, not until morning. Neither my high school French nor my apprehensive English was understood by anybody in the liquor store. I wanted to call Marc.

Funny how just a few miles back, I was hoping he was okay, and if there was anything I could do for him. And now I wanted him to swoop in here and make everything all right. Fix Vidalia. Put his arm around my shoulder. Rescue me.

Walking alone from the liquor store back to Vidalia, my shadow stretched almost across the narrow street. It would be alley dark very soon. Only because I was taller by more than a foot was I able to brush away a couple of urchins stabbing a coat hanger into the passenger door when I returned to Vidalia. They stood in a tight group out in the street laughing and pointing and seemed to grow taller as the street became darker.

There were no other options. I had to save myself. I locked myself inside Vidalia and rolled around on the floor while I changed into my bike uniform. I looked up and down the sidewalk and then crawled out dragging behind me my best cross-country bike, a titanium beauty. I'd have to leave all the rest for the street's scavengers. Sobbing on the sidewalk, I stuffed my tight jersey with spare tubes, patches, tire irons, and two pumps. My little wad of U.S. cash and useless deutsch marks was jammed deep into my Shimano shoes. I did sling one more spare tube around skinny shoulders like a bandolier. The last thing I wanted in this neighborhood was a flat tire. Tears welled in my eyes when I imagined what would happen to Vidalia, and to all my bike stuff. These were my most valued possessions, but I knew it wasn't a smart idea to camp out here for the night.

I didn't want everything to end here on this dark street. I wanted to win races. I wanted to be a champion! Mark died before he even got a chance to change the world. I'm not going to change the world by riding a mountain bike, but I do want to finish what I started, I thought. That would make Mark proud of me. He'd like that.

I was just locking the Kryptonite U-lock on Vidalia's sliding door when out of the shadows I saw a figure approaching. We stared at each other across a busted newspaper machine as I fumbled with my helmet's chin strap.

There was a flicker in his eye. This is it. Baggy pants. Gold on his neck. Backward baseball cap. This guy was older than the urchins, taller too. I am not going to get out of here. I forgot what the color schemes were for gangs: blue and red, or all blue, or all red, who was who, and what colors was I showing? He was wearing blue jeans and an oily green work shirt. What gang was that?

"Hey, I know you," he said, and broke into a broad smile. "Your name is Marla."

Yessss! He must be a mountain biker too, flashed across my mind. He must have seen me on TV doing that ESPN interview. Of course he would recognize me all dressed up in my official team uniform. I am a big-time pro mountain biker! I am somebody. I am not going to die on this nameless street in Los Angeles. My bikes looted and Vidalia raped. No! I am a famous international sports star!

"I know you. Do you 'member me?" he asked. I squinted into the dimming light. He was smiling at me. His shirt was new and pressed, but the material was stiff and heavy. It was smudged here and there with oil like a work uniform. A white rag, coarse, but still clean, dangled from the back pocket of his baggy jeans. He stood, smiling, in black workboots, not white leather gangsta-style basketball shoes. His hands were scrubbed all the way to the middle of his forearms where a ring of greasy dirt remained. Maybe he works in a bike shop around here somewhere! Maybe he is one the race mechanics on the circuit. That's how he knows me. Maybe he is a friend of Zap's, the magazine guy with the big earlobes? Or maybe he had caught my ten-second segment on the *Vicious Cycle* video that had recently come out? Only a few magazine issues back, there was a full-page photo of me all decked out in my leathers standing beside Marc's motorcycle with my cross-country bike affixed to the crazy bike rack he had rigged. I was almost as famous as Madonna, I told myself. Maybe I had signed an autograph for this guy at one of the wildly popular Lake Castaic races.

I am not really great at names. A shameful little secret is that Marc whispers many of them into my ear when I forget. "I'm sorry. I have forgotten your name. But I am glad that you remember mine."

"From the booze cruise," he prompted me.

My blank expression told him I had no idea what he was talking about. I had been clean and sober for a year now.

"Spring break in Jamaica," he gestured with his hands like he was drinking a beer and at the same time he sucked in his belly. "About ten years ago. I'll never forget."

I was worried about where I was right now, not where I might have been ten years ago. I was a completely different person then. Right now all I want to do is hop on my bike and escape. I am a world-class athlete.

"You were in the van full of Americans that was hijacked on the way to the resort. You won the beer chugging contest. On the booze cruise. You were famous. I'm Louis, 'member me? You asked me one time if there was any more ice left for the blender. 'Member?"

Louis ended up pushing Vidalia while I steered the few blocks to the small auto repair business he owned.

I didn't remember him. That week in Jamaica had been pretty crazy, but Louis had told me enough about the booze cruise, the hotel where we all stayed, and the kidnapping stuff to convince me that he knew me. At least the old me. What a small world. An even smaller world that he owned an auto repair business.

Louis worked all night on Vidalia. I crashed out on the couch in his office still in my bike uniform. He didn't even charge me a whole lot. Not even by 1971 VW camper bus standards. Early in the morning I was back on the highway happy, but a little humbled.

The mountain bike world is even smaller than the world of guys I had been on booze cruises with, I had to admit.

On the morning of this new day I realized that people might not think of you the way that you imagine. They might see someone else, someone different than who you know yourself to be. Just like I had with Louis—assuming the worst when he first walked up. I also thought that even if people did assume things about me, that was even less reason to care what people thought of my age. Whether or not it's crazy to race mountain bikes. More reason to try harder to become what you want.

As I got closer to Marin I realized how lucky I was to be living with the man I knew, Marc. The guy I knew that I was in love with. Why had I been hesitating to commit to this man? How much more time did we have to spend with each other? How much time would I need to say I loved him? How much more patient could he be? How much longer would he wait for me to figure out what I wanted from him? That what he had was already more than enough.

Down the Grapevine Grade into the dry, dusty San Joaquin Valley, I thought about what little time there might be left. How ironic that my life could just as easily have ended at a highway off-ramp as at an off-camber turn on the Kamikaze downhill course.

My dad had always planned on the time after he retired, time after we kids were grown, time after all the grandkids were born, to do what he wanted. He worked and saved and put off enjoying himself until later in life. Dad traveled all over the country and a large part of the world for his work. But he never really visited the museums or parks or theaters, etc. He was at work, he reasoned. There would be time later, after he retired, to go back and visit. Time after he retired to return to Scotland for a round of golf. There would be time later to take my mom to a show in New York City. And now because of his Parkinson's, it turns out he didn't have much time to play golf. More ironic that he might have plenty of time, but no ability to play. Mom and Dad had visited us in San Diego, and we had gone sailing for an afternoon, but my dad hadn't felt comfortable on the foredeck. My mom wanted him to enjoy the warm Santa Ana winds, but she was afraid that he might lose his balance if he tugged on a line too hard. Later we tried as a family to ride cruiser bikes along the beach boardwalk, enjoy the sunset, maybe get our feet wet in the surf, but my dad wasn't able to pedal his cruiser much beyond a wobble. He used to love to ride his cruiser bike, one of his few indulgences, and now that too was slipping away from him. Dad no longer would be able to do what he had so long planned for.

Along that lonely stretch of Interstate 5, buffetted by sidewinds and harassed by speeding big rigs, I putted on in Vidalia wondering about what I wanted. And how I would make use of my time.

I know I hadn't set out to do the impossible in mountain biking. Not impossible, like going faster than the speed of light. Not impossible, like looking at the same river twice or finding a circle whose diameter is greater than its circumference. But certainly what I was trying to do was improbable. In my thirties now, a woman competing in largely a man's game, disregarding my formal education, without the wholehearted support of my family, trying to be a world champion. Maybe I couldn't change the world the way Mark had wanted to: put an end to poverty and hunger and pain, stop the cycle of war and the trashing of our planet. Maybe I couldn't accomplish all those lofty goals like Mark had set out to do. But I could try my best to do this one thing: race a downhill bike faster than anybody else. I could try my best to do that, and when I reached the point where I could look in the mirror and admit I had given my all, then I would see what else there was to attempt in life. Maybe that was the important thing, to keep trying while I had the time. Maybe I couldn't make a difference in the world, but I would never allow myself to become indifferent.

As Vidalia staggered out of that long valley into the delta of San Francisco Bay, the road thickened with cars and the buildings stood tighter and tighter so that the grassy hillsides disappeared altogether under a wide expanse of concrete and steel and glass. I promised myself that I would with talk with Marc. Tell him how I feel about him. As the bay itself spread out as wide as the horizon just beyond, as Mount Tam and the promise of Marin's trails hung from the billowy clouds, I said out loud, "We have to change the name of our boat, *Indifference*. Change it to, *Difference* . . . or something else maybe."

I felt silly talking out loud like that. So I hunched over, my arms resting on the steering wheel, and thought quietly, "Even if I can only make a teeny difference in the tiny world of mountain biking it would still be worth trying. I've got to remember that the mountain-bike world is a small one. Still I'd much rather be known as a mountain biker than as a beer chugger."

The Faster You Go, the Bigger the Endo

Injuries to my ego, like being recognized for winning a beer-chugging contest rather than a downhill race, are not the least that I have suffered as a mountain biker. All injuries, however, are self-inflicted. The thing is, the better you become as a rider, the faster you go, the harder you crash. For a pro rider, injuries can end careers. A weekend warrior, or even a hard core expert racer who still puts in forty hours a week at the office, doesn't have to worry too much about an injury. The nine-to-five job usually comes with insurance. A pro ride usually does not. Even a really bad crash doesn't mean that an expert rider's paychecks will stop coming. That you could lose your house. Even if you lose your job during your recovery, you probably still have some marketable skills. A banged up, unsigned pro downhiller, typically does not. You'll be able to ride, with no pressure, when your body heals. A pro has to try to race the next weekend. So even though a pro might be a stronger rider, train with all the best equipment, and benefit from nightly massages, a pro is conversely weaker than any expert or sport rider. At the very top levels of competition even the lamest boo-boo like a bruised thumb might cause a mis-shift, resulting in a dropped chain, potentially bouncing you down the podium steps. A pro rider can't contemplate a season without some type of injury. For a pro rider the only insurance for a career-busting injury is a good education, the premiums paid in high grades, the policy kept up-to-date with refresher courses, and cashed in with a Rolodex of contacts made during your racing career.

On my right calf, the soft fleshy part, is a decent impression of a Shimano XTR chain ring. The teeth match up almost exactly with the scar tissue. A memento of one of my first single-track rides on Mount Tam.

At one of the Winter X Games a few years ago I fell so hard onto the concrete-soft ice pack that I still have a grapefruit-sized bump on my left butt cheek. For months afterward that bump cycled through all the lumpy colors of the bruising hematoma palette like a Lava Lamp.

Plates and screws were installed in my right ankle. A cadaver's posterior cruciate ligament now sits snugly in my right knee.

Both knees are missing anterior cruciate ligaments, but those were torn years ago playing field hockey in high school. It's surprising how little you need your ACL when downhilling. Except maybe when you need to dab a foot on the ground. I can't slip rings on my pinky fingers, which bend and twist like hickory twigs.

Of course there was my collarbone and a broken wrist

The simple task of recounting my injuries like this makes me wonder how many times my bell has been rung.

My first pro season, at the Iron Horse Classic in Durango, I played jingle bells with my cranium. At the foot of Chapman Hill beneath Fort Lewis College, there is a mountain-bike shrine of a course. It is old and eroded like an archeological remnant of what was once something great. Those rounded berms and steep descents are all that remain of what was once the roostmaster course. Recently some of those turns and banks have been rebuilt and reincarnated as part of a new NORBA Mountain-Cross course. Back when it was the old roostmaster I banged my head on that hard-packed dirt like a cathedral bell peeling for morning mass.

During practice again and again I lined up for a jump and on the landing I tried braking, and through the air I tried turning my wheel and no matter what combination of the two, each time I slammed into the hard-packed dirt. My friend Russell was living in Durango then, and he was embarrased for me. A small crowd of beer drinkers gathered to watch. Norm, who was visiting for the race, yelled encouragement each time. Each crash landing my head snapped around on my delicate Audrey Hepburnish neck like a rock in a sling before smacking into the red dirt as hard as Mexican pavers.

As the practice hour wound down Missy Giove rode over to see what the commotion was. I knew she was watching so I tried even more, but stacked even harder. The growing crowd of beer drinkers groaned and cheered the louder. Finally after I picked myself out of the dirt after a particularly nasty crash and stood with my front wheel in between my knees wrenching my twisted handlebars back into an approximation of perpendicularity, Missy asked aloud of the crowd, "Who is that chick?"

Norm, my old riding buddy, came to my defense and answered in his deep basso profundo for the whole crowd to hear, "That's no chick! That's Marla!"

I was so banged up and my head was so dizzy that Toby wouldn't even let me line up for the race an hour later.

But all in all I can't say that working in a science lab was any safer. Working in any medical facility by its very nature is like sharing a public biological bath of nasty airborne organisms, chemical solvents, toxic waste, and unfortunate "incidents." Besides, there is no cardiovascular advantage to working any office-type job, compared to mountain biking. Mountain biking is a natural stress reliever, but a job at a university research center is like a stint in a pressure cooker. Another consideration is that, if somehow while working as a researcher I exposed myself to a bit more radiation from those pesky X rays, or splashed one drop too many of acetone on myself, there really is no way to know. Usually exposure to toxins in the workplace is ambient and passive and never detected at all. Whereas in mountain biking, even though I am the cause of my own injuries, I do get the benefit of almost immediate feedback for doing so.

Prolonged Exposure
May Cause Discomfort

A top pro has other concerns to worry about. Another potential thorn in the heel to watch out for is exposure. Or, in my case, overexposure.

I fell in love with mountain biking because I was a girl who loved dirt. I guess that's why a few years after I turned pro Tom Floyd, the guy who owned the Cantina Mountain Bike Shop, the guy who organized the Wednesday night rides in San Diego's Sorrento Valley, surprised me with an offer. Subdivisions had sprung up on the trails behind his shop. Since those trails had disappeared he wasn't selling nearly as many bikes and components and the real moneymakers . . . energy bars. His small line of clothing, Cantina Clothing, was doing okay. But Tom noticed that, even though he only stocked relatively few items for women, the girls' stuff was selling a lot better than the boys'.

Tom wanted to begin a new clothing label aimed exclusively at hard-core women mountain bikers, realizing that its popularity would extend to even the casual rider. Maybe even to that holy grail of demographics, the fattest part of the consumer bell curve: the "lifestyle enthusiast." Tom realized that this market niche was not being served by the larger clothing companies. And he knew from his own sales that his female customers were loyal and that they would increase his sales by word of mouth. So his idea was to sponsor me. He was just starting out and all he could offer me was product—no money, just clothes.

I knew enough about business that I should counter his offer. I should drive a hard bargain. So I said, "Wow!"

"But maybe next year if things go as planned there might be some money for you."

I didn't want to say wow again so I stuffed my hand in my mouth.

Marc and I talked about the offer and how it fit in with what I'd contractually agreed to with Marin. Neither of us was quite sure about all the technicalities, but we hoped we could make it a win-win situation.

"But what if Bob thinks that my wearing 'Girls Love Dirt!' will benefit him? He'll probably say okay, right?"

"Yes. I mean you should definitely tell him about it ahead of time. Ask Bob if it'll be okay before you sign anything with Tom. But why would he say okay?"

"Well, what if I can get Tom to agree to put a Marin bike in any ad that I do for 'Girls Love Dirt!'? That way I can tell Bob I just got him thousands of dollars of free advertising."

Athletes are in a unique position to showcase a company's wares. In a nutshell that is how I get paid to ride my bike. True, there is some prize money for winning races, but the amount is not nearly commensurate with the door-sized check the race promoter hands over. An extreme athlete's sponsors pay to advertise their product on mannequins that move. If you win often, a sponsor might pay you to be a spokesperson for its product, like a mannequin who talks. If you are really at the top, lots of sponsors might pay for their products just to be associated with you.

It helps if you are in a sport that lends itself to such associations. Badminton, although an Olympic sport with a noble pedigree, really doesn't support a whole lot of pro athletes. For one reason or another companies do not want to create a link in the consumer's shopping budget between their products and badmintoneers. It also helps if the sport itself offers good opportunities for "signage." A good friend of mine is one of the world's top cliff divers, a sport that is certainly one of the most extreme, dangerous, telegenic, and dramatic ever. His main sponsor is Red Bull, and he joked once that he is glad that he only has one main sponsor since he couldn't fit another logo on his little, grape-smuggling, Speedo swimsuit.

Tom ran some really creative ads for the "Girls Love Dirt!" stuff, and I recieved boxes of socks and tee shirts and leg warmers, windbreakers and gloves. The clothes were great. But the best part of the deal was that the full-page ads in the bike magazines, with my name in big letters and a close-up photo, were more prominent than the smaller pictures of me that appeared in the same magazines when I stood on the lower rungs of a race podium. I was providing more exposure and representing my sponsors, Marin and Oakley, better than some racers who were beating me on a regular basis.

And it was a great reward when on the road or on the trail other women sporting "Girls Love Dirt!" socks or leg warmers gave me a thumbs up or a, "Hey, Marla!"

I wasn't the only girl who loved dirt. In Marin, and in lots of other places, there were bunches who did. It made good business sense for Tom to recognize that but, for other unfortunate business reasons, he wasn't able to capitalize on it.

The more you win races, the more companies want to sponsor you and the more you might be offered time in a video, and it gets complicated all the more. Often the athlete has very little control over the whole process.

My first season with Team Marin, I quickly learned how complicated things can get. I wasn't winning any races, but I did well enough that by midyear, Bob offered to double my salary for the following season.

By 1995 my commitment to mountain biking was really serious and I wanted be taken seriously. The video, *Vicious Cycle,* was just out and I was in a couple of scenes. During the week of taping, my teammate, Andrew Shandro, made a two-second joke about how he discovered my potential as a mountain biker while I was dancing as a stripper. The camera had been on. I learned that the camera always could be on. Better to act as though it will always be on when I am wearing my sponsor's logos. Anyway, of course, that snippet made the cut, and lots of people, other racers, possible sponsors, fans, thought I had been an exotic dancer!

"Not that there's anything wrong with that," Marc, my liberal spin-artist, had reminded me. "OJ's prosecutor had danced her way through law school."

Still, I was embarrassed. I had hoped to mail a copy of the video to Mom and Dad. I had thought the video would give them some idea of what I was doing as a mountain biker. The video would provide my friends from college back in Maryland an idea of what I had been up to since escaping out here to California. But I was afraid that some might believe what Andrew had said. Because of that joke I didn't want to send a copy of the video to anybody. That the video wasn't as large a blockbuster as *Pulp Fiction* was really my only saving grace.

I learned how delicate it was sometimes to maintain proper exposure for my sponsors when I did that VO2 MAX commercial. That was a corporate deal way out of my league. I had to hire an agent to negotiate that one for me.

Rob Wells, who later went on to become a huge hit on ESPN as a commentator of questionable taste, did a bang-up job negotiating the deal. But the VO2 MAX people were adamant that the bike I used in the commercial be "franked." They had wanted to supply me with their own clothes to wear and supply me with their own bike so the viewer would be compelled to focus exclusively on the logo of the VO2 MAX energy bar. Rob couldn't do much about their clothes. I had to wear them. But I got Rob to insist that I ride my own Marin bike, for safety purposes. I thought I had just snuck my Marin bike into a gazillion-dollar national-TV ad campaign, but on the weekend that we began filming I discovered what franking meant. It meant that two guys remove, strip, cover, and conceal any logo, insignia, or brand name on my bike.

At the end of that season, after all those TV ads had played a thousand times when Bob was telling me about breaking my contract, he mentioned that he wasn't pleased at all that I hadn't been able to sneak his bike into their ad campaign. That I had no negotiating position to force one of the world's largest privately-held companies, the M&M Mars Corporation, to bend to my will, that it was never in my contract with Marin that I couldn't ride any bike I wanted outside of competition, that Team Marin's manager had been a paid extra on the commercial and had seen how hard I really had tried to squeeze the Marin bike into every frame of footage, made no difference to Bob.

All he could say in the end was, "Well, you should have refused to do the commercial then."

All I could say back then was, "*Are you serious!*"

I had chosen to take a lump sum for doing the ad and it was just enough for a down payment on a house in West Marin. (The lump sum turned out to be a much better deal than residual payments every time the ad appeared, because as soon as enough people got a taste of those bars, the commercials were yanked.)

I guess Bob had become addicted to me providing free exposure for his company in the "Girls Love Dirt," the Shimano doll, and the ESPN X-Game ads and he felt burned about missing a score on the biggest ad of them all. Can't blame him, I guess.

It is really tricky trying to make everybody happy when the chance arises to go on the *Dateline* or *Today* show. But, the phone doesn't magically ring all by itself. I scope out media as much as I poach single track. A lot of work and compromise and finagling goes on to try to make sure that everything works out. Even then the athlete really doesn't have any control over which of the hundreds of photos might make the magazine. The one where your uniform is a complete blur sometimes is the only one that the magazine wants. The only way to make sure that a sponsor's logo isn't covered up by a boom mike, to guarantee zero tolerance for slipups, is to *just say no* to all those opportunities.

I couldn't say no to the chance to be written up in *Outside* magazine. Their cover story started out a lot smaller than that. At a local race a journalist, a nice-seeming guy, asked me a few general questions about downhilling. Andrew Tilin wasn't sporting blue hair, or flame tattoos on his forearms, but I pride myself on not judging people by their appearances. I spoke with him anyway. One thing led to another. The conversation was extended over a series of phone calls and then sooner than I realized I was seated in a leather makeup chair in the cavernous space of exposed brick, stainless-steel fixtures, and dramatic hardwoods of Gerry Bybee's studio in the swanky, artsy South of Market district in San Francisco.

The night before, the magazine's art director had called and asked me how I felt about posing nude. Marc jumped on the phone while I stammered. Marc ranted into the phone about how I was a serious athlete and how we didn't want mountain biking and myself depicted in some manner that did not reflect that. He knew how hard it had been for me to play down the stripper episode from that old video. I am so glad sometimes that I have Marc to help out. To watch out for me. To fight the good fight for me. A good while later Marc hung up the phone. From the kitchen I looked at him in our office closet, across the wide expanse of our seven-hundred square-foot cottage and Marc said, "Marla, just keep an open mind."

And that's what I was thinking, keep an open mind, as I sat in the makeup chair for the second go around of flashing lightbulbs. The art director had reviewed the head-on images of me sort of popping a wheelie. He liked that my hair was flying off to the side. He loved the low camera angle. "You know," he said, "it would look really cool to use one of these shots on the cover. I see you riding your bike right out of the page, sort of busting through all the print."

Marc was so nervous that he was trying to refrain from

speaking by popping catered sushi rolls into his mouth like they were M&Ms.

Wow, the cover of *Outside* magazine. I had never even been near the cover of any mountain bike magazine. Once, I made it onto the cover of *NORBA News,* which wasn't exactly the same as *Sports Illustrated* or *Time.* But *Outside* was practically the premier publication of nonball sports journalism. Maybe that doesn't sound like a big deal, but it really is.

"Although," the art director continued.

There is always some sort of "although." I climbed out of the makeup chair. I was feeling trapped in its curves.

"If we use that on the cover, how ever will we invite the reader into reading the story? What will make them curious to turn the page? I feel the reader really needs to see you as you truly are, without all the entangling accoutrements of your equipment. Andrew has drawn such an incredible portrait of the inner you, that I feel I have to try to capture a corresponding image just as revealing."

I had been keeping an open mind. In the back of that open mind it flashed that here was a chance to make the cover, and knowing how difficult it had been to get Yeti to ship me a catalog bike was almost too much to bear. A catalog bike is a perfect bike; flawless paint and museum-quality decals. Every component shiny with appropriateness, the rubber of its tires lusty with Armour All luster. Those Yeti bikes were in such demand, making it so hard to get a catalog bike in the middle of the race season, that Yeti hadn't shipped me one. That's why the images the art director wanted to use for the cover were more perfect than he knew. Of all the parts on my banged up and dented Yeti, the Manitou forks, which looked like they were sticking right out of the page, were the only things that appeared clean and crisp. Shot from almost any other angle I could potentially get in trouble from some of my sponsors. I really needed to guarantee that if any shot made the cover, it was this wheelie one with the Manitou forks in the foreground.

Everybody in the studio knew what question the art director was building up to.

There wasn't a sound in the room, except the crunch of Marc munching on a spider roll from the caterer's table, and even he swallowed silently.

"Marla, what do you think about posing for some artistic black and whites?"

The silence was broken by the crumple of cotton as I dropped my clothes to the floor.

Afterward for weeks I worried about the wisdom of my decision. What would my parents think? Would I be embarrassed? Should I be embarrassed? Would it backfire and would my sponsors cringe? After all, I was thirty-five years old when that portrait was taken. Would people get the wrong idea from Andrew's article, about why I mistakenly thought I might have AIDS? How would I feel about Sister Leodegard, my grade-school teacher, thumbing through that issue at the dentist's office?

As it turned out a few months after the edition hit the news-stands, I called the publisher wanting to buy a stack of them, and was told that they had sold out. They said that hardly happens. Could have been because there was a big story about the first *Survivor*-series TV show. Too bad, I only had two copies.

At the Interbike tradeshow, which was shortly thereafter, Yeti asked me to sign some posters that they had commissioned using the nude image. I agreed to be there bright and early the first day of the show one hour after the doors opened flashing a smile and armed with a Sharpie. But I was apprehensive. A lot of down-hillers didn't even know there was a naked picture of me inside the magazine because they only look at the covers. I didn't think that too many had actually read the article, but I was still leery of having my nude image floating around a convention hall in Las Vegas. I couldn't believe it when I saw the autograph line stretching along the outside wall of the exhibit hall. The guy first in line eagerly told me that he had claimed his spot an hour earlier. That there were almost as many women in line as men made me feel like I hadn't committed a blunder. More parents than I ever imagined asked me to sign for their daughters, and they thanked me for being such a positive role model of a strong, athletic, nontraditional-type of woman for their girls to look up to.

But all that exposure might have just as easily been a huge disaster if Andrew hadn't been such a good writer and if Gerry hadn't been such a master with his airbrush.

Chapter 9

The Myth and Reality of Pro Mountain Biking

"Must be nice to eat whatever you want, burning it up just by mountain biking like that," or "I wish I was a natural mountain-bike racer like you," and the phrase most common, "I need a new bike before I can really start riding." I have heard mythic comments like these from well-meaning people as I signed posters for them. Sometimes men made those comments, but just as likely it was a woman. Kids too. I simply smiled and signed, knowing that this wasn't really the time or the place to get into a serious discussion. I try to write an encouraging note on each poster and then shake a hand and smile for the next in line.

When people, men and women alike, tell me that they would like to have a more athletic-looking body, I cringe, because I feel like they are looking to me for some advice. As though I really had some special knowledge of the subject matter. Sometimes I think that they imagine that I have some secret recipe, a little pill that I can press into their outstretched hand, which they can swallow and presto . . . abdominals. Or that I could show them how to melt the pounds away by riding down some secret mountain-bike trails. The reality is that I do not possess a magical formula; as far I know any trail is as good as another.

I've never read any of those diet books. Not that I think those books have nothing to offer. It's just that I never made the time to read any. I am sure I would have benefitted years ago had I educated myself more about nutrition. Instead, as I went along I learned by trial and error what the nutritional needs are for a world-class downhill mountain-bike racer. It turns out that they are pretty much the same needs as for any healthy person. There are some basic medical or scientific principles that come into play, and beyond merely relying on those, I warrant no claims. In no way am I advocating that what works for me will work for anybody else. The basic idea applies to the vast majority of us. It just took me a lot longer than average to figure it out. And I am not even sure that I am right.

The primary myth is that a physical exercise like mountain biking can burn up all the extra calories that could possibly be eaten. Its correlative is that if you starve yourself, you will become more physically fit. Neither is true. There is plenty of science out there to tell you why, so I won't bother.

My imbalance was not too many calories going in, it was not enough calories for the work I wanted my body to do.

I have no experience with the former, but I have had some bouts with the latter. It doesn't make any difference which end of the seesaw you find yourself, if you are out of balance on either end, you are out of whack.

The underlying reasons why I wasn't eating properly are the common ones. They are the subject of afterschool TV specials aimed at teenage girls. They are sensationalized in the tabloid accounts of celebrities. The reasons are as much a product of our society.

I was a pro for some years before I found that the way out of my imbalance for me was to discard how I felt others saw me, and instead really focus on something that I passionately cared about. For me that was trying to win races. The result is that my thighs may be too muscular for some tastes, my biceps more defined than some mens', my butt more powerful than a horse's, but the reality is that I don't care. Aiming for an ideal, the silhouette of a Greek statue, for instance, was for me the wrong direction. To this day I don't know why I didn't recognize earlier one of the basic tenets of the science of industrial design, that "form follows function."

For my efforts I am grateful for the positive reinforcement I receive. Not only from the owner and CEO of my main sponsor, Team Luna's Gary Erickson, but also for the thumbs up I get whenever I walk through the Clif Bar company headquarters in Berkeley from the employees, men and women alike, as they hang from the climbing wall, or spin on their stationary trainers, wrestle with their telephones, and otherwise go about their workday in a healthy balance. Gary, a cyclist who still races on the road and in the dirt, and still escapes for century rides, understands that his employees will be more productive and feel more rewarded if they are also encouraged to seek a balance.

The example that those employees set for me is that long after I stop racing competitively, if that day ever comes, nutrition and exercise will remain an important daily consideration. A family emergency or a crisis at work may temporarily reduce that level of exercise and, correspondingly, nutritional needs may have to be adjusted. Just as likely an increased workload or the need for more energy may mean that nutrition levels need yet another tweak. Just because understanding the basic relationship between nutrition and exercise is not as complicated as rocket science doesn't make it any easier to sustain that relationship. I sincerely hope that others recognize that sooner than I did in my early thirties. After I am finished competing at a world-class level, maintaining that proper balance may require as much effort as I have ever expended racing a mountain bike.

There is nothing "natural" about being a mountain-bike racer except for the desire. I don't know why every person in the world hasn't embraced this sport. Why there isn't a ribbon of single tracks connecting each of us in our communities to every other, I can't understand. But there is nothing natural about the racing part.

Understand that I was never a "natural mountain-bike racer." There is nothing natural at all about climbing onto that saddle when your legs feel like they have fallen asleep on you. Nothing natural at all about wanting to win more than the racer ahead of you. Crawling out of a warm bed onto a cold and dark floor, even then aware that one of your competitors is pulling on a pair of chamois a second earlier than you, and that you may not catch up until the sun has risen and then set again on that same day. Recognizing that every disadvantage, every limitation, is really an opportunity to try harder is what keeps me going.

How many of us will ever be the best in the world? There will always be another, usually many others; faster, stronger, ultimately first. One mountain biker can never be the fastest, in absolute terms, since the measure is relative. If you have ever been to a NORBA downhill race and seen how casually the timing sequence is adhered to, and how emasculated the course marshalls are, the shifting yellow course tape, and some of the "Canadian lines," you'll understand why I have learned to not focus too much on official race results. Maybe all the Red Bull free, riding competitions are the way downhilling should grow. I really don't believe in racing against others. I enjoy the fun of it, and it pays, but I have not been deceived by thinking that I am racing against anyone but myself.

Downhilling for me is an exercise in personal satisfaction, the measure is if I tried my best. Did I do all that I could to race as fast as I could? I have won races during which I did not try my hardest. (I admit they were small local races, I could never win a NORBA without having given one hundred percent). But I took no pleasure in those wins knowing that someone else's flat tire or a loose dog running on course, rather than my own effort, might have decided the day. So I give it my all such that after most races I ride away as happy as though I had won, because in my heart I knew that there was nothing else I could have done. The perfect run is a myth, the reality is the effort.

Because that is universally true for any level of endeavor, I never have felt hindered by not being a "natural born mountain biker," or a "natural born scientist." None of us are naturally born anythings. Some of us have big feet (I don't. I have really cute petite feet, except for those bunyon scars. . . .) Some have big hands, others big ears, and still others big trust funds. Nonetheless as athletes, we all start from the same line. That line is a baseline measure of strength, or power, or the circumstances of our birth. All those things we have no control over. The same line that we all start from measures something that we do have control over and that no one has any influence on at all. That baseline from which we all start, measures how much each of us is willing to try.

And how much we are willing to try is in no way dependant on expensive equipment. Don't get me wrong. I am a bike geek! Meaning that I obsess over my equipment. By obsessing I do not mean that I clean with a Q-tip and wipe my bike stuff down with lambswool. I don't have a green velvet wall display of gleaming *grouppos* from which I select my daily drivetrain. Nope. The affection I show for my bike stuff is demonstrated by the dents and dings and baling wire that holds it all together. I am a pro mechanic's nightmare. I'm still not sure of the difference between the various colors of Loctite, but I really do believe that good equipment helps. Great equipment helps even more; I hunger and thirst for the trickest stuff. But all that cool stuff should not affect how hard I am willing to try my hardest to race fast.

Because I didn't know anything about bikes and parts and how they all fit together when I first fell in love with mountain biking, I've had to educate myself. In the beginning I would have gotten failing grades. I used to clean my bike by letting it soak in a pool overnight. For a few years I used two different floor pumps, one for the skinny nozzles and one for the fat ones, because I didn't know that all pumps come with interchangeable little gizmos for both kinds of inner tubes. But since then I've come a long way baby. At least the equivalent of a GED in bike repair. I'm still not great at repairs, but I can usually MacGyver a way home with a multitool and a sharp rock. At home I try to keep Marc out of my Park Tool drawer, but I dip into his boat tools just as frequently.

The proof that I care about my equipment is that now, on my workbench, I keep a range of scales from my days in the lab and I weigh each component twice. The first time right out of the box, and the second time right after I've gotten it muddy and all scratched up. I average the two and write it down in my training journal. Sometimes a few fine adjustments are required. Marc got me a Dremel tool for our anniversary. Since we're not married we celebrate our anniversary whenever West Marine or Home Depot has their yearly clearance sale. I use the Dremel tool to shave grams off my stuff when I think that my team mechanic is not looking. Equipment is so important that every speck of aluminum swarf counts.

That's why my moves from team to team were never based on salary considerations. I've taken a beating in salaries. A yearly graph of my team salary during the years that I have raced as a pro would approximate the ups and downs of my high-school crushes during my senior year. At least twice in my pro career I have followed my most lucrative salary to date by moving to another team that would pay less than half. I have turned down money plenty of times from various equipment makers. Why? Because of my obsession with equipment. This might cause some jaws to drop in different circles, but I have even paid for some equipment. Not with just Red Bull and Luna Bars, but with cash.

I've also "paid" for my equipment by signing onto a smaller team deal if the bike was better. And it has worked out every time. It was easy to sign with Yeti for less than half than Marin had been paying me, because the bike was so much better. When Yeti wanted to change the direction of their program, rather than find a "big team deal" for a lot of bucks, I happily hopped onto Team Foes, accepting a two-thirds reduction in pay, just so I could race on the same bike that Missy was using. But the best move I've ever made was in 2001 to Team Luna and the chance to ride a Santa Cruz.

The money wasn't the issue since Team Luna offered to pay me quite well. My only concern about the team was riding as the only downhiller on a primarily cross-country program. In effect rather than signing with a big downhill race program, even though Team Luna is a huge, I would be signing onto a relatively small downhill race effort. A large proportion of Team Luna's focus would naturally be on Alison Dunlap, the cross-country world champion. It turns out that I had nothing to worry about since Team Luna anticipated and took care of every racer's needs. Massages every night, top mechanics, supportive staff, and overall incredible professionalism. And this season, Kathy Pruitt, a former junior, and future senior world champ is joining the team, and I am looking forward to training with her. Maybe I can learn something.

The Santa Cruz bike was so good that I felt taking advantage of an opportunity to race on one far outweighed the small disadvantages of not racing out of a "downhill pit." To win races I really don't need all that downhill stuff you find on other race teams: a bunch of hopped up Z-50 motorcycles for scooting around the venue, a flatscreen TV for video games, some toy radio-controlled cars ripping under foot, loud head-banging speed-metal music vibrating loose all my pivot bearings, and Snap-on Tool calendars hanging from the walls that make my poster seem Victorian.

I really do believe that my Santa Cruz V10 is best bike on the mountain. By far it is the best pedaling bike, I have ever had the pleasure to ride. A lot of people, even other racers, mistakenly think that downhillers do not pedal. That we just "coast" down the hill like we are kids rolling down the driveway on a cruiser bike to pick up a newspaper. I pedal. Anybody who wants to win pedals. I don't want to get into too much technical detail about why the Santa Cruz virtual pivot-point design allows me to pedal efficiently, almost like I am on a hard tail, but understand that pedaling is important. Yes, I am racing downhill so gravity does help, but the bike itself weighs nearly forty pounds, and with all my pads and helmet and gloves as added bulk, I really have to crank those pedals in order to fly through the air for those big jumps. I have to spin those pedals to start again from a near standstill in a technical section. The only way to make up for a boo-boo through a rock garden, is to put your head down through the straightaway, like your sprinting against Mario Cipollini, the world's best, and pedal! pedal! pedal!

Part of the reason why the Santa Cruz bike is so good is because the owner of the company, Rob Roskopf, pedals one himself down race courses. There aren't too many bike-company owners who poach one of their pro rider's number plates, hop on a bike, and grab a couple of quick runs on a world-cup downhill course. Before getting into the bike business Rob was a top pro skateboarder, and so he knows firsthand that the best way to research and develop products is on a race course. I really respect him for that.

But the big myth of the recreational rider, the lifestyle enthusiast, is that in order to ride they need to buy an expensive "ride." That they are justing wasting their time riding the bike that they already own, instead they should stop riding completely, or not start at all until they have bought a titanium, custom fit, hand-painted, MIT-engineered, not-available-in-stores-yet bike. Even pro riders succumb to that belief. After all, it's a lot easier to blame the bike than yourself for any performance disappointments. Some guys are so upset about their disappointing lack of performance that they blame their saddles!

Of course I want the benefit of the best equipment, but like anyone else, I have to pay my dues to get it. But equipment does not win races, effort does. I try to balance that effort with the nutrition required to get me out of bed in the morning so I can train even harder, to go faster.

Chapter 10

Living a Mountain-Bike Fantasy in a Real-World Environment

Making the most out of your equipment is important, but so is taking advantage of the natural resources where you are riding. Marin County where I have lived for almost five years now is unnaturally abundant with resources for a professional mountain biker. The network of trails is famous, the weather allows all-season riding, and the bike community is competitive and supportive. Since living here, I've discovered that there is another network, a power girls' network, that is as much a resource as any watershed or mountain-bike park. All resources require some nurturing. There is no perfect place to live and train. I hope to leave a resource, such as the network of trails, the network of girls who don't mind getting dirty, in a healthier condition than when I first encountered them.

Before I had arrived at the birthplace of mountain biking, Marin County, Marc had tucked our boat into a slip in Sausalito, and had already checked out some houses to rent. In my third season as a pro, I was getting paid some decent money, enough to be able to afford living on land. Marin would be a little bit colder and a lot rainier than San Diego. The boat really wasn't near the best trails that Mount Tam had to offer. I needed more space for all my bike equipment. Damp salt air is not the best environment for delicate components and thin-wall tubing. Besides, the remaining work Marc needed to do on our boat to ready it for an around-the-world bike trip was in rebuilding the interior. That work, he said, would go smoother and faster and cheaper if we weren't trying to live on her at the same time. For all these reasons we rented a ground-level apartment in a big rambling hillside house.

The morning of my first day in our small apartment I woke determined to make the most of my time in Marin.

Fairfax is the last small town at the farthest end of a long sun-splashed valley. Any further west and you'd be in West Marin, where there are almost as many cows as there are telecommuters. The town of Fairfax is a tiny junction of two roads: one, the Bolinas Fairfax Road, which switchbacks over the mountain, and the other, Sir Francis Drake, which loops along the San Geronimo Creek around the mountain's base. Both roads end up more or less at the same point near the ocean, at an old hippie town famous for hiding the road signs that announce its presence. Fairfax is one of those small towns independantly famous for a few things at once. The town is a special place for mountain biking, yet the mountain bikers largely aren't aware of the town's musical cult status, and most of the music lovers rarely acknowledge the mountain bikers. Van Morrisson, the Irish balladeer famous for songs like, "Moondance" and "Brown-Eyed Girl," used to live here in town. Elvin Bishop, the ageless blues man, lives just over White's Hill. At each end of town there is a VW bus repair yard, an indication that Fairfax is Dead Head Central. Most of the band, their roadies, support crew, and groupies live nearby. Everybody, however, worships Mount Tam.

The hot tub, the Californian cultural contribution to hydrotherapy, was invented within the Fairfax town limits. The town's residents need a permit to remove any tree on their own property. All forms of pesticide sprays are banned within the town. The town boasts two forms of medical care: a natural birthing center for midwifery and a dispensary for medical marijuana. Fairfax is at the crossroads of two cultures: Fat Tread and Dead Head. I couldn't imagine a more perfect place to live.

I didn't want to sleep this morning. I had a big ride planned for my first day on Tam. Marc usually is up with the sun. He is also blessed with the ability to sleep through fire alarms, earthquakes, and other disasters. A disaster for me is a shaft of sunlight disturbing my slumber. A disaster for him is an after-breakfast invitation to be dragged up and down single tracks lost in the woods all day spurred on only by the chirp of my voice, "I think it's this way, come on!"

The night before I had kept Marc up late pointing out to him on my newly purchased Mount Tam trail guide all the thin squiggly lines that I had planned to ride the next day. Trails whose names I had seen in magazines: Hoo Koo E Koo, Zig Zag, and Benstein. My finger cranked up the blue ink of a trail through lightly-drawn concentric circles of elevation. Then my finger skittered atop ridgelines, before plunging down the mountain's slopes. The cracked nail of my index finger strummed the surface of the map hesitating at a multicolored junction of trails. Continue on down or climb up again? How can I traverse this spine, to get over to that side of the ridge? Mindful to not let my heart rate drop out of zone two, I impulsively pushed my finger through the trail junction off a blue continuous-line trail onto a blue broken-line trail for no good reason other than I was curious to see where it would take me. In the current issue of *Bike* there was an article about the "new paradigm" trail. It was an illegal trail, built by mountain bikers for mountain bikers. I wanted to find it and ride it. My map stated in large type above one of its folds that trails were clearly marked and not all were legal for mountain biking. Before shutting off the light I folded the map along its creases and stuck it under my pillow.

Thus this morning I softly kissed Marc's snoring goatee and crawled out of my sleeping bag. No need to take the map from under the pillow. Who needs a map when there is an opportunity to get lost in the woods? In the empty living room of our apartment I pulled on my chamois and top. Marc was on the other side of the closed bedroom door still asleep. I was sad that there was no use asking him if he wanted to ride with me. He'd say no. He wouldn't want to slow me down he'd say. I'd have more fun without him. I'd ride by myself today. That's the best way to enjoy exploring.

I understood what he meant when he said that mountain biking was my thing and he didn't want to pretend that we were sharing it. That he wanted me to get the full credit and self-satisfaction of having done it by myself. He's right in a way. Sometimes at a local race when he is unloading my bikes from Vidalia, another racer will ask him about the trail conditions. Even though Marc might be wearing construction boots, jeans, and a wool sweater, and I would be standing right next to him, helmet to shoes a real rider, the question would be addressed to Marc. Tiptoeing across the living room to the bathroom I was thinking how honest Marc was whenever he handled those questions by saying, "She rides, I watch."

I pulled my race-light titanium cross-country hard tail from the wall. Quietly as I could I untangled my bar ends from the assembly of lights, bells, horns, and coffee-thermos holder on the handlebar of Marc's commuter beater. Marc would be waking up soon enough and riding his bike to look for work in Sausalito as a bartender. Good tourist volume there, he had told me.

I didn't want to be late for my first day of work on Mount Tam. I rolled out the front door into the bright red morning and coasted down the tiny hill across the street to a doorway on the corner from which wafted coffee aromas. The shop's windows were steamed by roasting beans and I couldn't see inside. Two kinds of coffee shops exist in the world. One sells cups of cafeteria brew, free refills, to cops and truck drivers hunched over oval plates of steak and eggs. The other sells pint glasses of Ethiopian Heaven to cyclists, graphic artists, and earthie crunchies who daintily nibble bagels or scones. I could tell which kind of coffee shop this was by the pile of bikes tangled up against the floor-to-ceiling windows. The coffee-shop buzz was about a huge forest fire somewhere at a place called Mount Vision. I wasn't that interested. I didn't know where Mount Vision was. I was going to ride some single track on Mount Tam.

Tanked up on a mocha with fat-free foam, and an extra espresso shot, I pedaled up Bolinas Fairfax Road to the spine that runs the length of Marin like a bumpy outgrowth of the San Andreas fault from the coastal wine country of Sonoma to the north, south to the foot of the Golden Gate Bridge and the mouth of the bay. During the climb the microclimate changed at least three times, from warm and sunny, to cold and foggy, to windswept and smoky. From the ridgeline if I looked left I could see through giant redwoods the dot of Alcatraz and three bridges spanning the blue of the bay. Fog obscured San Francisco and Angel Island. If I looked over my right shoulder, over windswept meadows of wildflowers, the wide Pacific below washed the shores of Stinson Beach, the Headlands, and Drake's Bay. Far off toward Point Reyes, on another ridge, divided from the ridge on which I stood only by the jurisdictional lines of different park agencies, a smoky forest fire smoldered. Far from that fire and yet shielded by it, I was all alone on the road, dying to hop off it onto some single tracks.

But I was still wary of getting caught. The map had explained that most of the trails that are fun to ride on Mount Tam are not open to bikes at all. Only to hikers and sometimes horseback riders. As a kid I was a little skateboard rat. Back then, as today, most sidewalks and parking lots and any other place that was fun to skate were also verboten. But that never stopped me from grinding. It just made me more careful. And careful was what I wanted to be as I decided which forbidden trail I would poach on Mount Tam.

Yes, I am admitting that I have ridden illegal trails. I understand how excited people can get over this "criminal" act, but many of these same people "roll their own," cheat on their taxes, rip those little do-not-remove tags off their pillows. In the great scheme of things I do not think riding a bike through the woods, responsibly of course, is any worse for the environment than driving your car to the gym for an aerobics class.

I kept my eye out for a trailhead and made sure that no car was visible on either stretch of the lonely road, and then I bunny-hopped off the asphalt onto a path in between two fallen logs and ducked under some overhanging branches of oak and Monterey pine into the green and brown shadows of Mount Tam's canopy.

That day I rode for hours on both sides of the ridge, deliciously lost on single track made sweeter because it was forbidden. The woods were empty that day. No people. No hikers, no bikers, no rangers, nobody. "What is the big deal?" I thought. "What is all the fuss about illegal riding and getting caught and stuff?" Those magazines must have been exaggerating. I couldn't believe it. I was getting paid to ride past these beautiful streams, around mountain lakes, up steep slopes and down rocky slides. Hours later under a fireplace-red sky riding the last stretch home on the road, I was giddy thinking that those trees would be my office!

I couldn't wait to go to work again tomorrow.

The next morning, again early but the sky not as red, in the coffee shop, made bold by my second cup of coffee, I asked some of the guys in baggy shorts and Lycra shirts about some trails that I couldn't squeeze in the day before.

"You don't want to ride those trails today," said the shorter one. He was holding onto a bike called a Weasel.

He could tell that I didn't understand what he was talking about.

"It's Saturday. Who wants all that aggro? All those crowds and maybe a ticket?" he explained.

"But," I protested, "I rode all day yesterday. On Coastal, Pantoll, even Northside."

"That's 'cuz yesterday was a Friday. A workday," explained the taller guy. He had a beat-up hard tail.

The short one, "What do you know about work?" punched the tall one in the arm. It turns out that my first ride on Mount Tam really was special. The Mount Vision fire on nearby Point Reyes had been burning for days. The television newscasters had warned everyone that an expected wind shift threatened Mount Tam, and they advised everybody to stay off the trails. All the rangers had been diverted to fire suppression. It had been a workday so most of the hikers and equestrians had someplace else to be. On those trails on Mount Tam it had been a fantastic workday for me.

Defensively the taller one raised his arm and tried to ignore his tormentor. "Not as many hikers."

"Yeah, and the fire probably means the rangers are all busy," chimed in the third guy. "Hey, are you a pro?"

A dead giveaway for a suspected pro is if their name is stenciled on their top tube. I was such a "neo pro" back then that I didn't know it was much cooler to sit on your name while hanging out with "grommets." These guys were grommets—kids, or young guys who ask questions as much as they ride. They ask for free front forks, but will be satisfied with a pair of worn grips. They ask for any used bikes that you might have lying around, but don't really understand that pros have to return most bikes at the end of each season. They ask how you become a pro, but can't appreciate how much riding "a lot" really is. Grommets glom in groups of two or three during the week or in gangs uncounted during the weekend. Some have jobs and a few shave their chins. They race, they ride around, they spend most of their own money and a lot of their parents' on bike stuff. Grommets want to be pros someday, but until then are content to be seen with a pro. They are the future of the sport. And it is sad that they are not found everywhere. Marin is thick with them. Until they grow up and buy their first new car, then mountain biking loses a lot of them and doesn't get most of them back until they reach their thirties when they realize they have been transformed into . . . yuppies. These guys were full-grown grommets; young expert-class riders with no clue as to how to live a normal life or how to turn pro.

I don't want to embarrass these grommets by revealing their actual names, because eventually they did grow up to be real adults, with nice girlfriends and cool jobs. But I do want to thank them for showing me during the next year all the trails that weren't on any map guide. I would have ridden with them more except for one thing. Okay, maybe two things.

TV and weed.

My parents had tried to restrict our family's TV viewing to one hour a day, so I never developed the nasty habit of staring at it for hours at a stretch. Marc and I hadn't had one on the boat and we had no plans to buy one for our apartment either. I really believe that in life you can accomplish amazing things if you don't own one.

These clueless grommets all shared an apartment above a cafe and when they weren't riding they were doing two other things: getting baked and staring at the television. Whenever I breezed over to their place to start a ride their TV was so hot to the touch that you could fry an egg on it. The combo of those two drugs, weed and television, are synergistic.

But those grommets got me started on the right track in Marin.

Marc and I eventually did buy a futon to sleep on. It didn't take long for Marc and I to fall right in among the rest of the Marin community. Marc was not even considered much of a liberal by local standards. And I was just one of many bike "geeks" shopping in the organic health-food store. We pulled Vidalia into the garage from which she was seldom to emerge since we were able to take care of all our errands—shopping, visiting the Marin offices, commuting to the boat—all by bike. To help with the rent we posted an ad on the bulletin board of the town's vegetarian restaurant. Less than a week later Marc and I had a roommate.

Adam's face telegraphed that he was a nice guy. Almost-white hair, like Scandinavian Birch, pulled into a tight ponytail except for a few strands that fell onto the smooth of his cheek. Blue eyes blinked from behind small hippe-type wire-frame glasses. He was relieved that I liked bikes so much that I hadn't minded at all when he asked if he could bring his unpainted aluminum mountain bike right into the house. That's one of the great things about real hardwood floors: it's easy to sweep the dirt or mop the mud a couple of times a day. Adam rode his bike everywhere too but he also owned a helicopter. He had come to Marin to "find himself" at one of the nearby retreats like Spirit Rock, the Vedantic Center, and the Slide Ranch. That seemed New Agey to me. But I admitted that I, too, had come to Marin to find myself on Mount Tam. Adam was the best kind of roommate, clean and neat, quiet and polite: a trust-funder who wasn't around very much.

Because Marin is such an expensive place to live, the team mechanic, Frank Trotter, eventually moved into the breakfast nook in the kitchen. I had initially offered him the other bed-room that Adam was maintaining as a spartan retreat for sleep only. But since the rent for the whole place was $1,500, ten times what I had paid in Baltimore, five times what I had paid in Durham, and three times what I had paid in La Jolla, I wanted five hundred for that bedroom. Frank grew up in a hippie com-mune in Grass Valley high in the Sierras. The kind of rent I was asking for bugged his eyes out, so he said he'd look around and find someplace cheaper. Housing in Marin county is tough to come by. It's one of the most expensive places in the country de-spite the fact that most of the houses hang off the hillsides in precarious perches, buried under a blizzard of leaves, their foun-dations swept by a torrent of winter streams. More than a few houses lack even narrow dirt roads, but instead are only accessi-ble by footpaths. Waiting in line at the recently restored Fairfax cinema it's hard to discern if the couple beside you are million-aires or working class, sheep farmers or corporate headhunters, software developers or aspiring artists. After a month of bunk-ing down in the supply room at the Marin Mountain Bike of-fices, the breakfast nook seemed to Frank like the best deal available.

He chipped in a couple of hundred bucks toward the rent, built himself a sturdy loft bed with a desk underneath, and walled it off with a thick cotton curtain. He was tall and rangy, like you'd imagine a cowboy nicknamed Slim to be. His hands were calloused like a cowboy's, roughed up from the thousands of tire changes, the piles of links snipped out of chains and the nicks from the business end of wire cutters, head-tube reamers, bottom bracket chasers, and crank pullers. His hair was dark with rich reddish hues and curly, but his natural small-town shy-ness kept his curls hidden under a baseball cap. A loose tee shirt, baggy khaki shorts, wool socks, and leather sandals completed his outfit day in and day out. Freckles were scattered across and remained on his brow long after he wiped away the sweat and grease of a day's work. A vegan, Frank stuffed the fridge with his blue-green algae and set his bucket-sized wooden salad bowl beside the sink and felt right at home.

That's Fairfax.

Frank and I were at parallel points in our life cycles. He grew up surrounded by prime mountain-biking country in the Sierras. He had wanted to be a pro cross-country racer too. Frank is a very strong rider and had done well at many local races, but after a few seasons of getting knocked off the podium at the bigger races he decided that, if he wanted a life in the professional mountain-biking world, he would have a better chance as a pro mechanic than as a pro rider. My rookie season earning a salary, had been Frank's rookie season "interning" as a mechanic. This year Marin was paying him, but still he had racked up some debts paying his dues the year before.

Internship as a mechanic is the most common way of landing a job in the pits as a pro. A team agrees to take you on, usually under the supervision of a more experienced wrench. The team pays for your travel and lodging and meals during the six months or so that make up the race calendar, during which the intern has the opportunity to make the most out of washing muddy bikes, building knobby wheels, setting up and breaking down the team's tent and truck at the pit area, shuttling the racers to and from the airport, driving across all of North America for days at a time and dealing with whiny racers and strict guidelines from the home office. If the intern doesn't screw up, or doesn't smarten up, a team might offer him a salary for the next season. Pro mechanics take great pride and are very competitive about getting their racers on the podium. Some make such a great contribution to their company's race programs that during the off season they work as product developers, writing and reviewing sponsorship proposals, and in the marketing and sales departments. Other mechanics look forward to a winter of waxing skis and tightening snowboard bindings at some of the same ski resorts that we race in during the summer months. Frank would go onto work for Trek, and then Gary Fisher, and just recently the Giant mountain-bike race teams. I am happy to say he's done well for himself, having bought a house in Colorado and building himself another one in Idaho. Not bad for a guy who used to live in my breakfast nook!

Marin is a place where a mountain-bike dreamer can go hoping to make it real. Like Hollywood or Wall Street. The coffee shop, the nexus of the sport, is only a fifteen minute ride from the fire road of Fairfax's Repack Race, recognized as the first mountain-bike race ever. Sitting at one of the coffee shop's crowded tables it's not a big deal to see big-time riders, like Susan DeMattei, Olympic medal winner and local high-school graduate, riding past the window. Anne Trombley is another Olympian mountain biker raised drinking from water bottles filled from the taps of the Marin Municipal Water District. So is Joe Murray, multiple NORBA champ hall-of-famer and one of the founders of VooDoo Bikes. Sara Ellis, a former top pro spins past the coffee shop on her way to her new business: a spinning class and fitness center in Mill Valley. Gary Fisher, arguably the inventor of mountain bikes, prefers the ambiance at the Roastery in San Anselmo, the village farther up the valley. Gary still puts lots of miles on the trails and on the roads, riding distinctly in the colors of his company. You can't miss his long legs pumping away on his latest twenty-nine-inch toy. Julia, Gravy's partner in Gravy's Wheels, the boutique wheel builder who takes care of my own, stops by the coffee shop every morning. In the coffee shop fueling up for a morning ride there is a good chance that you'll come across an editorial in the local newspaper by Joe Breeze, arguably the other inventor of the mountain bike. Joe often editorializes about trail access and the right to claim a lane on the road, and the responsibilities attendant to those rights. World champion downhiller Myles Rockwell, one of the founding gang of the Marin Outlaw Bikers, also graduated from the local high school, and although you don't see him around much, the guy ahead of you in the refill line might tell you that "I used to kick Myles's ass down the mountain all the time, but I thought mountain biking was just a fad and instead I got into hanging drywall."

That too, is Fairfax.

I rode to the coffee shop every morning to "wake up" for early solo rides or to meet some new friends who promised to show me some secret single tracks. Many mornings Marc would ride to the coffee shop with me before he continued on his way to Sausalito. His tips were no longer the main source of our income, but now were devoted to finishing the restoration of our sailboat. I never did get around to asking him about changing her name, *Indifference,* to something else . . . oh, I don't know, more . . . inspirational. But I was finding it easier to tell him that I loved him. Saying those words no longer panicked me into flight mode. Marc has supported my racing in many ways. He was always looking for another way to help me win. On his bike poking around Sausalito down by the boat docks Marc came across Paolo's custom bike-frame shop.

At that time Paolo was bunking out part time in a converted train car, half of which was crammed with a Bridgeport milling machine, a Miller Tig welder, and an imported Italian marble frame-straightening table. The rest of the time Paolo's tolerant girlfriend opened her house in Mill Valley to him and his burgeoning brain. Marc swears, and I have come to believe, that Paulo is a genius. Paolo Salvagione was just one of the many independant, small, custom frame builders who either got their start in Marin like Charlie Cunningham, Joe Breeze, Gary Fisher, Mert Lawwill, and Otis Guy, or saw their end there like many more unknown and unremembered. Marc convinced Paolo to take him on as an apprentice frame builder. For a couple of years Paolo agreed to let Marc pester him five days a week before the happy-hour crowd at the bar required his attentions. Marc learned a lot from Paolo about not only the material and manufacture of bikes but more importantly about the Bay Area's bike culture.

One of the first things about our new neighborhood that Marc learned about in Paolo's shop was Critical Mass, an underground movement in San Francisco that had begun a few years earlier. It was born out of the frustration that all road cyclists feel about being denied our fair share of the roads by the mass of cars and the mess of urban design. Individual cyclists in the city are often unable to cross traffic to make left-hand turns at stop lights. They are denied the right to take a whole lane to make turns, and on narrow streets have little room to avoid the opening of parked cars' doors. More than a few cyclists are killed each year. I have been hit by cars at least five times, totalling my bike twice, and requiring trips to a doctor three times.

So in San Francisco on the last Friday of each month thousands of cyclists converge at the Ferry building on the city's waterfront, at the edge of the financial district, about a mile from the tourist zone. At five o'clock a horn sounds and a ride begins through the city streets that can last for hours. This was something that Marc, as Captain Commuter, could really get into. He enjoyed outfitting his bike with all sorts of lights and whistles and even mounted a powerful marine foghorn on his handlebars to do battle for his rights endowed to him by the traffic code. As a former bike messenger I really thought Critical Mass was a lot of fun. During those few hours the safety of riding in such large numbers was empowering and exhilarating. I've seen unicycles, tricycles, ice-cream vendor bikes all riding together. Single speeds and fixed gears. Tandem bikes. Folding bikes. Old ladies and nutty professors. Guys wobbling around astride complete DUI setups. Drag queens and punkers. Moms, dads, and kids. Bluehairs and skinheads. There are always a couple of nudes sprinkled about. Handlebar lights, blinking lights, thumb bells, clanging cow bells. One guy mounted a small camping propane tank to his water-bottle mount and in between his bar ends flamed an array of gas burners upon which he roasted hot dogs as he rode around town. A chase group of the Sisters of Perpetual Indulgence usually flash their calves riding around on Mary Poppins-type bikes. A contingent of Dykes on Bikes always makes a strong showing. The Recumbent Brigade with their low center of gravity seems to provide the nucleus around which the Critical Mass swarms. For the most part we cyclists obey the traffic laws, but anarchists always abound on bikes, so often the message that "Bikes Belong" on the roads is lost on the evening news reports. But it's fun to ride anyway. We usually sailed our boat over to South Beach Harbor or Pier 39, and made a whole night in the city out of it. We would ride around until the critical mass of thousands was reduced to a superficial rout of stragglers, and then Marc and I would pedal to Chinatown for a late-night snack before coasting home to our boat for a night's sleep.

The Day La, another underground ride, was a similar kind of protest, but a private one. This time on single track. Many of the same mountain bikers who waited in line for custom mountain bikes from builders like Paolo, and riders who would never think of upgrading their original equipment Bridgestones, assemble at a predetermined secret location together at four-twenty a.m. the day of the winter solstice and of the summer solstice, the shortest and longest days of the year, respectively, to poach one hundred miles of single track on Mount Tam and beyond. Like Critical Mass, the actual route of the Day La is kept

secret until the last minute and after a few hours of riding de-
volves into a freestyle free wheel fest. The Day La almost always
takes twenty-four hours to finish, and though I have started it a
few times, the longest I could hang with those guys was about
twelve hours.

Mountain biking on single track, especially on rides like the
Day La, is derided by other trail users, hikers, and equestrians as
abusive and harmful to the environment. Similarly the car commuters wrongfully accuse cyclists of slowing down traffic and
blame them for their own two-wheeled deaths because they did
not yield to a metal bumper. If you were able to hover in a helicopter above Mount Tam, and compare the harm done to her by
mountain-bike single tracks to that caused by hikers and equestrians, you would see that bikers have left a much smaller im-
print. Most bikers ride up and then ride down the mountain's
trails that were often first carved by deer. The vast majority of
hikers do not begin their hikes up the mountain from their back
door. Instead hikers drive up roads paved over the mountain and
park their cars on numerous asphalt lots scraped into her sides.
Each rainfall washes many thousands of pounds of pollutants, in
the form of dripping oil to the toxic dust of spent brake pads,
from the asphalt surfaces into the lakes that are the country's
primary water supply, and the reason for which the park system
on Mount Tam exists. I don't even want to describe the mounds
of horse manure that have no place to go but to end up in the
water system or in my lungs as I pedal through choking clouds
of horse-pucky dust.

From a few feet above the tree tops you can't see single
tracks, but the encircling asphalt roads appear as scars, and the
parking lots raw wounds on the leafy green mountain itself. No
cyclist has ever left a bloody deer carcass at a trailhead or a pile
of poo at a scenic stream crossing. I do not understand how

parking lots are an improvement to the mountain; and single track, a desecration.

This hiker-biker war has spilled from the op-ed pages of the *Marin Independent Journal* onto the trails themselves. Sometimes piano wire has been strung across bike trails, neck high, intended to cause serious harm to people whose only "crime" is riding their bikes in the woods. Too many people trying to use a limited resource. That in a nutshell is the problem of trail access on Mount Tam. All trail-users love the mountain, but a lot of us are misguided in our attempts to preserve its resources. A simplistic solution, I think, is to rip up the parking lots and allow the meadows and trees to reseed. Close the paved roads to all but fire trucks and ranger's vehicles. Allow anybody who can "climb" the mountain to use its trails. Instead of banning bikes from the trails that crisscross the mountain, try banning cars from using the roads that strangle the mountain. I bet Mount Tam will be the better for it, and its users more happy about it.

Even the little town of Fairfax is beset by the same problems as Tam: too much traffic on too-narrow roads all coming and going to the same place at the same times. Fairfax, as small as it is, more hippieish than most, as green as it gets, still has a rush hour. A geographic reality that impinges on the fantasy of Fairtax is that there are only two roads that lead in and out of the town. In the morning before the sun rises, the main road, Sir Francis Drake, which leads to the highway and on to San Francisco, crawls to a standstill with single occupant SUVs. On my single-speed bike I can zip past dozens and dozens of idling commuters at a time, fueling their frustration. At the peak of the morning work commute, the swarm-to-school crush chokes Sir Francis Drake even more as SUVs stop at the school to disgorge kids one at a time.

Fairfax, I realize, as much as I love it and have come to know it, will never be Amsterdam. The canals that carry the freight in that city could never be built here. The light-rail trains that move the people there, here were ripped out and paved over years ago. At one time not very long ago, someone living in our cottage in San Geronimo could walk the few minutes to the train station and climb aboard. The train would steam through a tunnel at the base of White's Hill, which Marc is always grumbling about having to climb. The road over the hill washes out every winter in the rains. The train would come out on the other side of that hill and stop in downtown Fairfax right where a parking lot now straddles the town. The train chugged on down the Center Boulevard stopping along the way at every village, cutting through a hill again at Camino Alto, past Mill Valley, all the way to the foot of the Golden Gate Bridge in Sausalito. Fairfax, already more likely than most towns in America to duplicate the European transportation model, still has a long way to go. Various bike groups over the years have tried valiantly to open these old abandoned train tunnels to bike traffic. I haven't given up hope.

I know that trying to fix these problems in one fell swoop is beyond me. It is beyond any one indivual. Even the real-world concerns are too much for a goddess to address. I have been so selfish in pursuing big-race wins that I haven't contributed much to any solutions beyond a few talks given to organizations like ROMP (Responsible Mountain Biking People) and other groups. I've donated some time to trailbuilding and maintenance for the Marin County Bike Coalition (MCBC). I really have enjoyed the few rides that I have shared with Marlyn Price's organization, trips for kids. There is a network of organizations like IMBA (International Mountain Bike Association), Bikes Belong, and Debbie Hubsmith's Safe Routes to Schools program that are working toward solutions and accomodations for bikes on the trails and on the streets. I know it is hypocritical to be an honorary associate junior member of the Marin Outlaw Bikers and the MCBC at the same time, but what is a gravity goddess to do? I know I could do more. When I go to Fairfax to shop it is almost always by bike with a messenger bag over my shoulder or a B.O.B. (Beast of Burden) blue trailer behind me, rarely in my bus. It's a little thing, I know. But riding a mountain bike has taught me that progress is made not in big strides, but in little circles.

Even Marin County, a bike lover's fantasy, a gravity goddess' logical abode is a work in progress. But I feel like I fit in here, something that I never felt in San Diego, Durham, or Baltimore.

Marc and I have lived in Marin for a few years now, and not long ago were lucky enough to buy a one-bedroom cottage on a tree-covered hillside beside a seasonal stream above the San Geronimo Creek, a fifteen-minute road ride from Fairfax. A little longer for Marc. Our little house is on a dirt road, carved into the northern slope of the woods that flank Mount Tam. We bought it despite its small size, lack of parking, and susceptibility to electrical blackouts whenever a strong wind brushes a tree limb into a power line. We bought it because of the backyard.

The backyard was a bramble of poison oak, wild blueberries and their protective thorns, and second-growth scrub tress, all of which choked the few native redwood, madrone, and oak that stood despite the legacy of clear-cutting years ago. The San Geronimo Valley was the site of the Bay Area's first stream-powered wood mill. A history that is honored equally by the valley's downstream Samuel P. Taylor State Park and by the upstream Paper Mill Saloon, which blinks red neon on the site of the original mill founded by Mr. Taylor. The slope behind our house is nearly three quarters an acre, shaped like a natural bowl. Shaped like a natural free-riding jump course, I thought, the moment I first saw the property.

Right after we purchased the house, we purchased a couple

of pygmy goats from a farmer's auction and Marc set them to work "clearing" my jump course. After those pygmy goats and their progeny had had their fill of poison oak and thorns, and after I retired them to an organic farm in a valley farther west, and Marc chopped down all the dead and dying trees, I slowly built a respectable series of double jumps, berms and banked turns, rock drop offs, stutter sections, chicanes and I have plans for still more. While I was digging those jumps one shovelful at a time, the grommets came out of the woodwork to help. Despite Marin's reputation and the Tamarancho Bike Park's renown as a mountain-bike mecca, there are actually very few places for kids to mess around on bikes.

Some summer afternoons while I am away racing, Marc says there are as many as a dozen kids in the backyard digging and jumping, snacking on Luna Bars, and drinking Red Bull. And not watching TV or huffing gasoline from a paper bag. Part of a *Dateline* TV show was filmed in my backyard. It's been the site of a couple of magazine shoots, and a mock location of the IMAX documentary film *Top Speed*.

I keep wanting to write off part of the property upkeep as a business expense. In our small kitchen we have discussed how much a double jump should qualify as a tax deduction, but Marc is too chicken. Besides, he says, I would then need a rider on my homeowner's policy to cover a business use if some grommet stacked too hard. What earthly intrusions on a goddess' concerns!

The day we bought our house it stretched to a maximum size of 610 square feet. Over the years Marc has added a glass-walled mud room. He has opened up the ceilings, put in some gable windows, and added a small loft. Somehow up the steep flight of wooden stairs and into our bedroom he even dragged an upright piano. It's still small but compared to living on a boat we think it is San Simeon.

The neighbors are very tolerant and understanding people. As it turns out Marc and I aren't home very much. I am gone for weeks at a time in the summer while racing. During the off season almost every weekend I find myself living at some trailhead in my VW camper bus, which compared to living on a boat is still sort of big. Since Marc works until late at night, he usually crashes on the boat and rides back home in the late morning to play with power tools or to help me stack logs in the backyard for a new whoop section. But I don't think that we have been around to enjoy our neighborhood in the same way as our neighbors have. Someday I hope we will.

For now I am happy that from my backyard I can hop onto legal trails and ride ridgelines all the way to the top of Tam. From the front door of this small house, which we have christened Estate of Indifference, I can hop on a narrow redwood-lined street to pedal to Fairfax to shop and play. When we lived in the small town of Fairfax we used to think of nearby San Francisco as the "the city." Now that we've lived in San Geronimo, which is only a church, a post office, and a very fine creekside restaurant, we joke that Fairfax is "the city."

Perhaps a big part of the reason why I liked Marin County so much was because I was able to tap into a network of other riders. In Marin, for the first time, I didn't feel like the odd girl out. In Marin there were mentors to learn from and examples to aspire to become and accolytes for me to teach. It also just happens that a large number were women.

One of the most adventurous women I know lived in the same dorm room with me in Maryland. She should have shared the same house with me in San Diego. It is my fault that she didn't. I suppose there are reasons why I believed then that women aren't supposed to be "extreme." That only a special few should even try. I don't know why Kathleen Tubridy's snowboarding, surfing, and rock climbing wasn't extreme enough for me. What conceit I had that blinded me to the existence of other women who were probably surrounding me my whole life and doing extraordinary things.

It used to be, before living in Marin, that I thought women like my first coach, Doreen Smith Williams, were as rare as I thought myself to be. Especially in San Diego, I wasn't aware of very many women who liked to ride their bikes in the dirt. Certainly there were, but in San Diego I never found a critical mass of women riders that had reached the point where we no longer felt we were competing against one another for attention from the boys. It was the boys' attention, in the form of sponsorship, that we all craved. I thought Doreen was a great coach not only because she really helped me but because her coaching skills were validated by the number of men she coached. Back then it was important to me, more for real, more legitimate, for her as a coach and for myself as an athlete, if we both operated under a male stamp of approval. Those kinds of views really didn't change for quite a while.

Jacquie Phelan, whom I could now count as a neighbor in Fairfax, certainly loved the dirt just as much as I. By the time I had made it to Marin, Jacquie had retired from racing, been inducted into the hall of fame, and had founded and for many years been president of the Wombats . . . the Women's Mountain Bike and Tea Society, and was beginning to teach herself how to play the banjo. I knew her largely through her pseudonym, Alice B. Toeclips, under which she wrote a wonderful column for *Bike* magazine, which is to say I hardly knew her at all.

She is still a strong rider, I have come to find out. And she still rides that custom aluminum Cunningham frame that her husband, Charlie, built years ago for her to win races on. She is as unpretentious as the simple, unpainted bike that she rides. And yes she is as unique a person as her bike. She favors polka-dot leggings when she rides. Practical for keeping warm through all of Marin's everchanging microclimates. Practical too is the fanny pack that she always carries stuffed with the right tools, energy bars, etc. On single track she wears a helmet, but while riding errands she might wear a straw bonnet securely fastened with a chin strap. As an athlete she has been a big inspiration to me. Because I knew that she was faster than most of the guys she had raced, she had my immediate respect.

I thought I had been the only professional woman to ever come out with a nude mountain-bike poster, until Marc showed me a much older poster of a much younger Jacquie, mud spattered and coyly crouching in a poster for Rock Shox. Not to say that being the first to strip your clothes off is anything to toot your own horn about. But had I known that Jacquie had already dealt with some of the issues like embarrassing potential sponsors, losing credibility with other women, and the spectre of exploitation, I would have asked her how she handled it all. Having known Jacquie for a few years now, I am not surprised by anything she might have said.

Jacquie Phelan is the reason why today I can say I am a professional mountain biker. She created the "professional" part of women's mountain biking by asking for and demanding equal pay for finishing faster than most of the "professional" men during the grueling, long, point to point, up and then down, cross-country races of NORBA's early years. Jacquie was a great racer, but a cross-country racer, and she knew enough about her own limitations as a rider that she couldn't help me at all with downhilling.

But she did say there was a lady down the street who could coach me, Blair Lombardi.

Rather than take Jacquie's advice and give Blair a call, I bought a motorcycle instead.

Instead of immediately taking advantage of Blair's insights into the biomechanics of downhilling, I got sidetracked throttle-twisting motorcycles for a few years, thinking that was a faster way to achieve better results as a downhiller. I was right about the faster part. My downhill skills have improved greatly in the high-speed sections. Jumping sixty feet on a motorcycle makes jumping twenty feet on a downhill bike seem not so bad. And trying to hold onto a dirt bike for a three-hour hare scramble or for two tanks of gas on a mototrack is an incredible muscular workout. But it is difficult to reconcile throttle-twisting with being green. Riding a dirt bike makes me feel the same way a Sierra Club member feels driving a Ford Excursion to work every day. And motoing doesn't really help my slow-speed skills for downhilling.

You would think the slow-speed stuff would be easy. The hard part you would assume must be the big drop offs and the long jumps. Yes, they are difficult, but not as frustrating and not as confidence-busting as blowing a slow-speed section like a tightly wooded, rocky switchback. Sitting in the dirt, your ass on the ground, looking up at a twenty-five-foot drop off that you just blew, at least makes you feel like you are wrestling with a giant—that your opponent is worthy, and that you must respect his size, by calling up all your gravity-goddess powers. Lying belly down in the dirt with your bike in a tangle, eye level with a gnarl of twisted tree roots and a jumble of loose rocks is just humbling. Most of the time you don't even know which root took you down. Sometimes a branch at shoulder height, that you never even thought twice about, ambushes you to the ground. All in slow motion, which makes it even more unbearable, because as you fall, you have time to think about how you just lost a race. One good thing about stacking a big jump is that often you don't have time to think about anything. You are just riding along . . . zippety doo dah . . . at forty miles an hour approaching the lip of a blind-landing jump, then in the air . . . la di da . . . oh there's the landing up a head . . . better shift my weight a bit . . . and then the next thing you see is stars. You often can't think at all for quite a while. "Race? What race? I'm just taking a nap here on these pine needles," I've said more than a few times to course marshalls. But the thing is if you can't make it through the slow stuff without dabbing, without dismounting, you start worrying about being able to handle the big stuff too. And then pretty soon you can't ride at all.

So Blair is right when she says most of it is in a racer's head.

I'd seen Blair at the races, and of course had bumped into her at the coffee shop a time or two. She appeared to be like any other woman of a certain age in Marin. Healthy, active, well-educated, passionate about a particular issue. At races I often rode by Blair standing just on the other side of the yellow caution tape. Under the wide brim of her crumpled safari hat, Blair would pick out an unassuming spot where all of us racers were having a bit of trouble. Usually it was a slow-speed, technical section.

When Jacquie suggested I speak to Blair about coaching I didn't think that there was anything she could do for me. I really didn't think I could learn much from another woman. I was, after all, already one of the top ten women downhillers in the world. Besides, I wasn't the youngest kid on the mountain, and Blair was even older than me! What could she teach me? Never thought for a moment what a sexist and ageist question that was. My blinding focus was on results. But I had lost enough seconds during my races in these slow, technical sections that I finally, sheepishly, asked her for some help.

Blair, too, lived in Fairfax, and had raced mountain bikes as well. But after she retired from racing she went on to study the biomechanics of balance and proprioception that winning mountain-bike racers utilize and others don't. Her coaching methods are embodied in the Lombardi technique. Gradually I have come around to appreciating her methods. She could provide me with valid physiological reasons why my elbows should be carried a certain way through a turn. She explained to me why my head should be positioned another certain way while riding through a really technical section. And the training drills that she devised to develop these skills were targeted and specific. I have really benefitted from her coaching over the years. Blair has also coached other big-time pros, like Jimena Florit and Missy Giove. Too bad there aren't more guys with enough self-confidence to take her advice like top pro Colin Bailey. Too bad that perhaps I didn't have enough confidence in myself to take her advice earlier.

I wish Mount Tam was such a magical place that there was some vernal pool from which I could drink, some spring waterfall under which I could bathe and so banish the dreaded arm pump. But there isn't. Blair is not a magical seer and she knows no incantation she can whisper in my ear to magically improve my balance. I would have to develop it through hard work. Build the muscles to maintain the equilibrium that my brain required to navigate those tricky, slow sections. No, there is no way to improve one's physiology other than by hours spent in the gym. So this winter before my tenth summer racing as a pro I have been working with a power and strength coach, Lisa Huck, concentrating on developing and improving my trunk strength . . . the small-balance muscles along the stomach and back, hips and shoulders. Lisa has been putting me through all the paces while I sit or stand balanced on a large inflatable ball, or while I repeatedly throw a sand-filled ball up against a wall.

Training hard enabled a girl from Fairfax to make the Olympic cross-country mountain-bike team in each of the last two Olympiads. Susan DeMattei raced to a bronze medal in Atlanta and Anne Trombley raced in Sydney. Maybe there is something special about the water on Tam. The next Olympiad will be in Athens and two girls from Fairfax have a pretty good shot to make the team: Mary McConeloug and Rachel Lloyd.

What are the odds that a small town like Fairfax could consistently produce such a bumper crop of Olympians? Has a critical mass of women racers finally developed?

Before the last Olympics in Sydney, I was in between team deals and flirted with the idea of applying for Lithuanian citizenship so I could race for their national team. My mother's mother was a Lithuanian, and since seceding from the Soviet Union, Lithuania has established a fairly liberal standard for dual citizenship. I never really pursued it, but I thought about it more than a few times. There's no way I could make the U.S. cross-country team, and since downhill is not one of the events, I am resigned to never competing in the Olympics. But Marin's past Olympic athletes and potential future athletes have inspired me nonetheless to train harder to win downhill races.

Even though there is no Title IX program for mountain biking at Marin's high schools or colleges, it seems that a network of more experienced women riders has created fertile soil from which newer women riders can sprout and race at an early enough age to develop a very deep base of fitness. Most cross-country racers, especially the women, do not come into their own until their early to mid thirties—the powerband for most of the top women racing today on the cross-country circuit.

For some reason the guys can win cross-country races at comparatively young ages. Except for the ageless Thomas Frischknecht, who has been a contender every year since the innaugaural world championships, not too many guys are a threat past the age of thirty-five. Ned Overend is in a special category all his own since he can longer claim to be thirty-nine and he is still winning XTERRA races. Come to think of it David "Tinker" Juarez is no spring chicken either and he wins the twenty-four-hour races all the time. But more commonly by their mid thirties, most guys are too pooped to pop for a big win.

These younger women have inspired me, and mentors like

Blair and trailblazers like Jacquie have shown me that perhaps the real magic of Marin is that it is a perfect fit for square pegs. It's nothing new to say that Marin is a state of mind. Hot-tubbers and stoners have been saying that for years, four-twenty dude.

Thesis/question: *How does a mild-mannered research scientist transform into a gravity goddess?*

Answer: The same way an extreme, high-speed gravity goddess transforms into a laid-back, single-speed, single-tracking, on-a-boat-living, sailing siren. Because she wants to.

PART III

Conclusions

Chapter 11

Stage 6—Goddesses Don't Retire, We Just Ride Away

Over the years that I have been a pro downhiller Marc and my plans for a big bike trip on a sailboat have grown more ambitious. When we first thought about this adventure we imagined that we would be flat broke. Now we think that when I am done racing we will happily be only partially broke. A few years ago we sold our thirty-seven-foot fiberglass sloop *Indifference,* and bought a fifty-two-foot-length overall steel ketch which we have also named *Indifference.*

The only difference between the two vessels, of course, is that this larger boat needed as much renovation as the last, but has cost more. But it hasn't been too bad. Marc has turned out to be pretty handy for a guy who didn't have any callouses on his fingers until he turned thirty.

Every fall for the last few seasons Marc and I have taken an annual vacation shakedown cruise in preparation for the big adventure. October and November offer the best sailing weather along the coast of California. I have no big races during that time. My body recuperates better and is ultimately stronger for each race season if I give it some downtime.

The first year's cruise was planned as a leisurely week's downwind sail from San Francisco to the island of Catalina where Red Bull was hosting its annual athlete retreat. We planned on attending the Red Bull events for a couple of days and then sailing on down to San Diego to visit my brother John and his family. Marc said the round trip would take less than a month. Taking a break would prevent me from falling into that nasty hole of overtraining as I prepared for the upcoming 2003 season. I made Marc promise that he would build special, dedicated, mountain-bike storage somewhere on the boat, so if we landed somewhere I could hop off instantly for a ride.

Marc agreed and added it to his list of renovations. He estimated that it would take him a month or so to get the boat ready. Just in time for a post-Interbike departure.

A few days before Interbike my mom called. It seems that the best time for our annual family portrait—as determined by some maternal divination process never fully explained to me— was the span of a few days in between Interbike and the Red Bull retreat.

There wasn't much I could do about it, I explained to Marc. He was sympathetic.

"Will we still have time to sail to Catalina? I told the Red Bull guys that we would take them all out for an afternoon."

"Huh."

"I have to go to Baltimore. I can't get out of it. That week works best for all my brothers and their wives and the kids. I don't know. I guess because we have no kids my mom thinks we can just pick up and go anytime. I'll make it as fast as I can."

"Well, would I have to go?"

Tricky question. Marc and I still are not married. My parents' great hope is that either Marc will magically wake up some morning to a large private practice as a pediatrician, or that some morning I will magically wake up married to some guy who already has one. The subject of marriage rarely comes up in our house or at my parents'. Both households it seems are more comfortable "blending" two open bottles of olive oil, rather than "marrying" them. Since my parents still hold out hope for Marc's conversion to medicine he is in a gray area as far as family portraits are concerned. Because my dad's Parkinson's is slowly getting worse I certainly want to visit home every chance I get. Marc does too. At holiday dinners past, whenever the maternal announcement was made that it was time to take a family portrait, Marc diplomatically retreated to the consular confines of the kitchen bathroom until he was sure all the flashbulbs had gone off. This holiday season Marc and I were planning to see how the portrait situation has changed since my brother Chris was now officially living in sin with his girlfriend, Luisa. Would there be room for both of them in the kitchen bathroom, or would they be allowed to remain in their chairs for the portrait? But now having to make a special trip just for the portrait really brought the issue to a head.

I stood in our small kitchen sizing him up. Did he not want to come with me? Was he the one not willing to make a commitment? Why not? Did he not want to commit to me because of the "bump" on my butt since the X Games? Strange twist. Before I was the one with commitment phobia.

"I was planning on going to Interbike with you, but if I go to Baltimore I won't be finished with all the new plumbing on the boat."

That was reassuring. A practical concern.

"No. You don't have to go with me. Can you get it all done in time?"

"No problem. When you get back we'll just have to sail from the bay straight to Catalina. No stopping in Santa Cruz or Monterey or Santa Barbara, that's all."

After my trip home Marc picked me up at SFO and we

headed straight to the boat. Marc told me that the boat was practically all ready. Just a few details that we could take care of on the way. If we woke up early enough we could ride the out-going tide right through the Golden Gate.

Because I was so hungry after the cross-country flight, we stopped for dinner. We got to the boat late. We woke up late. We started our sailing trip late. If this was a race and my pre-event routine was seriously disrupted, I would be in major trouble. But this wasn't really a race. Except of course that we had to get to Catalina in time for the Red Bull event.

The fog wasn't too thick as we untied the lines but as Marc hoisted the sails it grew so soupy that I couldn't even see the Golden Gate Bridge.

"Mark, the compass is stuck. Did you fix the compass?"

"No. It's not stuck. The whole boat is steel so every time I weld on a new pad eye or cleat or remove a hatch or something, the compass loses its balance and just acts crazy."

"Oh. So how do I know which way to steer? I can't even see the bridge."

"I'll set up the GPS."

"You don't have the GPS on yet?"

"Just give me a second."

"What about all the lats and longs that we have to put in?" I was rembering what a pain it was to punch the strings of digits lifted from the paper charts that the GPS needed to define the destinations we wanted to sail to, or maintain a safe distance from the things we wanted to avoid. The fog was a wet blanket thrown over my head. I couldn't see anything. I could steer by the GPS if the exact location of the center span of the bridge was programmed into the unit.

"Did you punch in the way points already?"

"They should be in there from the last time we took the boat out."

Our home on the ocean, the new *Indifference*. (*Author*)

"Are you sure?"

"Yes. No problem. Just let me plug it in." Marc was fiddling with the GPS unit's power cord. "For some reason the batteries won't work."

I was sailing by sound approaching one of the world's busiest harbor entrances, into a tide and swell, dangerous shores on either side, and I was getting a little concerned.

"There," Marc triumphed, once the GPS was plugged in and the unit came alive. "Just give it a sec to warm up."

As we neared the mouth of the bay, the water color changed, and it began to swirl like saltwater taffy in our wake. The wind had freshened. That's when I found out that the batteries failing in the GPS unit had erased its memory. All the way points we'd entered were gone.

"It's not foggy over Oakland or over Alcatraz," Marc said. "We can see Angel Island and the big buildings of the city pretty well. We'll just line up a buncha points on land, match 'em with points on this paper chart, and where the lines all cross is where we are. If we know where we are, then we can use some of those points to line up which way we're going. If you look backward and keep some of those points lined up, then we can sail forward." Marc spread out the chart on the wet deck and weighted down its corners with coils of line, his rigging knife, and a flashlight.

I turned around and stood facing the opposite direction from where we were headed and tried to keep the rolling boat tracing along the imaginary line on the damp chart.

"I'll go forward and stand on the bowsprit to make sure we don't run into a fishing boat or somethin'," Marc said. "I'll blow this horn if we are gonna hit anything."

That was reassuring.

It seemed like crossing under the bridge against the tide, billions of gallons of sea water a second were trying to push us back into the bay. Sailing blind in the fog and guessing from which direction the sounds of other boats were coming took hours.

When we were finally clear of the bridge, and we were far enough off shore that we could finally take a left and head south, it started to rain. It rained for the next twenty-four hours. We took turns hand steering, a few hours on and a few hours off, nonstop. We wore the same clothes, ate food grown cold by the time we got to the bottom of the bowl. Marc had disconnected the CD-stereo system while he was messing with the running lights, so all we had was a hand-crank radio that I had bought in

South Africa a year earlier at a race. It was an airport gift for Marc. Now we cranked it up for thirty seconds every half hour so we could hear scratchy National Public Radio broadcasts.

The windows dripped water right over my head whenever I crawled below to nap on one of the berths. "I'm gonna caulk those first thing," Marc promised. His assurance gave me no sleep.

The stove swung violently whenever I tried to make coffee. It was supposed to swing level, slowly and under control, as the boat heeled over in the swells and wind. "I have to position the lead ballast in that stove a little lower," Marc observed.

The mizzen sail flapped violently, and the boom whipped dangerously from one side of the boat right over our heads to the other side whenever the wind shifted quarters astern. "I gotta rig a preventer," Marc commented, "at'll take care of that, no problem."

After twenty-four hours at sea I finally had to go "number two." All the number ones had been taken care of in the time-honored tradition of walking up to the head of the boat, crawling as far out as possible on the bowsprit so that you were way out over the water, then dropping pants and holding onto the stainless-steel railings of the pulpit.

"Marc, did you finish installing the toilet?"

"Yes," Marc hissed with a hint of indignance. "The toilet works perfectly."

"Perfectly?"

"Perfectly."

The toilet that Marc installed was the simplest kind in the world, he told me. Simple because it had no moving parts, he explained. It doesn't use electricity and will never wear out. Simply move the handle back and forth, which drives a pump that efficiently flushes the toilet into the holding tank by creating a vacuum. I was on guard, but it worked fine.

"It worked!" I exclaimed as I climbed the companionway ladder back into the cockpit.

"You sound surprised."

"Not surprised, proud. Just proud of my little handy boyfriend." We were approaching Point Conception now and the rain was behind us. The sun was a bit stronger. We were bounding along sailing downwind just south of Big Sur. Ahead of Point Conception we could see blue cloudless sky. Dolphins were swimming right alongside of us, playing with us. Pelicans were dive-bombing into the water all around us. On their backs sea otters floated like vacationers on Barcaloungers as they munched on oysters. Whales puffed their spray in the distance. The wallowing swell of their mass rolled through the small windwaves without making an additional ripple.

About halfway around the point, the swells grew as the wind picked up. Marc said that we should have tried to sail past the point in the middle of night when the wind was asleep. It was just after noon and the wind was flattening every wrinkle out of our sails.

"Marla, what do you think? Should we drop one of the sails?"

From bow to stern we were flying the biggest sail, called a genoa, then the smallest, the staysail. Then the mainsail, and finally the mizzen. With all this canvas up we were still only going about five miles an hour. That's about the best a cruising boat can do.

"No way. We are just crawling along. Finally the wind is picking up and we are starting to get somewhere."

"Okaaay," Marc draws out the last syllable of his capitulations when he is nervous. Like the extra inflection is some kind of muted defiance.

It wasn't long before the wind was lifting the caps off the waves. Since the wind and swells and the boat were all traveling in the same direction the speeds were deceiving. Pretty soon the sails were so taut that Marc couldn't drop them. Also, the swells were now so big that I had to line up the stern relatively square with the swell, otherwise the boat would turn sideways, quickly throwing all the plates and coffee mugs, bags of food, and Marc's tools all over the cabin. That posed no real danger, just a mess. But the farther we rounded the quicker the wind increased, the bigger the swells rolled, and the faster I had to spin the wheel. After an hour it wasn't safe on deck without being clipped into a harness so that a rogue swell wouldn't just flip the twenty-two-ton boat like an empty beer can. A couple of times we were surfing down the face of the swell at fifteen knots, which is like Indy car speed for sailboats. At the bottom of the trough I had to spin the wheel because the sails were still full of wind and if the boat and the sails weren't headed in the same direction there was the slight chance that their directions would part ways.

That's called a dismasting.

Not a good thing.

If at the top of the swell I wasn't lined up to surf straight down, the buck of the wave, then the swell, would grab the keel as it rolled under it. Gently at first and then with more force until the swell had turned the boat completely sideways. The next swell a few seconds later would slam right into the side of the boat knocking it right onto its side.

That's called a broach.

Also, not a good thing.

Maybe the swell would even tip the boat right over.

If the boat tips itself back the right way up, that's called a roll.

That's making a good thing out of a bad thing, but you still don't want it to happen.

Marc knew about these things only by reading books. I knew about them from experience. I had forgotten over the years how white-knuckle some sailing can be. Suddenly hurtling down a mountain seemed somewhat tame.

An hour or two later we had made it all the way around the point. The wind had dropped and the swells had subsided. The sun hung lower in the sky, but shone much stronger. We peeled off the layers of waterproofing, the woolies, and Polartec so that I was wearing only my sports bra and shorts. Marc stood bare chested grinning with his arms folded across each other just below his chin. He put one leg up on the cabin top. He looked like a stocky Horatio Hornblower. Marc first and then I took a solar shower right on deck. We had been awake now for almost thirty-six hours and I had started out already jet lagged. The warm fresh water and soap was refreshing.

Marc fired up the barbecue and we wolfed down some shrimp-and-salmon skewers. We ate almost everything in the icebox since most of the ice was now just cold water. Our boat doesn't have refrigeration. Too complicated.

"Marc, let's anchor somewhere off Goleta and get some sleep."

"*Okaaay.*"

He had been a little right about the sails. The last five hours would have been a little less white-knuckled if we had dropped at least the Genoa sail.

"Why don't you want to anchor? Don't you want some sleep?"

"Sure I'm beat too. But I didn't have time to fill the hydraulic lines with fluid. If we drop the anchor, we have to raise it by hand."

"So? The other boat didn't even have a hydraulic windlass. We always cranked it up by hand."

"But this boat is much bigger, so the anchor is twice as heavy and instead of rope we have chain that's a half-inch thick. That stuff weighs a ton."

"Well, do you want to keep on sailing to Catalina? That's at least twelve hours away."

"No. We'll anchor. But there's a lot of kelp around here. We have to be careful."

"Okey dokey. How about that spot right there." I was pointing to the sandy beach that was directly off our port bow.

Marc went forward to drop the sails. I started the engine so we could maintain steerage as we lost our wind power. The sun was dropping to the horizon quickly now. The greens and browns of the Santa Barbara coastline came into focus. Trees emerged distinctly from the beach. Large rocks popped into view. I could almost smells grapes ripening on the vine. But I was really beat.

Marc directed me to the spot where he thought the bottom would be clear of kelp. As the sun slanted its prettiest oranges and reds we splashed the anchor into the oil-black water. Marc cut the engine and began tidying the mess our marathon sail had made of our decks. I popped an Ambien and crawled into my berth. Warm and exhausted.

I remember Marc kissing me on the cheek and telling me that he was going to sit on deck and have a beer. Make sure the anchor was set, he said, before he crawled into bed too.

It seemed only a minute later that he was yelling in my ear and shaking my shoulder, "Wake up! Wake up! I need you to steer!"

The cabin was pitch black. What was he yelling about? I rubbed my eyes and looked toward the companionway hatch. The sky was full of stars and the moon was bright. Marc's voice was echoing all over the boat. I could hear his feet pounding on the deck as he scampered about. "Wake up! I need you!"

I climbed the stairs and crawled onto the deck, still deep in Ambien land. Ambien makes you really silly if you fight the urge to sleep. I felt like giggling when I couldn't figure out what was going on.

The engine was running. The ship's wheel was sloshing back and forth slowly. The boat's bow was fixed it seemed in one spot while the stern was making lazy circles around it. Mark was kneeling on the bow and pulling up the chain one foot at a time by heaving and hoing a bar on the anchor windlass. I looked toward shore. The beach was a distant shore of twinkling lights. I held my hand to my face and giggled.

Later, when I was off my Ambien cloud, Marc told me that the anchor had set in a giant clump of kelp. He didn't notice it because he was so tired. Everything seemed okay so he finally fell asleep right on deck. During the night the motion of the boat woke him up. He said he looked up and realized that somehow we were miles off shore, drifting with no lights on except for a tiny kerosene anchor light hanging from the rigging. The shore breeze had blown us away from the beach, but there easily could have been a sea breeze that would have pushed us right onto the beach.

That's not a good thing.

Marc said he ran up front and began raising in the seventy-five feet of chain, but it was slow going. There was a big jungle of kelp wrapped around the anchor. That's when Marc noticed that we were drifting real close to one of those oil platforms that dot that section of coast.

He started the engine but he couldn't steer the boat at the same time he was raising the anchor. Without me to put the engine in reverse and back away from the oil platform, and allowing him to raise the chain without its links banging away on the steel hull, we might have been in trouble, he said.

I giggled for a second. Marc is such a worrier.

We made it to Catalina late Saturday night. We were supposed to take everybody sailing on Friday afternoon, so that wasn't too bad. Red Bull treated us all to a great breakfast and then we played games in the surf all day. On Sunday night Marc and I hosted about thirty extreme athletes on board for Red Bull and vodkas, and stacks of pizza boxes.

The next morning we had Catalina all to ourselves. We dinghied our bikes ashore and rode from one end of the island to the other on our single speeds. The single speeds are so much easier to carry in the dinghy. Don't have to worry nearly as much about the damage saltwater can cause. Fewer cables to snag. Marc stayed pretty close. On the final climb he actually outsprinted me to the scenic-vista wooden bench. He has a surprisingly strong first seven cranks. We never once got a glimpse of Los Angeles. All we could make out was a brown smudge of clouds. But from the rocky crags of the island's peak we could see our happy little boat, just a speck, anchored in the harbor.

This easily could be some little bay in Baja. We could sail around the world and ride wherever we wanted.

"Sure we could," Marc agreed.

"But you'll have to build me a stationary bike. Something on gimbals like the stove so I could ride even when the boat is sailing."

"No problem. I could even rig it so you power a small 'fridgerator to keep the beer cold."

"Let's try to keep it simple okay?"

• • •

When it is time to retire from racing I know that I will be riding even more single track than I have been able to ride lately. I am relying on Marc, however, to tell me before any of my sponsors do that the time has come to stop racing. I am so deep into racing still that I may not see that my spot on a pro team may deserve to go to a younger rider who hasn't yet had the chance to benefit from the opportunities that I have. If this 2003 downhill season turns out to be my last, I can honestly say that I have raced my best. My parents are proud of my efforts. It took them a while but they finally came around. My mother even recently posed for a magazine shoot with me. My dad is holding out for residuals, I think. My brothers, John, Dave, and Chris, are now talking smack and trying to rope me into joining them on Team Streb to race in a twenty-four-hour race sometime this season. We'll see about that.

Marc and I have sailed down to San Diego and back a few times since that first trip. We've added a radar so we won't get lost in the fog again. I have promised to not pop sleeping pills until the anchor has really been set. Marc's restoration of our boat is behind schedule and overbudget, naturally. But we are confident that, shortly after my last race, whenever that is, our boat will be packed up with two mountain bikes and tubes and patch kits and all the stuff we'll need to explore some new trails.

I have been looking forward for some time now to a great adventure in Baja. I'd like to ride my bike down along the coast at the same time the gray whales are migrating south to the Sea of Cortez. It would be a lot of fun to ride the whole coastline using our boat as a big sailing sag vehicle. My old San Diego friend

My brothers, members of the future Team Streb (left to right), Chris, John, and Dave. (*Author*)

Russell, who now owns the best bike shop in Durango, the Durango Cyclery, heads down to Baja every winter. He tells me that there are miles and miles of trails down there. I want to see for myself.

And I've never ridden across Australia before. Or along the length of the Great Wall in China.

We have rented out our house in Marin to a couple of really nice people, even though one of them is pretty much a roadie. We are living on our sailboat in Morro Bay, which is exactly halfway between Los Angeles and San Francisco. Just before I signed with Team Luna I bought a fixer-upper duplex house in one of the small neighborhoods that ring the estuary. I used the money from the IMAX movie *Top Speed* as a down payment. Marc is fixing it up one apartment at a time. We are trying to live simply. Getting acquainted again with living on the water. Rowing back and forth to shore for ice for the galley's icebox. Marc is readying our boat for our big sailing adventure, while I am preparing for another season of racing downhill.

My ninth winter as a pro downhiller is easing into my tenth summer. When I first began I said to myself, "I'll try it for a year and see what happens." Every new season since then I say the same thing. I recommit myself to the discipline. I train for the rigors and I hope to do the best that I can.

The first race of the year, the 2003 Red Bull Race Down to the Middle of the Earth, has just wrapped up. Racing mountain bikes seven hundred feet underground in an abandoned salt mine in the old East Germany, I placed second to the world champion, Anne Caroline Chausson. Same results as the last Race Down.

In the spring I plan to be at the Sea Otter a few days before most of my competition shows up. I'll walk the course. Talk to some of the local riders about the mud, the morning rains, and the afternoon sun. On race day I'll be at the top of the mountain dialing in my suspension.

Getting to the top is the easiest part of my race. It's the going downhill that's the real challenge. Like Marc told me that first time I raced with him: The important thing is to just keep making circles.

Marc and I out for another shakedown cruise aboard *Indifference*. (*Author*)